OTTAWA BOY

AN AUTOBIOGRAPHY

by Lloyd Francis

Published by

GENERAL STORE
GSPH PUBLISHING HOUSE

Box 28, 1694B Burnstown, Ontario, Canada K0J 1G0
Telephone (613) 432-7697 or 1-800-465-6072

ISBN 1-894263-30-8
Printed and bound in Canada

Layout and Design by Derek McEwen
Printing by Custom Printers of Renfrew Ltd.

Canadian Cataloguing in Publication Data

Francis, Lloyd, 1920-
Ottawa boy

ISBN 1-894263-30-8

1. Francis, Lloyd, 1920- 2. Canada. Parliament. House of Commons–Biography. 3. Canada–Politics and government–1963-1984. I. Title.

FC601.F73A3 2000 328.71'092 C00-901300-8
F1034.3F73A3 2000

TABLE OF CONTENTS

Part 1

PREFACE

IS IT AN ACT of vanity to write one's memoirs? Who will want to read them? It is possible that some browsing historian some day will want to read my observations on what happened in 1982 when six MPs tried to prevent a vote taking place in the House of Commons and I was presiding as deputy Speaker, or my observations during the Long Bells. Some aspiring politician may find my anecdotes interesting—after all, every man or woman in public life has to accumulate a quota of these and to use them judiciously, carefully choosing the time and audience. Perhaps others can profit from my mistakes, since I never did become a cabinet minister, although I did have other successes. However, it has been a thoroughly enjoyable experience—as a student, in business, four years in the Royal Canadian Air Force during World War II, as a graduate student and member of a university faculty, as a public servant in Ottawa for nine years, as president of the Professional Institute of the Public Service of Canada, as a municipal politician, a member of Parliament, Speaker of the House of Commons, and ambassador to Portugal.

I have travelled to many countries in Europe, Asia, Africa and Australasia and seen many different places and peoples. They were all interesting. In the words of Tennyson's Ulysses, "I am a part of all that I have met."

Politicians rarely talk about their travels, because a merciless press always labels them "junkets." But, to my mind, the Canadian public would be ill-served by backbench MPs who never met a member of the parliament of another country, who never saw the results of our aid programs abroad, who never attended a session of the United Nations or visited our peacekeepers, who never attended an international trade conference. In these days of globalization, Canada plays a significant role on the world scene. Most of our cabinet ministers graduate from the backbenches and this is where they learn what it means to govern. I profited a great deal from my trips and have tried to explain why. My political career was funded by a fortunate investment in real estate, which I also describe. My hobby of polishing stones intrudes into my story in many places.

My choice of constituency was, perhaps, unfortunate. I always contested the seat in which I lived, starting with the huge, sprawling constituency of Carleton, which had voted Conservative since Confederation. I won it for the Liberals for the first time in 1963, and afterwards contested Ottawa West, which had been carved out of it. When the Liberals instituted the policy of bilingualism in the public service in 1963, this English language seat contained many bitterly unhappy voters. Prime Minister Pearson's pledge that the careers of unilingual English-speaking public servants would not be impaired was viewed as a cynical, deceptive political promise that was never meant to be kept.

For a constituency that had voted for the same political party for nearly a century, the change was incredible. In the nine federal elections between

1963 and 1988, the voters threw the incumbent out. This could hardly be due to my performance. Rather, it reflected a deep anger at the sitting MP, regardless of political party. I contested nine elections between 1962 and 1984, winning every second time. Does this merit a mention in the *Guinness Book of Records*? Beginning in 1988, Marlene Catterall has won the seat for the Liberals in three successive elections and the deep anger that motivated many residents appears to have subsided.

In brief, this is a frank and uninhibited story of my life, as well as a record of some events that took place. I am indebted to many people who reviewed parts of my manuscript and offered suggestions that corrected the deficiencies of my memory. For my period in the Speaker's chair, Messrs Arthur Silverman, Philip Laundy and Robert Desramaux were particularly helpful. For review of problems arising out of the application of bilingualism in the public service, Mr. Leslie Barnes assisted. Messrs Jack Osborne and Dick Splane commented on the section dealing with my work in the Department of National Health and Welfare. Claude Bennett recalled days at City Hall. My old friend, Frank Marchington, commented on our campaigns.

Finally, I am forever grateful to my wife, Mary, without whose patience and assistance my task would never have been finished.

FAMILY BACKGROUND

Both my parents were born in England and emigrated to Canada as teenagers. On both sides, they were probably of French Huguenot descent.

My father, Frederick Roland Francis, was born in the district of Armley of the City of Leeds, Yorkshire, in 1892. His parents, Ada Mary Raby and Robert John Francis, had eight children, of whom three died in infancy. The Francis family had moved north into the Midlands at the time of the Industrial Revolution. Generations back, I believe they were immigrants from France whose original name was Lefrançois.

My grandfather, Robert John Francis, had been a coal merchant and his business failed. In desperation, he emigrated to Canada about 1903, securing employment in Ottawa. My father and his older brother Sam joined him in 1905 and the rest of the family came later. Family relationships, however, were stormy and Grandfather returned to England. The Ottawa telephone directory for 1917 shows a listing in the name of my uncle Sam at 22 Hawthorne Avenue, where presumably the family were living. Grandfather died in 1924 and is buried in Loughborough, Yorkshire.

Under my grandmother's direction, the family quickly put their roots down in Canada. Aunt Ada, the eldest, married a railroader and lived in Montreal. Not having children of her own, she had my brother Jack and myself stay with her for part of our summer holidays, a most pleasant experience for boys who lived in the country. Uncle Sam worked for the Canada Metal Co. and later left to establish his own very successful business in Toronto. He married an Ottawa girl, Violet Hooper, who was especially kind to me. Together they had a son and a daughter, Fred and Irene. Aunt Doris married a federal public servant and made her home in Ottawa but had no children. Uncle John was an office worker and at one time a purchasing agent for the E.B. Eddy Co. He married late in life and was childless. His widow, Helen, died in 1996.

My father, Roland, trained as a machinist and worked in a munitions plant during World War I. As the result of an industrial accident, one eye was damaged and later replaced by a glass one. This led to a total change of employment. He and Uncle Sam unsuccessfully attempted to establish a business assembling an early type of vacuum cleaner based on mechanical, not electrical, principles. My father then decided to go into the poultry business for reasons that I do not understand, since he had no knowledge or experience in this field. The business did give the family a living for twenty years, but it was hard work.

In 1918 he married my mother and I am the first of three sons, followed by my brothers, Jack and Lyle. My mother, Mary Dyble, was born in the village of Knutsford, Cheshire, in 1889, the second youngest of twelve children, four of whom died in infancy. Knutsford, as you might judge from the spelling, was where the Danish King Kanute was alleged to have crossed a stream. My maternal grandmother, Mary Ardern, was married in 1865, at the age of eighteen, to Arthur Dyble[1] in Manchester Cathedral. During World War II, when I was attached to the Royal Air Force, I spent a pleasant leave in Knutsford and was impressed by how clear her mind was, although she was by then in her mid-nineties. She told me that she had married a bricklayer from Cornwall whose family spoke French and had come from Brittany. Her husband died in 1917.

One of Mother's older sisters, Mabel, had emigrated to Canada and was living in Ottawa. Grandmother Dyble decided that my mother, Mary (who had lost a beau on a training voyage to Scandinavia with the Royal Navy), should join Mabel. At the age of eighteen, Mother came to Ottawa. Mabel then took off for Western Canada and married a wheat farmer in Saskatchewan! Mother stayed in Ottawa, became a dressmaker at Murphy-Gamble's store and lived at 18 Spruce Street with a family named Stanley-Smith, who treated her as one of their own.

Mother's family was typical of the large families of her generation. Two sisters, Maggie and Louie, married in Cheshire and had no children. Hettie (Lisetta) married a Welsh postmaster and raised four daughters in Carnarvon. Lizzie married and had four children, two of whom stayed in England and two emigrated with her to Canada. John went into business in Manchester, married, and raised three sons, one of whom came to Canada and for some time shared a partnership in the poultry business with my father.

---

[1] The family name Dyble has always puzzled me. Was it an Anglicized version of the French word "*diable*," as in Isle du Diable?

James Arthur Dyble emigrated to Australia, where he settled near Brisbane, became a shoemaker, and raised two children. Presumably he was in touch with his maternal uncle, James Ardern, who had emigrated to the same area some three decades earlier, become a sheep farmer, and fathered a family of ten children. Mother corresponded with her brother Jim for some years, but lost touch with him after the Second World War.

MY CHILDHOOD

I was born in Ottawa on March 19, 1920. When I was eighteen months old, my parents sold their house at 467 Parkdale Avenue and purchased a frame two-storey house with five acres of land on the Bowesville Road (now Riverside Drive) near the Hog's Back falls of the Rideau River. This was to be the poultry farm.

The Bowesville Road, which extended from the city limits at Billings Bridge to Bowesville about four miles to the south, was built initially by a private company as a toll road. It was later taken over by the Suburban Roads Commission. I can still remember the man we called "Joe" walking the road twice a week with a hand-drawn cart in which he collected manure from the teams of horses that went from the farms into the city daily.

My mother, Mary Dyble, circa 1915

In 1927, the aviator Charles Lindbergh, after his famous trip across the Atlantic, visited Ottawa with a number of his associates. One aircraft crashed on landing and the pilot was killed. The level field where they landed adjacent to Bowesville was for many years known locally as "Lindy's Field," and later became the home of the Ottawa Flying Club. During World War II the farms of Bowesville were expropriated for a military airport, and still later the Ottawa International Airport was added to the complex.

We lived in the country, a mile and a half from Billings Bridge, where our post office was located. I can still remember vividly the sound of water falling from the Hog's Back falls of the Rideau River, half a mile away, drifting across the evening calm to our house. Opposite us on the other side of the road was the McMahon farm, rented as a dairy operation to successive tenants—Tom Saunderson and Milton Russell in particular. Beside us were two small holdings, carved as was ours from the original McMahon farm. The Frasers had ten acres, the Grahams, like ourselves, five. The Grahams were an older couple, and Mr. Graham worked as the school caretaker. Mr. Fraser was an Inspector in the RCMP and his family of five included three roughly my age.

The McMahon farm was not really good farmland. Tom Saunderson, a Northern Ireland Orangeman with a family of thirteen, supplemented his income with an ice business. Large blocks of ice were cut from the Rideau River above the Hog's Back dam by hand with huge saws and guided by poles to a machine-operated device that pulled them out of the water, loading them onto horse-drawn sleighs. The work was dangerous, but getting soaked in the cold water was the worst that happened to anyone in my recollection. The blocks, frequently two-and-a-half to three feet thick, were carried to a tall ice house, packed in sawdust and stored for the summer trade. Jimmie and Herbie Saunderson, and other members of the family, worked at these tasks, sometimes in bitter cold and frequently when they should have been at school. The invention of the electric refrigerator in the 1930s destroyed the ice business as it had been known.

Looking back, I now realize how fortunate we were to be raised in such a district. We swam in the dam above the falls, from the boom logs that

The Francis family, 1925: Lloyd, Jack, Lyle, Mary and Roland

linked five piers that Colonel By, the builder of the Rideau Canal, had constructed at great cost after his initial dam failed. These piers are all gone now. We went fishing in the rapids below the dam and played on the huge timber slide that also channelled sluice water so that it would not erode the base of the dam. The slide, too, no longer exists. One season we built a raft, which we kept by the boathouse on the McMahon Farm, and which enabled us to fish for rock bass, black bass, perch, sunfish and suckers from the stumps in the dam near Mooney's Bay. The Graham and Dowler farms had extensive bushlands, where we found wild flowers in the spring, picked wild raspberries in July, and snared rabbits in the winter to supplement our larder at home.

The Barnes lands faced our place diagonally on the other side of the Bowesville Road. A magnificent grove of mature basswood trees in the spring attracted birds that nested in their branches. Behind the one-storey frame house stood an apple orchard with some forty trees. In 1930 the property was purchased by Joseph Lafrance, a butcher from Hull who wanted his family of six children to learn English. Mr. and Mrs. Lafrance spoke very little English and my parents never spoke French, but they were friends. We always bought our meat from them. The Lafrance children learned English and I learned some French.

The City of Ottawa has now grown to absorb the whole area. Where we lived is now a parking garage. An apartment building stands where we played scrub softball, and adjacent to it is now a shopping centre. That part of the McMahon farm on the other side of Riverside Drive is a public park. The old Perley quarry where we hunted frogs and mud turtles in the summer and skated in the winter, has been completely filled in and the Terry Fox Centre built not far away.

The magnificent Vincent Massey Park at Hog's Back was created through the foresight of the National Capital Commission, in particular that of the late Douglas McDonald[2] when he was director of Planning. Part of the lands are leased to the Municipal Department of Parks and Recreation, who maintain a popular public beach, created on the old Graham and McMahon Farms. To do this they had to remove all the stumps and haul in many tons of sand.

ELEMENTARY AND SECONDARY SCHOOLS

Mother told me that my fifth birthday was on a Friday and I would start school the following Monday. The red brick schoolhouse contained a single classroom in which one teacher instructed all grades from beginners to high school entrance level. A solid basement under the classroom had separate playrooms for boys and girls. We had an outdoor well, with a hand pump, and separate old-fashioned outhouses. In the summer, garden

[2] A tape of an interview that I conducted with Mr. McDonald before his death is now deposited with the Ottawa Public Library.

plots for flowers and vegetables provided practical instruction in agriculture.

Miss Copping was my first teacher. Eighteen years later, while attending Initial Training School for Aircrew in the RCAF, I was riding the streetcar home to my new bride. A woman came up to me and said: "You must be Lloyd Francis. I have watched you and you have the same expression on your face that you had when you sat in the front row in public school." It was incredible that she could recognize me, but she was a highly intelligent woman and at that time functioned as personnel director for a small arms plant.

Miss Margaret Meagher, later Mrs. Wallace, was my second teacher. School was every minute a pleasure, and I could not understand why anyone would think otherwise. When the lesson for my grade was completed, I listened to the lesson for the grade above me and then the lesson for a still higher grade. Miss Meagher accelerated my promotions so that I did six normal grades in three years. I was sad when she left to accept a promotion in an Ottawa school. She later became a principal in the Roman Catholic school system of the City of Ottawa. There were no separate schools in School Section #7 where I attended—Catholic and Protestant students benefited from excellent Protestant and Catholic teachers. Sons of the Orange Saunderson family proudly proclaimed their Irish origins with the Catholic Mears boys. Parents elected three school trustees at the annual meetings which, from all accounts, were pleasant social affairs.

Primary education in a rural school in Ontario at that time leaned heavily on the basics of reading, writing and arithmetic. We also learned the names of different breeds of cattle and horses, and studied the elements of botany in order to understand plant growth. We did not have the options like music or shop that were offered in urban schools.

When I entered Glebe Collegiate in September 1930, I was not quite ten-and-a-half years old. Is this still a record for the Province of Ontario? My teachers thought it was at the time. Perhaps it would have been better if I had delayed a bit, because I was not a match in social or athletic development with my classmates. Academic grades were something else. I was the first graduate of School Section #7 ever to go to university, and my brother Jack the second. In those days, it was taken for granted that when you reached sixteen you got a job—on the farm, in a store, or in an office. But my parents encouraged me to go on.

At that time, Gloucester Township had no high school of its own and paid for its students to attend Ottawa schools. Most went to Lisgar Collegiate, the first to be built in Ottawa, or else to Ottawa Technical School or the High School of Commerce. Glebe, a new school completed in 1922, was much closer to where we lived. Still, it was over three miles away. In the summer, I bicycled. In the winter, I shared a taxi with at least four others (ten cents a day per person) and walked home afterwards.

At Glebe, we had daily timetables, moving from one classroom to another every thirty-five minutes. Perhaps it was explained to us, but I did not comprehend. At the end of the second day my homeroom teacher, Mr. Irenus Mix, patiently took me aside and wrote out the sequence of where I was to be, and when. Small for my age and shy, and coming from a one-room country school to Glebe with over 1,200 students, I felt very much alone. The teachers—Mr. Elliott, Miss Burnette, Mr. Shannette and Miss Jones (later the wife of Senator John Connolly, a good friend)—understood and were patient. Also, I made friends, with some of whom I kept in touch for many years.

Meanwhile, life became more and more difficult at home, for these were the years of the Great Depression. My father's income fell sharply. At the age of thirteen, I took over a paper route from a neighbour who had started it, delivering newspapers that I picked up in Ottawa South to families living on the Bowesville Road. In the summer, by using my bicycle, I was able to extend delivery to many summer cottages at Hog's Back. After my tenth birthday, I spent every Saturday with my father (with time out to look after my papers), delivering eggs and chickens to families in Ottawa. We prepared everything in the morning, set out in early afternoon and frequently did not come home till after nine o'clock in the evening. Sundays were generally free (when I did not have to attend Sunday School) and so were some days in the summer when we did not have to clean out chicken pens or do other chores. We killed our own chickens and plucking them was no fun.

Even though we usually had a hired man, there was an endless amount of work to be done. My father was a mechanic, and did his own carpentry, roofing, plumbing and electrical work. He converted an old two-storey shed to a building in which he stored and partially raised baby chicks, hatched in the Petersime incubator in our basement, prior to selling them. In 1927 the building burned down. In 1930, the long single-storey henhouse burned. I suspect electrical problems were responsible. Despite his financial losses, my father re-built a better henhouse and in 1931 created a huge three-storey cement block uninsulated barn into which we moved. It was fine in the summer but the winters were indescribable.

In addition to the poultry business and the chick hatchery, we had a small retail store on the first floor of the cement block building, selling ice cream, chocolate bars and soft drinks. In front we had two gas pumps and also sold oil. For a time, my father also ran an ice business.

Looking back, I suspect that only the poultry business and chick hatchery made any money. Obviously, not one of the three sons in the family wanted to earn a living this way. The life was especially hard for Mother, who looked after the family (including the hired man), made the clothes for her sons and helped in all the businesses.

I graduated from Glebe in the spring of 1936. The guest speaker at our graduation ceremony was the Hon. C.D. Howe, minister of Transport. I was the valedictorian and talked about the mess the older generation had made of things, with the depression and threats of wars. It was our duty to do better. A trustee of the Board of Education, Mrs. Thorburn, congratulated me and predicted that some day I would be an MP. Having been named after the British prime minister, Lloyd George, there was no doubt in my mind that being an MP was what I wanted to do.

My mother also made sure that we did not neglect our schoolwork. My favourite subjects were mathematics, languages (Latin, French and Spanish), English and history. In fifth form I was one of three silver medallists in the school with a grade average of over ninety per cent, but when I applied to the University of Toronto, I was refused entrance. I was only fifteen years old. However, after repeating fifth form, I won a scholarship to University College.

THE UNIVERSITY OF TORONTO

That day in September 1936 when I boarded a train for Toronto will live in my memory till I die. A new and exciting life lay ahead. My scholarship provided me with free tuition and $300, enough money to pay my expenses for the year. My father's brother, Uncle John, met me at Union Station, and I stayed with my mother's sister, Aunt Lizzie, her daughter Annie James, whom we all called "Jimmie," and her husband, Gordon. They were kind beyond words.

University College was non-denominational and at that time received many graduates from Harbord Collegiate, not far from the campus. These sons and daughters of newly arrived immigrants included many brilliant and determined achievers who made a great contribution to Canada. The comedians Wayne and Shuster, for example, started their careers at Harbord and I knew them well. University College, as the oldest on campus, also attracted a share of graduates from Upper Canada College and other distinguished private schools.

My first year was designated Social and Philosophical Studies, combining political science and economics, sociology, psychology, history and philosophy. We registered in our particular specialties in second year. Some names still stand out in my memory—Professor Lorne Morgan in economic history, Professor Griffith Taylor in geography, Professor Brett in philosophy. Medieval and Renaissance history was taught by several individuals who made the invasions of Europe from the east and the story of the Renaissance and Reformation exciting and alive. A Pass Course in anthropology (as opposed to the other courses that were designated Honour Courses) was taught by Professor Steve Hart. We studied the fossil records of early mankind and their place in the theory of evolution. It was a great year and I earned first-class honours.

That summer, I returned home to work for my father, earning four dollars a week and my room and board. In September, I was short of money to pay my year's expenses and he gave me $70. We had some sharp words. My father was a short man, not much over five feet tall, with a violent temper that often exploded without warning. I resolved never again to spend more than a short visit at home.

A fellow student, Paul McGillicuddy, suggested that we share a room on Sherbourne Street, which we would have free in return for doing some chores, including looking after the furnace. Paul also had some other part-time work. Frankly, I don't think we did the work expected and were politely invited to leave at Christmas.

Paul was just a fair student, registered in Sociology, but was very active in extracurricular activities. We shared reporting for the undergraduate newspaper, *The Varsity*, and ran for various offices in the undergraduate Literary and Athletic Society. In his final year, Paul became president and the representative of University College on the campus-wide Students' Administrative Council. At the same time, I was elected literary director and speaker of the University College Parliament.

After graduation, Paul McGillicuddy enlisted in the RCAF. He became an air observer and served with a squadron of Boston Intruders. They were diverted to provide part of the aerial escort for the Dieppe Raid and his aircraft was shot down by an enemy fighter. Paul was wounded by a cannon shell and died in hospital in Littlehampton, after being pulled out of the sea. I interviewed the nurse who attended him when he died and reported back to his family in Canada. I also spoke to his pilot, a fellow called Buchanan from Ottawa, who was bitter that his aircraft, painted black for night intruder raids, had been diverted to a low-flying daylight operation and therefore was an easy target for enemy aircraft. Buchanan was lost on operations shortly afterwards. I named my older son after Paul.

It was through Paul that I met Harold Beveridge. The two of them wrote a brief on behalf of the Canadian Student Assembly for a system of national scholarships. Beveridge was brilliant but unstable—he worked hard, played hard and drank hard. One day I met him while having a snack in the Campus Coffee Shop and, by way of conversation, mentioned that I had a date with a young freshie we both knew. He said that he had a date also and suggested we get together to make a foursome. I was not keen—Harold's breath smelled of alcohol and I did not always approve of his choice of girlfriends. Mistakenly, I humoured him, suggesting that he call me at my room. Not hearing further from him, I proceeded to Margaret's home only to be met at the door by her frosty father demanding to know what I had planned for the evening. It turned out that Harold had called her home and asked for Lloyd. Lloyd was also her father's name! The details of the conversation were not repeated, but I gather it was some time before Harold discovered which Lloyd he was talking to! I do not believe I was ever able to explain that I was a truly innocent party to Harold's schemes.

The Canadian Student Assembly was planning a convention in Ste.-Anne-de-Bellevue, Quebec, for January of 1940 and Harold and I were on the committee. One night I was travelling north on a Yonge Street streetcar, only to be joined by Harold in his usual state of inebriation. He asked me to make sure he got off at the stop for the Davisville bus. Why? I shuddered when he explained that he had a date with Iris Matthews, who also worked on the CSA committee. I had the impression that Iris came from a distinguished family of Baptist teetotallers.

The next morning, curious to know how his date had turned out, I called on Harold in his room on St. Charles Street. He was in a vile mood. It seems that he was still leaning on the doorbell when the front door was opened. He entered, took off his coat, but dropped a mickey flask from his coat pocket, which broke on the floor. He was promptly ejected.

Harold Beveridge had a curious career. After the war, I met him briefly while he was lecturing with the Workers Educational Association in Toronto. He had married a fine girl of Finnish origin from Northern Ontario and they had a son, but the marriage broke up. Rumour maintained he had gone pub-crawling one evening with his small son and left him behind in one of the bars, which would certainly be enough to discourage any mother. Harold was reported to have emigrated to Czechoslovakia for some kind of employment, although to my knowledge he was not a communist. My friend Don Blackley, then a professor of history in Edmonton, met him on the streets of London during one of his sabbatical years. Harold was most secretive about his activities. I suspect he died of alcoholism and is buried somewhere in Central Europe.

Harold was not the type of person to choose to live in a university residence, but I wanted to do so and at Christmas 1937 I entered the newly established Campus Co-operative Residence.[3] It occupied the back part of a huge old residence on St. George Street, owned by Victoria College. While there were students from all faculties, most were registered in Arts and nearly all of these in Victoria College. Several went on to be ordained as ministers of the United Church. Each resident had to do so many hours of work per week cleaning, cooking or washing up and the quality of the work was zealously inspected by a committee. I recall that room and board cost us four dollars a week! Mrs. Mimms, our housekeeper, was a warm, caring person with a faculty for resolving problems, which she had been obliged to learn to do as a widow with a family.

The "Co-op" taught me a great deal. There were the usual pranks. One night we collected all the alarm clocks we could find and hid them in Rowell Bowles' room, set for 2:30 a.m., 3:00, 3:30, and so on, at half-hour intervals.

With rare exceptions, the members were hard working and clean living. Two senior medical students, Harvey Hamilton and George Nicholson, were natural leaders. Campbell Dowd from Ottawa took an Arts degree before his MD and practised as a surgeon in the state of Washington. Art Dayfoot became a missionary in the Caribbean and raised a family of six.

---

[3] Some fifty years later, the Co-op held a reunion and it was a pleasure to meet old friends. Now co-educational, it has expanded to several houses and owns its own properties.

Art Fox, also from Ottawa, became a professor of Spanish at Queen's University.

In this period, I grew physically and socially, but my grades suffered. However, I still managed to stand near the top of second-class honours in my second, third and fourth years. Extracurricular activities included Hart House debates, the Social Problems Club and left-wing politics. Mr. Thoms at high school had introduced me to Marxism, and had taken me to meet Norman Bethune, the Canadian doctor who served on the Republican side in the Spanish Civil War and later went to China where he died and is revered as a martyr. In the thirties, there were many Marxist sympathisers on all university campuses. Residents of the Co-op, however, were nearly all supporters of the Co-operative Commonwealth Federation, the predecessor of the New Democratic Party. I can recall visits from Agnes Macphail, Canada's first woman MP, and M.J. Coldwell, the national leader of the CCF. Elsewhere on campus, Trotskyites and Stalinists pursued their relentless vendettas. I was attracted by the Stalinists and, looking back, wonder how anyone could have swallowed the nonsense about Stalin's purges that we repeated.

In the summers of 1938 and 1939, I obtained employment as a clerk with the Department of Education in Toronto. In those days, all students wrote examinations for Middle and Upper School subjects and the papers were marked by teachers hired for the purpose. Clerks were required to record marks, deliver the papers for marking and gather them for storage afterwards. In my second summer, I was the timekeeper for the examiners and responsible for their expense accounts. One day, reviewing the files, I was horrified to discover that I had demanded from a middle-aged spinster a receipt for her "birth while travelling on the train." It was, of course, normal to require a receipt for a "berth." To my relief, nothing came of it.

This was my introduction to the world of political patronage. Each member of the provincial legislature was given a quota for summer jobs. A classmate tipped me off that all I had to do was to write to my local member and ask him, since it was unlikely that as the representative of Gloucester Township, he would have many other requests. My father was a well-known Conservative and it worked.

In the fall of 1939, Hitler's panzers marched into Poland and World War II began. The mood on the campus slowly changed. Professor Harold Innis (a classmate of Mr. Thoms, my old high school teacher) gave us unforgettable (but sometimes incomprehensible) lectures on communications, which Marshall McLuhan later credited with inspiring his research. Vincent Bladen gave a course on economic theory with extended lectures on Adam Smith. Professor Brough Macpherson, who had studied under Harold Laski in England, taught Political Science. We were exposed to some of the most brilliant minds in academia but they were approachable, sympathetic and capable of inspiring their students.

Lloyd, 1940

MONTREAL

In May of 1940, blessed with a Bachelor of Arts, substantial debts, and a desire to see more of the world, I accepted a job with Canadian Industries Limited in Montreal. My pay of $100 a month was above the average of our class—some received as little as $65. Officially, my job was described as Clerk, Sales Statistics Department, General Chemicals Division. Our office was in CIL House, Beaver Hall Hill. I prepared market studies for specific chemicals, based on reports from salesmen in the field and other sources, all of which were punched onto cards. They were stored in a large room and sorted by a Hollerith machine—a huge cumbersome predecessor of a modern computer.

This period of my life brings back only pleasant memories. I liked the people with whom I worked, but did not really want to spend the rest of my life analysing markets for chemicals. As the result of a crush I had on one of the secretaries, the supervisor called me into his office to say that I should either cease dating Miss Black or he would have her transferred. (She did not want to be transferred, so that ended the matter.) Still, I saved enough money to pay off my debts and help my younger brother Jack, who was entering his freshman year at Toronto.[4]

At first, I roomed with Aunt Ada in Notre Dame de Grace in the west end of Montreal. This was far from work and far from the social life downtown. Many of my friends lived in a fabulous rooming house run by a Swiss family at 3480 Durocher Street. Two old houses were joined to accommodate some thirty roomers, including two fellow graduates from Toronto also working at CIL. I joined them, registered for night classes at Sir George Williams College (now part of Concordia University), and

[4] Shortly after the war broke out, my father abandoned the poultry business and got a job in his old trade as a machinist. After finishing high school, Jack worked with my father in the same shop. In the fall of 1940, he began his studies at the University of Toronto with assistance from myself and younger brother Lyle. My father, as a result of his quarrels with me, strongly opposed Jack's further education. Jack eventually became a professor of Food Sciences at the University of Massachusetts in Amherst, Mass., and enjoyed a distinguished career. Lyle trained as a machinist and later supervised a maintenance section for the National Research Council.

enjoyed the life of a young single man with some money in his pocket for the first time. I can remember one night, after a dance at the college, offering to see a young lady home, assuming that she lived in the west end. To my shock, she lived in Pointe aux Trembles in the extreme east end. Not able to afford a taxi, I relied on the street cars and arrived back at Aunt Ada's in time to shave, wash and leave for work. Needless to say, that romance ended promptly.

At this time, Tom Fairley, the son of Professor Barker Fairley of the German Department at University College, became a close friend. Tom, who had graduated at the same time as myself, worked for the Canadian Press. We spent many pleasant evenings together, and I remember him introducing me to two well-known hangouts for the younger set in Montreal—a downtown pub called Mother Martins and a night club called Rockhead's Paradise.

France had fallen in 1940 and, in the fall of 1941, Hitler invaded Russia. Many were enlisting. Tom, who had trained with the Canadian Officers Training Corps at university, accepted a commission in the army. I was attracted to the air force. At that time the government issued a general appeal for young men with good educational backgrounds to train as radar mechanics with the Royal Air Force. I reported to the recruiting depot, and underwent a physical examination. I have, since birth, had extremely low blood pressure and the medical examiner checked his reading three times, then announced: "Under no circumstances would I let you fly."

That settled the matter. I enlisted for training as a radar mechanic.

THE RCAF

New recruits were sent to Manning Depot in Toronto, since for some reason the depot in Quebec was closed temporarily. This was fortunate for me, since I had family and many friends there. Also, I started to see a girl I had known (but not dated) as an undergraduate, and who later became my wife. She was employed as a service representative with Bell Telephone and later told friends that I was attracted because I could call her without having to pay a nickel for a phone call!

We were housed in the buildings of the Toronto Exhibition Grounds. At night we slept in bunk beds in the old sheep-pen, to be awakened at six o'clock every morning for seven o'clock parade and inspection. Woe betide anyone whose brass buttons were not polished or was caught unshaven or needing a haircut. Pete Landry in the bunk above me was an artist: he laid out his clothes in a sequence before retiring so that he could sleep late. In one continuous smooth motion, he would slide into his clothes and emerge ready for parade when he jumped into his boots on the floor.

This was six weeks before Pearl Harbor and many Americans were enlisting with us. When lights were turned out at night, men would shout: "Who is from Virginia? Who is from the Carolinas?" It seemed that every state in the USA was represented, but by far the most frequent was: "Who's from Texas?"

During the day we drilled in squads, back and forth as far as the Tip Top Tailors building. We received shots to inoculate us against lord knows what, clothing and a kit bag to hold all the items we had to account for. We could buy soft drinks, chocolate and other items in the canteen, where the juke box seemed to be always playing *You Are My Sunshine*. While I still love the tune, I always think of the Manning Depot canteen when I hear it.

In late November, I was posted to the University of Toronto for a three-month course offered by the Physics Department. We were taught the basic principles of energy, the theory of alternating and direct currents, and the transmission of radio waves. In high school, I had opted for languages ahead of science and this was an opportunity to make up for some gaps in my education. The classroom work was easy, but when it came to building working models of radio receivers, I found I did not have the same facility for working with tools that others had.

I can still remember December 7, 1941, when I heard on the radio the news of the attack on Pearl Harbor. I was waiting for Uncle Sam and Aunt Vie to pick me up for a dinner at their home. This came as a brutal shock and we all wondered how it would affect the war.

Early in 1942, I was posted to the radar school at Clinton, Ontario, and assigned to the class known as CAN 34. The RCAF had agreed to supply the RAF with 5,000 (later the number was increased to 5,800) trained mechanics to staff its radar installations in the air, on ships and on the ground, in all theatres of war. A few had gone overseas before the station was built, but more than eighty per cent trained at Clinton.

Clinton was originally staffed by RAF personnel but, by the time I arrived, the commanding officer, as well as most of the staff, were Canadian. We were, however, introduced to some RAF practices that were hard to accept. For instance, each airman was issued with his own knife, fork and spoon (known as our "irons"), which we were supposed to carry with us for use at every meal. Outside the mess hall was a tank with live steam fed through it, where we were supposed to wash our irons after every meal. On top of the tank, a layer of scum usually formed and many of us were reluctant to wash our irons in the tank, preferring to do so in barracks. On occasion a sergeant was posted to make sure we followed the proper procedure and to place us on charge if we did not.

The staff in the mess hall were from the RAF, and they were accustomed to different rations than the usual Canadian issue. They did not know what to do with peanut butter and let it pile up in stores. They even boiled macaroni in a light sugar sauce and served it as a dessert! Most of us did not believe that the staff on this particular station observed the proper standards of cleanliness.

Matters came to a head when a group of Americans were posted to Clinton for training. After twenty-four hours, they were complaining to their superiors, their families, their congressmen. Two limousines from Ottawa with high-ranking medical officers made their way to the Airmen's Mess and condemned it on the spot. New messing staff were transferred from Canadian stations and conditions improved immensely. The system of irons continued but the tank was kept clean.

Ten per cent of the graduates from Clinton were commissioned, but I was not. In the spring of 1942, I sailed from Halifax aboard the *Letitia*, a Cunard liner converted to a troopship, on which my mother had sailed to England ten years previously for her only visit home since she had emigrated to Canada.

We were part of a convoy, with destroyer escorts, and the *Letitia* was crowded beyond belief. At night, we slept in the dining room, with one level in sleeping bags below the tables, one on the tables, and a third in hammocks above the tables. The ones who bedded down early had to wait until the others got up before they could go to the washrooms. The food was revolting. To this day, I associate kippers with the partially cooked ones served to us on that trip.

In mid-Atlantic, submarines attacked our convoy. We could see depth charges going off in the distance and the destroyers altering course to chase their targets. To the best of my knowledge, no ships in the convoy were lost, although we could never be sure how many ships were travelling with us. If we had been hit at night while bedded down, the losses would have been horrendous.

We landed at Greenock, in Scotland, and then travelled by rail to Hastings on the south coast of England. After a few days, we were moved to Bournemouth. I learned later that this was to clear Hastings as one of the ports for launching the Dieppe Raid. From Bournemouth, I was posted to 96 Squadron, RAF, at Wrexham in North Wales.

Our squadron used Beaufighters to combat enemy raids at night. In particular, its assignment was to protect Birmingham, Leamington and Coventry. Coventry had already been badly hit, but there were still industrial installations functioning. Later, we were moved to Honiley in Warwickshire.

Graduates from Clinton were assigned usually to one of three branches of radar (at that time called Range-Direction Finders, or RDF for short). I worked with Aircraft Interception (AI). Others were assigned to Aircraft to Surface Vessels (ASV). The third category was a land-based system for early warnings on enemy raids, Chain Home (CH), which proved invaluable in the defence of Malta. All of us were expected to service a device for distinguishing friendly from enemy aircraft, called Identification: Friend or Foe (IFF). Numerous other systems, each with its own acronym, were developed later.

Radar installations and radar equipment were guarded most carefully, and assigned the highest degree of security. We were instructed not to discuss our work with anyone not in our trade, not even fellow airmen in the barracks. If you removed unserviceable equipment from an aircraft, it was your responsibility to stay with it until it was stored in a secure area.

Canadians were simply assigned as needed to RAF installations, and treated on the same basis as other RAF personnel.[5]

This created some problems. RAF mechanics had more experience, and occupied all the NCO and officer positions. The RAF had not placed the same level of education as a requirement for radar, and it was hard for many Canadians to take orders from NCOs they did not respect. Our scale of pay was higher, but we could not draw it on the station, only in the deferred pay accounts kept at Lincoln's Inn Fields in London. Our uniforms and shoulder badges[6] were different, and the Canadian badge for LAC (Leading Aircraftsman, really first-class private) did not have the square-patch background of the RAF.

The Australians had solved these problems by making their uniforms a different colour, dark blue. No one expected Australians to be like the RAF, and service policemen left them alone. Canadians, however, were subject to continual harassment on some squadrons. Some of my friends simply gave up, and put on RAF uniforms with a Canada badge on the shoulder. RAF policemen did not object to this, conceding the same privileges to all colonials from Antigua, Dar-es-Salaam, and the other outposts of the Empire.

One night I was on duty during an alert and had to replace the transmitter on an aircraft. I stayed with it, waiting for a lorry to come at dawn to take it to security in the workshop. As we were loading it, the squadron leader in charge of "B" Flight approached on a bicycle. I cannot conceive what was on his mind, but he was belligerent and hostile. Did he think we were engaged in some kind of black market operation?

"What is the purpose of this trip?" he demanded of the driver. We were stunned, but the driver, a small, slight man, was a match for him.

In a slow, deliberate manner, he reached down, pulled out some papers and read: "Orders, signed by Flying Officer Laidlaw. Proceed to end of north runway, meet LAC Francis, pick up equipment and take to security workshop, sir."

"How many miles has this vehicle been driven this morning?" Again, in the slow, deliberate fashion, he replied: "0600 hours. Speedometer reading: 12345. Present reading: 12347. Two miles, sir."

Since he was getting nowhere with the driver, he turned to me and pointed to my LAC insignia. "Why have you defaced your rank? Take that bastard thing you have on your arm off and put up a proper square badge."

---

5 Prime Minister Pearson described the determination of the Canadian government to create fighting units in all three services under Canadian command, in contrast to the experience of the First World War: "In the early months, however, it was difficult to remove the impression that we were once more supplying men and formations for 'imperial' forces under British management . . . "
Mike: The Memoirs of the Right Honourable Lester B. Pearson, Volume I, The New American Library of Canada Limited, 1973, p. 146.

6 The RAF called the symbol on their shoulder badges an eagle, but many of us called ours an albatross.

He then proceeded to reprimand me in a loud voice, threatening to put me on charge, and left. I was devastated and returned to barracks. There were perhaps six Canadians on our squadron, including a man who would qualify as the original Philadelphia lawyer, Frank Russell. Frank announced that the situation called for his talents.

Frank's memorandum to RCAF Liaison in London deserves a place in the annals of literature. We all signed it. He recounted how six lonely Canadians on 96 Squadron, without even their own NCO, had been systematically persecuted. In particular, LAC Francis, in the presence of witnesses, had been ordered by Squadron Leader Young to remove his "bastard" LAC badge and replace it with a square patch RAF issue. LAC Francis was publicly reprimanded and threatened with being placed on charge for the sole crime of wearing Canadian-issue uniform and insignia, which he continued to do proudly. Frank went on to recite the time and place of a series of other incidents, where the service police took exception to Canadian uniforms.

It happened that I was to go on leave shortly afterwards, and the commanding officer called every Canadian in for an interview. On Russell's advice, each one gave his name, rank and regimental number, and invoked the Geneva Convention on prisoners of war, refusing to answer any further questions. (Russell argued that, since we had been ordered to remove our Canadian uniforms, we had grounds for arguing that we had been treated as enemies.)

Nothing happened. None of us was questioned again. Squadron Leader Young was posted to another squadron. All of a sudden, the service police left us alone.

Twenty years later, when I was the deputy mayor of Ottawa, and attending a reception at the British High Commission, I learned that a new military attaché had arrived, Air Commodore Burns. Was he the former commanding officer of 96 Squadron? I asked. Yes. I would very much like to meet him, I told the social secretary.

Air Commodore Burns invited my wife and myself to dinner.

Lloyd wearing badge of radar mechanic and leading aircraftsman (LAC) rank, 1942

While the entrée was being served, I asked: "Just what did you do with Squadron Leader Young at Wrexham?" The response was slow. He stopped, looked at me and asked: "Were you one of those damned Canadians?"

On learning that I was, he went on. "I received a screaming communication from RCAF Liaison. What were we doing with our Canadians? I called all of you into my office but none of you would answer any questions. Half a dozen men do not act like that without some reason. I called in the service police and found out about the problems with your insignia and told them to leave you alone. Then I checked out Young. He had not been with my squadron long but he was a bastard, who tried to log his night flying at three o'clock in the afternoon. I got rid of him. That seemed to end the matter." If Frank Russell is still alive, I hope he reads this.

Years later, I was part of a delegation of Canadian MPs attending a conference sponsored by the North Atlantic Treaty Organization in London. Seated beside me at the dinner table was the wife of a senior RAF officer. She remarked that it was a pity that Canada, under Paul Hellyer's guidance, had abandoned its blue uniform for air force personnel. She thought it would be just fine if all Commonwealth forces used the same colour. I told her of my experience, adding I was determined that Canadians would have a uniform markedly different from that of the RAF, even if it had to have pink polka dots on it!

Although life on 96 Squadron improved after Young's departure, working conditions remained difficult. For some six months, I worked a shift of twenty-four hours on, followed by twenty-four off. Two of us were on each shift. It was not bad if you had no alert, since we could take turns sleeping. If there was an alert, however, you could be exhausted when your shift was over. We were the only ground trade working such hours, possibly because of the shortage of radar mechanics.

One night, after an alert, I was coming off at about 7:30 a.m., looking and feeling like the wrath of God. A new warrant officer in charge of maintenance, noting my Canadian insignia, caught me.

"Why were you not on daily parade at 7:00 a.m.?" he asked.

"Special signals, sir, we are exempt," I replied.

"We will see about that."

The next morning, a paragraph in Daily Routine Orders simply stated that Special Signals were to report every morning for parade at 7:00 a.m.

One of our men, Johnny Murphy, was a former steelworkers' union steward from North Sydney, Nova Scotia. "Do you know anything about this, Francis?" he asked. I told him what had happened. "Well, as they say, you laid an egg. But we had to deal with bastards like that in the steel mill."

Murphy was an experienced and very capable mechanic whom I came to like very much. You crossed him at your peril. He had been placed in charge of a shift doing regular maintenance and inspection of aircraft, after specified hours of flying, in the service area that we called "echelon."

Murphy's rank was the same as the rest of us, namely LAC, but he was generally recognized as the leader of his group and later deservedly received his commission.

The RAF had elaborate manuals specifying what you did after fifty hours of flying time, after one hundred hours, and so on. If we had done everything according to the book, we would have needed four times as many men. Murphy pulled out the book.

"Francis, break the seal on the transmitting aerial on that aircraft and look at it," he ordered. One of the things that I had learned was that you never, never ever broke a good seal on a transmitting aerial, since it was so hard to re-establish. "But, Murph . . ." "You heard me. That's what the manual says."

By the end of the second day, Murphy had five aircraft out of operations and Flying Officer Laidlaw came over to find out what was going on. Every available man in our unit was working like a Canadian beaver. Laidlaw was no fool and he and Murphy understood each other.

"Murphy, please tell me what the hell is really going on here."

"Too much work, sir, I haven't enough men."

"You seemed to get along well enough up to this point. What has happened?"

"That was before we had to re-organize all of our work schedules, sir."

"Why did you have to do that?"

"For one thing, every one of our men now has to report at 7:00 a.m. for daily parade, sir. I had to pull all of our men off work for an hour-and-a-half this morning."

Laidlaw got the point. The next morning a short item appeared in Daily Routine Orders, to the effect that Special Signals was excused from daily parade at 7:00 a.m. Two days later, all of the aircraft were operational again. I shudder to think of what might have happened if Laidlaw had not known how to handle Murphy, or if we had had an enemy raid.

On the whole, I enjoyed life on the squadron and made friends. One in particular, a Welshman named Eiron Rees, invited me to his home in Newport, Monmouthshire, a county detached from Wales by Edward I centuries ago but still claimed by the Welsh. The countryside was new and different, and everywhere we went people welcomed us. The warmth of their hospitality made up for the institutional frictions between RAF and RCAF, which we learned to take in our stride. When working with Welsh tradesmen in echelon, there was always a tune being carried. You may not have been able to see who was singing, but you could always hear them.

The airdrome at Wrexham kept sinking and had to be repaired constantly. We were told that mining tunnels existed below the runways where a number of miners had been entombed in a cave-in some decades before. Excursions to the nearby village of Llangollen, and north by rail to Llandudno on the coast, provided welcome diversions. The city of Wrexham had some good pubs, but that was all you could say for it.

Eventually, the airfield was abandoned and we were moved to Honiley in Warwickshire.

Honiley had much better runways and was a bigger facility. The countryside was totally different. On my bicycle, I could travel to Stratford-on-Avon, Coventry, the village of Knowle on the way to Birmingham and, not least, Kenilworth Castle. Climbing on the old keep, the crumbling walls and tower, and gazing over the surrounding fields, would have excited the imagination of any young man from the New World. Not far from the camp, I discovered a small chapel built in the time of the Crusades, carefully maintained for regular services.

My mother's home in the old village of Knutsford was no doubt typical of many in the Midlands, but was special to me when I visited Aunt Maggie's tobacconist shop, the farm where Aunt Louie lived, and especially the churchyard where so many of my mother's family are buried.

Every Canadian spent as many leaves as possible in London, visiting the Beaver Club, strolling in front of Buckingham Palace and in Hyde Park. Yes, we went to the Windmill Theatre where for the first time I saw a live nude woman on stage, standing perfectly still as required by the authorities at the time. (Times have really changed.)

At this time, the Allied air forces were building up their massive bombing offensive on German cities. After a raid, strange aircraft from other squadrons cluttered our runways. Hit by enemy anti-aircraft fire, they were guided to the most convenient aerodrome, and searchlights crossed in the sky. This use of searchlights in the blackout was dangerous since it offered an easy target for enemy intruders, but our Beaufighters were on guard and the German air force was suffering from its losses of trained pilots.

The lack of opportunities for promotion had a serious effect on morale of many Canadians. I have since learned that "Chubby" Power, the minister for Air in the Canadian cabinet, had a son in radar who kept his father informed. Chubby established a "shadow roster" promoting Canadians in the same proportions as the RAF personnel, but we could not put up our stripes until we returned to Canada. Chubby also insisted that quotas of Canadians be commissioned.[7]

In the summer of 1942, I heard that low blood pressure no longer presented an impediment for aircrew and volunteered for training. To my delight, I was accepted. In the days of unpressurized aircraft, low blood pressure was, if anything, an asset. While flying I felt good and was alert. On landing, however, it was an effort to get to my bunk to sleep it off.

Before returning to Canada, I had two short postings with two squadrons using Mosquito aircraft, a new type of night fighter with a plywood skin, many of which were built in Canada. At Scorton in Yorkshire we were in the midst of a bomber group and every afternoon we

[7] I am indebted to Mr. Robert Linden, who is writing a book on Canadian radar mechanics, for this information. Linden, using Canadian laws on access to information, has uncovered many of the blunt telegrams sent from Canada.

heard the drone of bombers climbing in circles to reach their desired height before crossing the coast to reach their targets on the continent. At Bradwell Bay in Essex, we were right on the coast, not far from occupied France. As protection from enemy surprise raiding parties, we slept with loaded Sten guns beside us, and never strayed far from our weapons.

The memory of one mechanic with whom I shared a shift has bothered me ever since. A Dutchman named Smals was anti-Semitic and his attitude on many things bothered me. His widowed mother had married a Britisher and made her home in the south of England. Smals was a keen amateur radio operator and boasted of his transmission facilities in his mother's home. One day he made reference to visiting Nuremberg, Germany, and I asked if a Hitler Youth rally was taking place at the time. His face turned ashen and he changed the subject. It seemed to me that he went out of his way to cultivate my friendship from that point. Was he a Nazi sympathiser? Did he transmit information to the enemy? I will never know.

In September 1943, I returned to Canada for aircrew training aboard the *Queen Elizabeth*. What a contrast! This time the ship was almost empty and we had private rooms. The big liner was fast and travelled without escort. Almost immediately on arrival, I was posted to Initial Training School in Toronto, in the old normal school on Jarvis Street.

On December 23, 1943, Margery Miller and I were married in Hart House Chapel on the university campus. Margery's cousin, Marion, and her engineer husband, Squadron Leader Bob Beale, held a reception for us and Aunt Vie baked the wedding cake.

Margery's father had been born in Dunnville, Ontario, and her paternal grandfather in the Canton of Zug, Switzerland. After service in the Boer War, her father had taken up a land grant in Alberta and late in life married Florence Weir of Hamilton. Florence was 45 when Margery was born, and she died of a ruptured appendix when her only child was nine. From that time on, Margery was raised by two childless aunts in Dunnville. I had met her when we were both undergraduates at Toronto, but we did not date until after she had broken a long-time relationship with a medical student from Dunnville, and I had broken one with a girl I had known since high school in Ottawa. We enjoyed a superb partnership that was only terminated by her death nearly forty-six years later.

Margery and I rented an apartment in Toronto while I attended Initial Training School and later Air Navigation School at nearby Malton. Air Navigation was much more to my taste than radar. The difference could be described as white collar work versus blue collar. The theory of radio transmission was not difficult, but repairing equipment using tools in a workshop did not come easily or quickly to me. In June 1944, I graduated, was immediately commissioned and posted as an instructor to No. 1 Central Navigation School, Rivers, Manitoba.

The Commonwealth Air Training Plan was in full swing, turning out a steady stream of pilots, navigators, gunners, bomb aimers, and all other required skills. A total of 131,000 aircrew were trained over four years, of

Lloyd wearing air navigator's badge, 1944

whom 18,000 were killed in action and 800 in accidents. Most of my graduating class saw service but later classes became part of an accumulating backlog and did not. In contrast, I have since learned, the enemy, both in Europe and the Pacific, could not replenish their skilled aircrews as the war progressed. Their superbly trained crews gave them an advantage early in the war, but it was a different story at the end of hostilities.

The choice of Rivers as site for a training camp was a good one. It enjoyed clear days, with very little precipitation, although we did have to wash out flying when temperatures exceeded thirty below. I have used a marine sextant on the prairie horizon with zero error. The town of Rivers, some four miles away, offered some off-base private accommodation for married personnel and indeed Margery left her job with Bell Canada to be with me in 1945 when she was pregnant with our son Paul. I will never forget how blue the prairie was when the wild crocuses emerged in the spring or how impressive appeared the valley of the Assiniboine some six miles to the south, as we cycled across it.

Social life on the base more than compensated for our isolation on the prairie. In addition to the parties in the mess and the poker games in the officers' quarters, were the discussions with men (and a few women) from all walks of life—geologists, engineers, teachers, foresters, you name it. I became editor of the station magazine, succeeding its founder, Dave Ritchie. *MTB*, short for the navigators' jargon of "message to base," was published once a month and had quite a reputation in Western Command.[8] Ted Mann, a fellow graduate of Toronto, later ordained as an Anglican minister, was my assistant. Doug "Ozzie" Wright, our cartoonist, and Don Aiken, our station poet, both distinguished themselves after discharge.

Events moved rapidly in July 1945. Our son Paul was born. The war in Europe collapsed. I was posted to a Ventura squadron base at Summerside,

[8] Thanks to the Rev. Bill Bates, a pilot at Rivers later also ordained as an Anglican minister, all of the issues of *MTB* were collected and bound. Dave Ritchie, Bill Bates and I participated in a November 1996 ceremony presenting a bound copy to the Commonwealth Air Museum in Brandon, Manitoba.

PEI. Patrols over the Atlantic were suspended and we were put on notice of posting to the Pacific Theatre. But then the atom bombs on Hiroshima and Nagasaki changed everything.

BACK TO UNIVERSITY

In October 1945, I enrolled as a graduate student in Economics at the University of Toronto. While overseas, I had debated going to law school and to this day cannot say why I chose graduate work, but I have never regretted it.

Professor Vincent Bladen, who supervised my M.A., was a good friend as well as a mentor. His main interest was economic theory, but in the immediate post-war period he established an Institute of Industrial Relations. The Veterans Charter provided us with basic income but I needed more than that to support a wife and small child. Professor Bladen found work for me with university extension classes and his institute.

During the academic year 1945-1946, the university was swamped with huge classes of returning veterans. Professor Innis's seminar on communications attracted large numbers. While he gave me gave me good marks on my papers, I must confess that I had difficulty understanding what he was saying at times. Still he was challenging, as was Professor Edgar McInnis of the Department of History. Among the veterans were many who went on in business (a vice-president of a bank), in academic posts (president of a Canadian university) and, not least, in the public service of Canada. Hu Harries became an international expert on energy and pipelines and later dean of a school of business and, still later, member of Parliament for Edmonton. Frank Genovese became Dean of Arts at Babson College in Wellesley, Massachusetts, and a close friend over the years.

Early in 1946, I wrote a general examination for the Department of External Affairs. In the spring, I was called for an interview in Ottawa but declined. By this time I had decided that, after completing my Master of Arts, I would pursue doctoral studies at a university in the United States. Professor Lorne Morgan arranged a fellowship at the University of California in Berkley, but I was attracted to Wisconsin, largely on the advice of Professor Harold Logan. Wisconsin was the home of Professor John R. Commons, and was well known for labour economics. To my delight, on the recommendations of Professors Bladen and Logan, Wisconsin offered fellowships to Frank Genovese and myself. We both accepted.

Wisconsin, like Toronto, was doing its best to cope with the large numbers of returning veterans. The only suitable accommodation we could find was fifteen miles from campus, on the second floor of a farmhouse, which we shared with Baldur and Helen Kristjansson, Canadians from Manitoba, who also had a small son. For a time, Baldur's brother Kristjan lived with us. I bought a second-hand car and we shared commuting. The owners of the farm, Wayne and Doris Weidemann, also had two small children. Wayne was a part-time preacher, which was more to his interest than farming. In our second year at Wisconsin, the Kristjanssons found accommodation in Madison, and Margery and I rented a basement apartment in the village of Sun Prairie, about eight miles from campus.

Professor John R. Commons, the father of Wisconsin's studies in institutional economics, had died the year before we came to Madison. His students included Professor Edwin Witte, under whom I did my thesis, and Selig Perlman, who had co-authored studies on the history of trade unions in the United States and written a brilliant little book entitled *A Theory of the Labour Movement*. Professor Paul Ellsworth taught international trade, Walter Morton and Martin Bronfenbrenner, economic theory. For my minor field of study, I spent one semester in the law school, with courses in labour law, contracts, and a course called "Law in Society," tracing the evolution of workmen's compensation in the state. Under the leadership of the Lafolletts, Wisconsin had been a leader in social legislation.

The introductory course in economics for undergraduates was taught by Professor William H. Kiekhofer, a disciple of the very orthodox Austrian School. A clear, well organized speaker, he gave his polished lectures in a huge lecture hall. Students were assigned to smaller groups conducted by us, the graduate assistants. We used Kiekhofer's own textbook, which was one of the best sellers of its kind at the time and no doubt provided him with good royalties. He deserved credit for the way he was able to supervise and make sure that the whole operation ran smoothly.

Other members of the department, however, could scarcely conceal their contempt for the failure of Kiekhofer to keep up with modern economic theory. Clearly, he had never read *Keynes' General Theory of Employment, Interest and Money*. In the fall of 1946 Walter Morton was beginning to call himself a post-Keynesian. While he lacked Kiekhofer's discipline and work habits, his seminars were stimulating. Morton had no patience with ivory-tower economists who could spout solutions for the problems of the world but declare that it was the responsibility of others, such as politicians, to implement them.

One day Morton announced that he had a solution to the world's food problems. "Feed them sand."

"But no one can eat sand."

"That is a problem for the nutritionists, not the economists," he replied, with heavy sarcasm.

In my second year, I became a teaching assistant to Professor Selig Perlman who taught a general course on the history of labour organizations. Born in czarist Russia, he lectured on medieval guilds, the structure of Russian villages (the Mir) and the miserable conditions that the industrial revolution imposed on workers in the United Kingdom. Out of all this he had developed a theory that workers in a modern state formed unions, not to change society and transform it into utopia, but simply to control their jobs. In earlier times custom and social tradition had done this for them. It followed, according to Perlman, that unions had to beware of intellectuals constantly striving to divert them to other objectives. This explained the innate conservatism of trade unionism in America, focussing on job consciousness and repudiating (with a few brief and ignominious exceptions) socialism, anarchism and other utopian doctrines. Professor Perlman's views made a lasting impression on me, particularly in the light of my earlier flirtation with Stalinists on the University of Toronto campus. The Marxist concept, based on its so-called scientific interpretation of history, of a class-conscious proletariat rising to destroy the chains imposed by its capitalist masters, was a gross and tragic illusion.

Marxism, however, continues to fascinate some intellectuals, due to the sheer magnitude and scope of its pretensions. Starting with the proposition that history can be explained in economic terms by understanding man's organization and technique for getting a living, it goes on to encompass a Hegelian dialectic and a labour theory of value. Karl Marx's book, *Das Kapital*, is still prescribed reading for students of economic theory. For all his brilliance, Marx was still a prophet who led millions of people astray.

For my doctoral thesis, I chose the subject of national emergency strikes, under the direction of Professor Witte. Professor Edwin Witte had been for many years Director of the State Legislative Reference Library in Madison, Wisconsin. In this capacity, he became a skilled legislative draftsman, as the State of Wisconsin in those years pioneered social legislation. In addition he developed an incredible knowledge of the administration of public welfare programs. In 1935 he was named chairman of an advisory committee of Congress responsible for drafting the *Social Security Act*, one of the most important pieces of legislation to survive the New Deal of Franklin Delano Roosevelt. During World War II he served as a member of the War Labour Board.

Using the powers conferred on the federal authority in wartime, governments in both Canada and the United States had attempted to resolve strikes paralysing broad sectors of the economy by seizing the companies involved. Usually the union leaders accepted this action as a good face-saving excuse to get back to work. I tried to examine, as best I could, how companies responded when they were returned to private ownership and concluded that seizures had not really had much effect. In a few instances, the strikes continued in spite of the government's action. This merely exposed, as Professor Witte frequently pointed out, the essential weakness of governments in a free society to deal with such problems. When the parties involved have made up their minds not to make concessions, the public must suffer until one side or the other yields. I spent some time gathering information on case histories of strikes, and did not receive my Doctor of Philosophy until 1955.

Wisconsin, like Toronto, was a place to make friends with fellow students. Many went on to brilliant careers in university, foreign service, and at least two took employment with the public service in Canada. At many different times and places, I have met fellow students from this period. Years later, when attending an international conference in Sanaa, North Yemen, I discovered that I had shared classes with the Arab Secretary of the Gulf Association of Petroleum Exporting countries.

The spring of 1948 was a great time to seek employment. Post-war classes of veterans abounded, and I had job offers from Grinnell College in Iowa, the University of Maine, and no doubt could have had others had I pursued them. The University of Buffalo, however, made an offer I could not refuse—to lecture in the Faculty of Arts and School of Business. The Dean of Business was Harold Somers, brother of a classmate at Toronto killed in the war. Also, Buffalo was only forty miles from Margery's childhood home in Dunnville, where her two aging aunts still lived. Margery never pressed the point, but I knew she was pleased.

THE UNIVERSITY OF BUFFALO

We arrived in Buffalo in August 1948 and stayed until August 1951. During that time we moved three times: from a flat on Greenfield Street, to the house of a professor on sabbatical leave, to a low rental project in Tonawanda. Our second son, Donald, was born in 1949.

My courses included Introductory Economics, Economic Theory and Labour Problems. My business subjects, personnel administration and job evaluation, required much more effort initially. For job evaluation especially, I was indebted to a fellow student at Wisconsin who had lectured to union classes and given me an excellent bibliography.

The department had chosen their younger faculty carefully, offering starting salaries above the market average. As a result, our social and intellectual life could hardly have been better. We also took advantage of being close to Dunnville, where Margery's aunts Sophia and Elizabeth were in their last years.

We visited Dunnville every possible weekend. Margery's aunts could have been the inspiration for the Broadway play, *Arsenic and Old Lace*, except that they had no bodies in the basement that we knew of. The Victorian virtues of industry, thrift and sobriety were supplemented by regular attendance at the Anglican Church. Grandfather Miller, born Johann Wolfgang Muller in Canton Zug, Switzerland (the family changed their name to Miller during the First World War), had captained a Great Lakes steamer in the days of the Erie Canal and received a decoration for bravery while evacuating some men under fire during a Fenian Raid. We still have his medals from the Government of Canada and the County of Haldimand. Two of his brothers emigrated to the United States. He died in 1930 at the age of eighty-eight and grandmother Sarah Rowe Miller died in 1945 in her ninety-seventh year.

When I came upon the scene, the household consisted of Aunts Sophia and Elizabeth, Grandmother Miller, and Miss Gertrude Rourke, a native of Brockville who taught in Dunnville High School. Miss Rourke boarded with them for all but five years of her entire working life. There were no men in the house. Aunt Sophia never married, but we discovered after her death that she had had a beau who had emigrated to the United States, attempted to establish a business, but was defrauded and lost everything. Aunt Elizabeth had studied elocution in Brampton, joined a stage company, and toured the eastern states. She spoke kindly of her husband, who had died of consumption during the First World War. After her death, we discovered she had previously been married but we have no record of who the man was, what he did or, for that matter, whether she was legally divorced. After her second husband's death, Elizabeth became a nurse and served as receptionist, assistant and household nanny to a local general practitioner.

It would be fair to say that there was considerable bitterness towards men in general in the household. Neither Sophia nor Elizabeth attended our wedding, but they did accept me after Margery and I were married. One day, Sophia and I were walking down the main street and a woman who ran a family restaurant, which proudly proclaimed it was "recommended by Duncan Hines," came up to say how pleased she was to hear the news about Margery's babies.

"It was not our Margery. She has only been married for five months," screamed Sophia. Unknown to me, a cousin in Buffalo, whose name was spelt Marjorie, had given birth to twins. I doubt that she ever spoke to that woman again.

Although never a smoker, Aunt Elizabeth developed emphysema, which crippled her. She died in 1949. Following the custom of the time, Sophia had her sister laid out for visiting purposes in the living room of their home. First, however, it was necessary to choose a casket and she asked me to accompany her to the undertaker.

"Sophia, I have just the casket for a gentle lady like Elizabeth," he purred.

Sophia went straight to the point. "How much will it cost, John?"

"Not much, Sophia. We will talk about that. Don't you just love this light purple tone, just right for a lady, I always say. Feel it."

"You are asking too much. And I don't like that colour. What else have you got?"

The sparring went on for some twenty minutes. John finally produced a casket with a scratch on it, which he made available at a reduced price. By placing the casket in a corner of the room, no one would see the scratch. The bargain was sealed.

Sophia did not tell her brother John in Alberta about his sister's death. John had visited the year before but his smoking and alleged dropping of ashes from his pipe had so infuriated Sophia that he had come over to Buffalo to spend a week with us. He was really hurt when Margery broke the news to him some time later.

Sophia and her brother were later reconciled and on the whole they were close, but Sophia was not an easy person to get along with. Margery told me that her father had considered marrying the widow who had become his housekeeper after his wife's death, but Sophia and Elizabeth had so violently opposed it that her father did not do it. The two aunts had even gone so far as to put words into Margery's mouth to the effect that a remarriage by her father would have hurt her!

I enjoyed a comfortable relationship with the students at Buffalo. The student newspaper conducted a poll on what students in the Arts Faculty thought of their lecturers and, to my delight, I was rated one of the best four. However, as the classes of returning veterans worked their way through to graduation, enrolment and university funds from tuition declined.

At this point, I received an offer of employment from Ottawa. To be technical, I was invited to enter a competition for a post in the public service. My academic qualifications and entitlement to Veterans Preference, a policy that gave an overwhelming advantage to someone with overseas service, made it unlikely that I would be rejected.

We left Buffalo with many regrets. It was hard to leave our friends on the faculty, including the Butlers who had followed us from Wisconsin, but Ottawa appealed to me for many reasons, not least the challenge of the work involved.

THE DEPARTMENT OF NATIONAL HEALTH AND WELFARE

We arrived in Ottawa in August 1951. By this time, we had two children, some furniture and my library, which made it our most complicated move to date. We had saved enough for a down payment on a house and Uncle John (who had by now moved from Toronto to Ottawa) had scouted the local market for us. On his advice, we purchased 2026 Carling Avenue, part of the Glabar Park subdivision, then in the suburbs without municipal services of water or sewer. Lots were 15,000 square feet, each with a drilled well and septic tank. Familiarity with the problems we later encountered proved useful when I decided to enter municipal politics.

My new job in Ottawa was in the Department of National Health and Welfare. As the minister responsible in the St. Laurent government, Paul Martin (the father of Jean Chrétien's minister of Finance) took the initiative in developing Canada's post-war social security programs. His immediate principal adviser was George Davidson, deputy minister of Welfare. I am not sure of the background behind the creation of the Research and Statistics Division, which served both the health and welfare branches of the department, but Paul Martin himself had to be largely responsible. The division served as an intelligence section, prepared to produce studies as required on possible new programs. Dr. Joseph Willard was chosen as its director.

Joseph Willard had been a fellow graduate in Political Science and Economics at Toronto in 1940. For medical reasons, he had not been eligible for military service and had taken a position with the Department of Labour, working on the *Labour Gazette*. Among other things, he had established and maintained a national Register of Physicians. After the war, he had completed a Doctor of Philosophy degree at Harvard, in the School of Public Administration.

By the time I joined the division, Parliament had already passed the legislation to implement, in January 1952, a universal pay-as-you-go pension, payable to everyone over seventy years of age with at least twenty years of residence. Universality was a new principle, which had been employed first in the family allowances program in 1944. Previous old age pensions had been based on need, using a "means test" dating back to the Elizabethan Poor Law in England. In many circles it had a bad name. Canada was breaking new ground. George Davidson's testimony before the joint committee of the Senate and the House of Commons, with supporting documentation from the Research Division, had been very impressive.[9]

When I joined Willard's team, there was still much to do on the welfare side, but health insurance presented the real challenge. We were to conduct long-term studies and I had responsibility for a number of them.

The Research and Statistics Division at the time was organized in four sections: Social Security under myself, Welfare Services under Flora Hurst, Health Services under John Macdonald, and Biostatistics under Gordon Josie. All four sections published reports from their investigations, which were sometimes undertaken as a result of a special request from the minister's office, from the Dominion Council of Health, the Canadian Welfare Council, the Canadian Association of Social Workers, or some other source. Some studies were ongoing and published results at regular intervals.

Gordon Josie's section included morbidity studies, undertaken in collaboration with the Dominion Bureau of Statistics. This was Bill Mennie's specialty. Gordon's staff also maintained the Physicians' Register, and did special assignments such as an examination of the functions of the head nurse in a hospital. John Macdonald's section tracked developments in provincial public health legislation and also included a special unit that reported on the expanding field of rehabilitation services.

Flora Hurst reported regularly on developments in the public welfare field, including child welfare services and social assistance programs. Residence requirements varied even more between provinces than they do today, in spite of the best efforts of leaders in the social work profession, and were frequently on the agenda of federal-provincial conferences (as they still are). Flora's section conducted a national survey to determine the demand for social workers in Canada.

My own section included Douglas Allen, who had an incredible knowledge of the public accounts, both federal and provincial, and of the

---

[9] *The Report of the Joint Committee of the Senate and House of Commons on Old Age Security*, June 28, 1950, is still a classic document, well worth reading today in the light of recent changes to the federal program.

British and American pension systems, both public and private, and their actuarial bases. Paul Martin wanted to know the latest estimates of total expenditures on health, welfare and social security in Canada. When he spoke to business audiences, he cited percentages of gross national product, emphasizing how stable they were. When it was a labour crowd, he cited gross amounts, the larger the better. We kept him informed.

John Sparks was responsible for our health insurance studies. A medical social worker by profession, he had studied at the University of Chicago and was one of the most dedicated men I have known in this field. We were to build upon the work that had been started a decade previously, during World War II.

The 1942 *Beveridge Report* in the United Kingdom had outlined a scheme of comprehensive social benefits, including health insurance. A comparable report under Professor Leonard Marsh followed the next year in Canada. At the same time, Dr. J.J. Heaggerty of the National Department of Health provided a blueprint for health insurance in Canada.[10]

Reflecting the public interest, Prime Minister Mackenzie King, at the 1945 Federal-Provincial Conference on Post-War Reconstruction, offered the provinces a comprehensive system of social security and health insurance in exchange for continued income tax rental agreements. These were set out in the Green Book proposals that were often referred to over the years, notably by the Premier of Saskatchewan, Tommy Douglas, to remind the Liberal government of its commitments.

In the fall of 1951, Sparks and I visited the Swift Current Health District, where the Government of Saskatchewan had pioneered a form of public medical care for all residents. We prepared a report, later published, describing the costs, services provided and utilization by the covered population. The provinces of Saskatchewan and British Columbia developed public plans for hospital insurance, and these were also described in publications. We surveyed voluntary Blue Cross, Blue Shield and co-operative plans in Canada and regularly reported on them. Our staff prepared special studies on health insurance in a number of foreign countries.[11] Members of our staff visited the Social Security Administration in Washington. In 1958, John Sparks spent a month with the Ministry of Health in London and I did likewise the following year.

Ministry staff were cordial and I was permitted to attend a number of meetings with regional officers. These were the days before computers and the ministry maintained mammoth clerical records by hand. Indeed, a town in the Midlands (whose name I forget), where contribution records

---

10 Dr. Heaggerty had also written a history of medicine in Canada, going back to the earliest settlements.

11 We prepared and released the following studies: *Health Insurance in Sweden*, January 1952; *Health Insurance in Denmark*, March 1952; *Health Insurance in Great Britain*, March 1952; *Selected Public Hospital and Medical Care Plans in Canada*, July 1955; *and Voluntary Medical and Hospital Insurance in Canada*, August 1955.

for social benefits were kept, was alleged to house the largest clerical operation in Europe. Medical specialists were salaried and attached to hospital staffs, which made the provision of doctors' services quite different from what happens in North America.

John Osborne, who had also done his MA at Toronto in 1946, joined my section in 1952 and later replaced Joe Willard when he became deputy minister of Welfare. John made an outstanding contribution to the development of the Canada Pension Plan. Dick Splane, also with an MA from Toronto and further work at the London School of Economics, joined us in 1952. He later served as executive assistant to the deputy minister of Welfare, George Davidson, and became director of Unemployment Assistance, a program later expanded to include programs for the aged, blind and disabled. Dick published a book on the administration of public welfare in Ontario and was appointed a professor at the University of British Columbia.[12] Many younger economists served with us for a short time and went on to other posts. Looking back, we had assembled a brilliant team and our studies certainly had an impact on the evolution of Canada's Medicare program.

The Department of National Health and Welfare had two deputy ministers—Dr. George Davidson for welfare and Dr. Donald Cameron for health. To help prepare the groundwork for health insurance, Paul Martin had brought into the department the deputy minister from Manitoba, Dr. Fred Jackson, who reported directly to Dr. Cameron. Fred had pioneered a form of public diagnostic services in rural areas, based on publicly operated laboratories. The principle of separate diagnostic facilities outside doctors' offices was later incorporated into the Canadian Medicare system. Fred was dedicated to the principle of universal public health insurance, but unfortunately suffered from ill health and was not as vigorous as he had been. It was a pleasure to work with him at all times, however.

Paul Martin kept a staff of speech writers busy. When I joined the department, Dan Wallace was in charge. A Rhodes Scholar from Nova Scotia, Dan was a prodigious worker who never believed in going home at five o'clock. Later, he was joined and finally replaced by George Carty, who had spent some years with the Public Service Commission. Don Emerson looked after constituency matters in Windsor.

In some ways, Paul Martin was a caricature of a politician. Every birth, marriage, death or school graduation in his constituency was the occasion for a note from Paul. Two clerks regularly scanned the newspapers and one signed his English letters for him, the other the French ones. If he had an hour to spare, he would dial numbers in his constituency at random, asking the surprised answerer how he or she felt about the government in Ottawa. Dick Jackson of the *Ottawa Journal* alleged that in one bar in Windsor, a

---

[12] Dick and his wife, Verna, recently both received the Order of Canada for their international studies.

parrot had been trained to say: "Vote for Paul." On one occasion, Paul Martin was caught in a trap of his own making. He had been at the United Nations Assembly with the Canadian delegation, and returned to Windsor to speak to the Rotary Club. On meeting a man he recognized, he asked: "How is your father?" The man replied: "Just as dead as when I received that letter of condolence from you yesterday." As they say, you can't win them all.

Paul Martin never lost an election in his constituency. He worked hard himself and set hard tasks for those who worked for him. On one occasion, George Carty thought Paul should speak to a local group in Windsor. Paul reluctantly agreed, but only on condition that he get some publicity out of it. George called an announcer from a local radio station, suggesting that this might be a scoop for him. However, when George proudly told his boss that the station would tape the speech and play large sections of it at convenient times, Paul asked, "Why am I not on a national network?"

So George called a friend from the Trans-Canada network of the CBC, informing him that the Honourable Paul Martin would be coming from the United Nations in New York to deliver a significant speech to a group in Windsor, and the network agreed to cover it. (By this time George had some ideas on how he could beef up the speech.) George then called his friend at the local radio station, explaining that the event was too big to hold for an exclusive and he could not stop the CBC network from covering it. His friend understood and thanked George for trying to do something for him.

Again, George broke what he hoped would be good news, only to be met with another query: "Why am I not on television?" In those days, the only television coverage for Windsor came from two stations in Detroit across the river. George was eventually able to get one of the stations to give Paul some coverage, but this time did not break the news to his boss until a half hour before the speech.

On one occasion, Paul Martin and George Carty were walking down Sparks Street in Ottawa and a man came up asking the question that every politician dislikes: "Mr. Martin, I bet you don't remember me?"

"Of course I do, but just give me a minute. You are not from Ottawa, are you?"

"No, I just came in from the Sault last night."

"It was five years ago in the Sault, and I spoke in a theatre. You were in the receiving line."

The man was overwhelmed. To think that the Honourable Paul Martin would remember him after such a brief encounter. He simply could not believe it. George was also impressed and asked how Paul could have possibly remembered. The answer was very logical.

"I had to establish where the man lived. The Sault made it easy for me. I have only been there once, and I spoke in a theatre after going through a long reception line. The odds were very high that that was the occasion I met him."

With all his foibles, Paul Martin was respected and loved by the employees of his department. We knew of his deep convictions and his determination to add programs to the Canadian social security net. The National Health Grants, for example, which had been established in 1948 to train personnel and help build the necessary facilities for health insurance, were substantially strengthened and extended under his guidance. The grants were paid out of federal funds on a project basis, under policy guidelines set by the Dominion Council of Health, a body composed of the provincial deputy ministers of Health under the chairmanship of the federal deputy minister, meeting every six months. Within the department, Dr. Fred Jackson was in charge of their administration. The departmental architect, Gordon Hughes, supervised the Hospital Construction Grants and had a substantial influence on the design and construction of hospitals across Canada.

In this period, Joe Willard frequently participated as a member of the Canadian delegation to the meetings of the International Labour Organization in Geneva. Once, during his absence, I was acting in his place as chief and received an invitation to speak on the work of the department. Being a novice and anxious to do the right thing, I wrote out my speech and took it to the deputy minister, George Davidson. George had a simple screening device for anyone wanting to see him. He would see you at seven o'clock in the evening, figuring you would only come if it was really important. I showed up and handed him my speech. Did I expect him to read it? No way. What were the rules for a public servant making speeches? There are no rules, I was told. I should go ahead. As I turned to leave him, he made his parting shot, "Remember, if you are ever criticized, you are wrong."

The speech was not an outstanding success, but I did not get into any trouble over it.

The Aid to Disabled Persons Program was approved by Parliament in June 1954, and implemented on January 1, 1955. It provided us with an excellent opportunity to see how a new program was born and how the Research Division, especially Joe Willard, prepared the necessary documentation for the minister. Apparently, the program was sparked by someone in the prime minister's constituency, who wrote to say that something should be done to relieve the family of so-and-so, whose child needed care but they did not wish to place him in an institution. There were some precedents in European countries, but in Canada at that time the only assistance available was public welfare.

The new program required a means test, in spite of the arguments in favour of universality which had led to family allowances and the revised old age pension. Tests for determining total, as well as permanent, disability had to be worked out and standardized. Administration would be provincial, but all provinces encouraged to participate through a formula of federal cost-sharing which would give higher percentages to poorer provinces. The program was instantly popular and from every point of view a success. In later years, it was folded into the *Canada Assistance Plan*, which, as I write, is in turn being changed drastically.

Meanwhile, most of the efforts of my section were devoted to studies of health care programs and estimates of the cost of providing them on a national basis. Professor Malcolm Taylor of the University of Toronto, who had spent some time in the administration of the Saskatchewan hospital insurance plan, published some pioneering studies that we followed closely. In his later years, he was designated Distinguished Health Scientist, the only recipient of this honour, to my knowledge.

The Health Insurance Plan of Greater New York developed a form of voluntary coverage based on group practise by physicians, frequently employed on salary, as opposed to North American fee-for-service private practice. Dr. John Grant of the Rockefeller Foundation in the United States published regularly on developments in the United States and Europe.

In 1957 the Liberal St. Laurent government was defeated and a Conservative minority government led by John Diefenbaker took office. The new minister of Health and Welfare, the Honourable J. Waldo Monteith, continued the work of his predecessor Paul Martin. The groundwork for the *Hospital Insurance and Diagnostic Services Act* had been prepared in a series of sessions of the Dominion Council of Health and federal-provincial conferences. The new government passed the federal legislation, which incorporated the tried and true way of eliciting provincial participation through cost-sharing grants. Two provinces—Saskatchewan and British Columbia—had proved that public universal hospital insurance could work. Diagnostic services had been a special interest of Dr. Fred Jackson, and made a logical addition to hospital insurance.

The Research Division, particularly my own section, had prepared countless memoranda on every conceivable aspect, including estimates of costs, descriptions of services to be covered, both in and out of hospital, and the merits of financing by premiums or out of general revenue. It was exciting to testify before the parliamentary committee, and to go through the draft of regulations with the solicitor from the Department of Justice on a line-by-line basis.

As nearly as I could tell, the only significant opposition came from the private insurance industry, which was going to lose business. I received some nasty personal letters from the secretary of the Canadian Life and Health Insurance Association. Blue Cross plans had seen the writing on the wall and were resigned to seeing the experiments in Saskatchewan and British Columbia extended to the rest of the country. The medical profession, with rare exceptions, welcomed the new federal-provincial programs.

In February 1960, John Sparks resigned from the public service to work for the provincial Department of Health in Saskatchewan and later for the United Automobile Workers in Windsor.

In 1960, George Davidson left his post as deputy minister of Welfare to become deputy minister to the Honourable Ellen Fairclough, who was having some difficulties with the Immigration department. George's experience and good judgment quickly showed. Still later, he became secretary to the Treasury Board, chairman of the CBC, and ended his career with the United Nations in New York. He died in 1996.

Joe Willard succeeded George Davidson as deputy minister of National Welfare. John Osborne became director of the Research and Statistics Division. In 1964, while the new Liberal government of Lester Pearson named Liberal guru Tom Kent to prepare the groundwork for what was to become the *Canada Pension Plan*, the division prepared numerous submissions for Kent and the parliamentary committee that followed.

I was not in the picture when Mr. Justice Emmett Hall conducted his investigations that eventually led to Canada's program of Medicare. The division certainly played its role with its studies over the years.

Subsequent federal ministers did not take the same interest in the division. Its staff was split, some being assigned to the Health Branch, others to the Welfare Branch. Joe Willard was removed as deputy minister and replaced by Al Johnson. It may have been some small consolation for Joe to be awarded later the Gold Medal of the Professional Institute of the Public Service of Canada, realising that the people who really knew him recognized his remarkable contribution. He died shortly afterwards in his early sixties.

BACKGROUND TO POLITICS

Early in my employment with the public service, I had joined the Professional Institute of the Public Service of Canada (PIPSC). It just seemed the natural thing to do. In those days, PIPSC would not for a minute have considered itself to be a union and we did not have collective bargaining. The institute was organized by professional groups, and I belonged to the Economists, Sociologists, Statisticians and Actuaries.[13] We had professional development seminars, annual meetings and, in the course of events, I made many friends in other government departments. Before very long, I found myself nominated for chairman of our group. Two years later, the retiring national president, who came from the same group, suggested that I run to succeed him. Joe Willard had no objections, and it was the easiest election I ever experienced.

In those days, the office of president was considered part time and therefore unpaid. In the course of my work, I was obliged to travel a fair amount in Canada and on many of those occasions I met with local chapters of the institute. The great majority of our members resided in Ottawa, but we were anxious to expand to serve all eligible members across the country.

---

[13] This group later seceded from the institute and formed a separate association.

Board of directors, Professional Institute of the Public Service of Canada (PIPSC), 1958-59; includes eight who served as presidents

The government had requested one of former prime minister Mackenzie King's private secretaries, Arnold Heeney, to report on the steps to be taken to prepare for collective bargaining in the public service. PIPSC responded by moving to larger quarters and engaging a full-time professional secretary, Les Barnes, who later became national president and remains a good friend to this day.

The high point of our annual general meeting in the Chateau Laurier Hotel was usually an address by the prime minister. Mr. Diefenbaker accepted, but was obliged to decline at the last minute. The minister of Finance, the Hon. Donald Fleming, substituted, to my intense relief.

That year, 1957-58, was a delightful experience, but I declined to run for a second term, because of pressure on my time from other directions. Later, when I resigned from the public service, the institute made me an honorary member and it has since invited me to attend its annual meetings. In 1994, when it sponsored the Canadian Medical Discoveries Fund to take advantage of tax incentives offered by both federal and provincial governments, I was invited to become a director. The fund was remarkably successful, raising over $200 million in its first two years. It made investments that carried medical discoveries from the Medical Research Council and Canadian universities to commercial applications.

CHANGING A CAREER

At this stage, I felt more and more that I did not want to spend the rest of my career as a public servant. I had enjoyed my term as president of the Professional Institute and had become involved with a number of community associations. I wanted a more active life dealing with people.

In 1954, using the proceeds from the estate of one of Margery's aunts, we purchased a summer cottage on the Big Rideau Lake, some sixty miles to the southwest of Ottawa. This became our quiet retreat from Ottawa and its hot summers. My parents had purchased a cottage on the same lake, which was not yet crowded and where we all enjoyed good fishing in its clear waters. With two and later three small children (Elaine having joined us in 1953), it was not fair to impose on my parents by using their cottage. It was one of the best decisions we ever made.

In 1957, again using the proceeds of Margery's inheritance, we invested in a successful land development in Bells Corners to the west of Ottawa. As a result, I felt it was then possible to take some risks in changing my employment.

Meanwhile, I became active in many community associations in the west end of Ottawa. With children in school, I joined the executive of the Woodroffe Home and School Association and later became the second president of the D. Roy Kennedy Home and School. As Ottawa extended its sewer and water mains to serve us, I was elected president of the Glabar Park Community Association. We were anxious to get rid of our individual drilled wells and septic tanks, which were blamed for an outbreak of hepatitis and had caused Margery to be hospitalized. I served on a committee to revise our zoning bylaw.

At this time our community had an interesting experience with petitions. Two of the streets in our subdivision were named after the developers. Petitions were successful in changing them to Muskoka and Kingsmere. Others sought to change Hare Avenue, which had been named after an old settler family, against the wishes of some. Two teams, shaking fists at each other, went up and down the street seeking signatures. When the matter finally came before the county court judge, the city clerk, Alf Hastey, was required to testify.

"Have you examined the signatures on this petition to change the name, and compared them with the list of property owners,

Mr. Hastey?"

"I have, your honour."

"What is your conclusion?"

"The petition has been signed by seventy-five per cent of the registered property owners. But, your honour, I also have a petition to retain the name of Hare Avenue."

"Have you examined it carefully?"

"I have, your honour. It also has been signed by seventy-five per cent of the property owners."

Everybody had a good laugh and the judge washed his hands of the matter, refusing to change anything. At least fifty per cent of the owners had signed both petitions! The moral of the story was plain, that some people can be persuaded to sign anything, and petitions should not always be taken at face value.

McKellar Golf Course, which was privately owned, offered open space that was highly desirable in our neighbourhood. When its owners made noises about selling it, the community associations rallied. We carried our fight to City Hall, only to find Mayor Charlotte Whitton solidly in league with a developer who wanted to build a shopping centre. We were able, however, to prolong the hearings and the developer backed off.

Robert McKeown of the Press Gallery, circa 1964—"a very special person"

I had spoken of my federal ambitions to a member of the National Press Gallery, Robert McKeown, probably the best friend I have ever known. His advice was to the point. How could I be sure that I would really like the life of a politician? Why not test the waters by running for alderman on city council? In any case, our ward would likely replace one of its two sitting aldermen, who had disappointed the community associations.

In the civic elections of 1954, I had supported an aldermanic candidate who narrowly lost. His candidacy had been promoted by a group at odds with Mayor Charlotte Whitton because of her quarrels with the school boards. In the course of that campaign, I met Frank Patten, a former principal of the High School of Commerce and later administrator for the Secondary School Board, who also became a close friend. Slowly, I was building up contacts with people who would help in an election.

In the fall of 1956, I decided to run for alderman. A member of the legal branch of the department,

Carlisle Hansen, had wanted to do the same thing but George Davidson had refused permission on the ground that Mayor Charlotte Whitton was already causing enough trouble for the department. I waited until seven o'clock one evening and went to Davidson's office to put the question bluntly.

"I have decided to run for alderman, sir. Do I have your permission or do I have to resign?" He gave me permission.

Unfortunately, the contacts that I had made were not enough to get me elected. I was defeated due to the last-minute entry of another community association activist who split the vote. But when I ran again in 1958, the results were quite different. I had done a great deal of house-to-house canvassing in parts of Carleton Ward where I was not well known and Bob McKeown had helped prepare my campaign literature. This time, no one split the vote and I was elected an alderman of Ottawa City Council.

OTTAWA CITY COUNCIL

I assumed office on January 1, 1959. That day Ottawa experienced one of its classic blizzards, and my telephone never stopped ringing. One call came from Britannia, a district in the extreme west end of my ward.

> "It did not take you long to mess things up, did it?"
>
> "What have I done?"
>
> "You know damned well what you have done. My street used to be ploughed first, and now it is the last."
>
> "This is my first day. I don't know what happened but I will find out and be back to you."
>
> "Don't bother."
>
> "I most certainly will bother. I will be back to you before tomorrow night."
>
> "You will have a hard job. At ten o'clock tomorrow morning, I leave for Florida."

This snowbird was named John Purdue, and when he came back in the spring, I sought him out. He took me over to see Mud Lake, on the eastern side of Britannia Road and surrounded by trees. If the bridge across the Ottawa River to Aylmer were ever built, Mud Lake would be sacrificed, and the community was vehemently opposed to such a plan. He pointed out where a sidewalk for the benefit of school children should be built. He wanted to know when they could expect city sewers, and get rid of a service to outhouses politely called night-soil removal, something I did not even know existed. He spoke to everybody and knew everything about his neighbourhood.

Early ploughing of his street was a status symbol to John Purdue and, really, a small reward for his efforts on behalf of his community. A few words with the ward foreman settled the matter. John and I became the best of friends and he continued to support me in federal politics.

I learned a lot about snow during my time as an alderman. Taxpayers want it removed so that they can use their streets in the morning, but do not want to be kept awake by the noise of equipment during the night. If it is dumped anywhere, no one wants to look at the dump. Therefore, the objective is to have it removed immediately, silently and economically to a place no one has to see. I eventually came to the conclusion that snow brings out the worst in all Canadians who are not enthusiastic skiers.

One Sunday morning an elderly gentleman called me to complain that there were two kinds of snow in his driveway—the kind that God had deposited out there and the kind that the city snowplow had just put there. He expected me to do something about the second kind at least, but that was difficult. Our civic budgets simply did not provide for clearing individual driveways.

Another long-time resident of Britannia was Eva Taylor, a retired schoolteacher who had spent some time in the National Archives researching local history. She told me that Captain LeBreton, an early settler who had been wounded at Waterloo but was a notorious land speculator, had given the area its name. The governor of the day, Lord Dalhousie, had anticipated the construction of the Rideau Canal and had stated his intention to buy the land from Dow's Great Swamp to the Ottawa River, on which Preston Street is now located. But Captain LeBreton beat him to it and raised the price by a factor of six! As a result, when Colonel John By came to build the canal six years later, he was obliged to use a longer and costlier route, terminating beside the Parliament Buildings below the Chaudiere Falls.[14]

Eva Taylor delighted in recounting such stories and, to all outward appearances, Eva was the very model of propriety; but I have heard her deliver some of the saltiest anecdotes you would never dream could come from her lips. Eva was a community treasure, and delightful.

During my first term on city council, George Nelms was the mayor, succeeding Charlotte Whitton, who had served from 1951 to 1956. In those days, a board of control of four persons elected by all the voters of the city formed a cabinet of city council. George, whose family had been neighbours on the Bowesville Road, had served for thirteen years as a trustee of the Ottawa Public School Board, and two acrimonious years on the Board of Control with Charlotte. When he decided to run for mayor in 1956, she did not oppose him.

George Nelms's term coincided with the most rapid period of civic growth Ottawa had seen for many decades. Campeau Construction, under Robert Campeau, and Minto Construction, under Irving Greenberg, were

---

[14] The LeBreton incident is recounted at length by Shirley E. Woods, Jr., *Ottawa, the Capital of Canada*, Doubleday Canada Limited, Toronto, 1980, pages 47 et seq.

registering subdivisions at an incredible rate; they grew into two of Canada's largest builders. Fortunately for me, this growth had spilled over to the Township of Nepean where Bill Teron was building houses in our subdivision. In a personal interview, George listed what he considered to be his most significant accomplishments:

- an agreement with federal and provincial representatives to share the costs of the Queensway;
- an express east-west route through the city;
- the construction of a second water filtration plant at Britannia;
- the construction of a major sewage treatment plant at Watts Creek in Gloucester Township;
- fluoridation of the municipal water supply;
- construction of a new city hall on Green Island;
- conversion of the municipal transit system from street cars to buses.

Truly this was an incredible agenda for any council. Three employees of the city had key responsibilities: Gordon Medcalf was the city solicitor, James Lowther the commissioner of Finance and Les Pilar (later Frank Ayers) the senior engineer. In addition were the normal budgets for street construction, traffic signals and street lights. Garbage removal was privatized in this period, at a considerable saving to the taxpayer. Meanwhile the school boards were busy building new elementary and high schools.

As a new alderman, I shared responsibility for Carleton Ward with Howard Henry. Howard had served not only on Ottawa council, but also on the council of the Township of Nepean, from which Carleton Ward had been annexed in 1950. Coming from an old Ottawa family, Howard had graduated from its schools and served as a fighter pilot in World War II. He was well respected and we made a good team.

Shortly after I assumed office, the mayor's mother died and he asked me to replace him at a ceremony for cutting the ribbon for the new Mutual Life Assurance Company building on Argyle Avenue. The audience included members of the federal cabinet and senior public servants from the Departments of Finance and Insurance, and the Treasury Board as well as local politicians.

Donald Fleming, the minister of Finance, spoke in glowing terms of the Mutual Life Assurance Company. (It has always puzzled me how some companies could assure your life while others could merely insure it.) He and his father before him had known personally every president of the company since its founding. The white-haired president of the board was visibly moved to tears. When it came his turn to speak, all he could say was: "Thank you, Mr. Fleming. I am looking at Brooke Claxton down there in the front row. If you ever need a job, Donald, come to us." Brooke

Claxton, a former Liberal cabinet minister, had recently been named an officer of another insurance company. Donald Fleming turned scarlet.[15]

In my first term as alderman, I played a part in initiating two new city policies. The first related to school sidewalks. New sidewalks were constructed as local improvements, which meant that the adjoining property owners had to pay their full costs. Two streets in particular gave me concern—Broadview and Woodroffe Avenues. Broadview had a high school as well as an elementary, both of which, in the absence of sidewalks, obliged children to walk in the streets. In the winter, this was especially dangerous. Woodroffe Avenue had only an elementary school, but had deep ditches on both sides.

From time to time, the Ontario Municipal Board held public hearings at which taxpayers who objected to local improvements could be heard. I appeared before one hearing on a sidewalk, to argue that there should be a formula permitting a school sidewalk to be charged over a benefitting area, not just the one side of the street. The board's representative agreed with me and wrote a judgment to that effect, giving me credit. The city secured permission by an amendment to the regulations under the *Municipal Act* and was able to initiate the construction of a number of school sidewalks, including the two that most concerned me.

On one occasion, I visited the office of the engineer in charge of the sewer department. On a map on the wall were a series of red pins. The engineer explained that each pin represented a basement that had been flooded in the previous six months. I noted that they were concentrated in the centre of the city. Why? Well, it seemed that the old sewers combined both sanitary and storm drainage and were badly overloaded whenever we had a heavy rain. Moreover, many sewers were very old, some of them even built of wood staves, and were in terrible condition.

The sewers not only had to be replaced, but also separate systems constructed for storm and sanitary drainage. Sanitary sewage would of course be treated in the new treatment plant, and storm drainage allowed to flow into the Ottawa and Rideau Rivers. The city's budget was already strained to the limit and there were no funds for Centretown sewers, despite the urgency of the situation.

I placed a motion before council that every new apartment building should pay a per unit fee into a redevelopment fund for the downtown sewers. As the population density of the central areas increased, so did the load on the sewers, and it seemed only fair that new construction should pay for at least part of the costs. At this time lot charges were applied to new subdivisions in the suburbs and I argued that apartments were just subdivisions in the sky.

---

[15] At this time, insurance companies, trust companies, banks and investment dealers were competing vigorously and the Department of Finance had the unenviable job of regulating them. The remarks of the Chairman of the Board of the Mutual Life could easily have been interpreted as an attempted bribe.

The commissioner of Finance, James Lowther, and the chief engineer, Frank Ayers, agreed and hired a firm of consultants to argue the case before the Municipal Board. No other city in Ontario had done this, but eventually the authorities in Toronto agreed. Ottawa was the first to institute this type of redevelopment charges and others soon followed.

Alignments on city council did not follow political parties. Suburban representatives often voted against those from the older neighbourhoods in Centretown, who were more concerned about recreation and social welfare than the expensive extension of water and sewer mains to new areas. Personal friendships counted a great deal, but when it came to committee assignments, plain old-fashioned horse trading proved the rule. I quickly learned how to score some points in getting the committees I wanted, by volunteering the information that I was not interested in joining the Exhibition Committee. There was no question that this committee, alone as far as I knew, provided some minor perquisites, such as passes for your friends to the annual exhibition and hospitality at the Florida quarters for a company with many of the midway concessions. The invariable response was surprise, followed by an offer to support me for whatever committee I wanted, provided I support them for the Exhibition Committee.

Woodroffe High School was built during my first term and my old high school buddy, Jack Merkley, was made principal. Jack, his wife Marion, and their four children owned a cottage near ours on the Big Rideau Lake and we were the best of friends. I offered an annual prize at Woodroffe commencement to the student who best combined intellectual and scholastic attainment. For the first two years, I made the usual (dull) remarks about how important both achievements were, etc. One year I thought I would spice my comments up a bit.

I began by stating that it was not the ones who bloomed early who often went furthest in life. That was safe enough. Looking back, neither Mr. Merkley nor I would have qualified for such an award. He had his locker opposite mine on the third floor, and I remembered well having to duck whenever he opened it to miss being hit by his tumbling books. The audience roared. They seemed very responsive, but how was I to know that he had given the whole school a lecture on the need to keep tidy lockers that afternoon? I went on to say that I was a good student but not much of an athlete, whereas Jack was a great athlete but, by inference, not much of a student. The students took it away, as they say. Jack eventually forgave me, but it was a lesson on the dangers of extemporaneous remarks.

In the fall of 1959, after only one term on council, I decided to run for the Board of Control.[16] It, together with the mayor, formed the cabinet of city council and was elected by the voters at large. At the same time, I resigned from the Department of National Health and Welfare. Two very

[16] The Board of Control system was unique to Ontario in Canada. It has now almost disappeared.

talented people, my journalist friend Bob McKeown and photographer Ted Grant, helped prepare my publicity and did a superb job. Since we had to cover the entire city, the campaign proved expensive. Fortunately for me, the Bells Corners development was going well and I could afford to pay for ninety per cent of my campaign costs. A few friends also made some modest contributions.

Another alderman, Don Reid, with whom I enjoyed good terms, also ran for the board. He had served for four years, compared to my two. We both ran ahead of the two veterans, Paul Tardif and Wilbur Hamilton, and when all the votes were counted, I narrowly beat Don Reid to head the poll and became the deputy mayor. Don did well in Centretown, where he had a furniture business, and in the east. Carleton Ward supported me massively in the west. The votes were as follows:

Francis	47,736
Reid	47,575
Tardif	41,591
Hamilton	38,611

George Nelms had decided in the fall of 1959 that, after four years as mayor, he would retire from public life. Charlotte Whitton saw an opportunity to come back. Her chief opponent was Controller Sam Berger and a bitter battle it was. I supported Sam, whom I had known on council and respected, since Charlotte's pugnacious reputation had put me off. However, when the battle was over and the smoke cleared, Charlotte won, yoking us in harness together.

LIFE WITH CHARLOTTE

There is no easy way to describe Charlotte Whitton. She was fiercely controversial, evoking strong emotions from both her supporters and her enemies, of whom she had many. On occasion she was brilliant, witty and charming. Then, moments later, her mood would change and she would be screaming like a demon. In a meeting she would cite fictitious sections of the *Municipal Act*, but by the time you looked up the reference to challenge her, she would be on to something else, confusing and wearing down her opponents. She could also be personally malicious, like when she referred to George Nelms's "artificial family" of four adopted children.

Alderman May Nickson warned me that when Charlotte sent you a document, to look for the most important items at the very end or in the footnotes. Anyone reading the documents in a hurry could miss them.

The Board of Control was responsible for preparing the agenda for the council's regular monthly meeting and Charlotte personally went over every line. On one occasion, I moved the paving of Woodroffe Avenue and it was carried by the board, even though the mayor opposed it believing it would benefit Robert Campeau's subdivision of Bel-Air Park. The minutes prepared for council contained no reference and I challenged them, calling on the secretary of the Board, Bob Gorman, to testify from his notes. Shaking like a leaf, Gorman confirmed that the item had been approved by the board, and it was reinstated on council's agenda.

Controller Wilbert Hamilton, who had served with Charlotte on previous councils, took me aside. "You have just signed that man's death warrant, if we don't do something. You have no idea how vindictive she can be." According to the *Municipal Act*, the board had jurisdiction over personnel matters. We found a position with the municipal markets, in a building removed from city hall, and offered it to Gorman, who readily agreed.[17] At the next board meeting, we introduced the motion and it carried.

During this period, Robert Campeau was developing one new subdivision of single family homes after another. It was of course easier for him if he had the co-operation of the Planning Board. In previous councils, Paul Tardif as senior controller had been the chairman, but because of my association with the Bells Corners development, I declined to take the post of chairman of the Planning Board to avoid any possible conflict of interest and chose responsibility for Social Welfare and Recreation instead.

Charlotte Whitton and Robert Campeau were mortal enemies. She believed that he was a devil ready to rape the taxpayers at every opportunity; she regarded Tardif as Campeau's instrument. At one of the in camera meetings of the board she took offence at one of Tardif's remarks and slapped, punched and kicked him.[18] He did not retaliate in any way and certainly I failed to understand how his remark could have been construed as offensive. When news hit the press concerning the assault, Prime Minister Diefenbaker had second thoughts about naming Charlotte as ambassador to Ireland.

Those who had appointments with the mayor had to pass in front of her secretary and through a glass door. Beside the door was a fixed glass panel and many bumped into it, by error. The commissioner of Parks recommended that a large potted plant be placed in front of the glass panel. Charlotte objected to the expense, stating that anyone wanting to enter to see the mayor should be able to see where they were going. Don Reid quipped: "Yes, but will they be able to see on the way out?"

Chief of Police Dolman took me aside one day to say that we should be careful at in camera meetings. He had reason to believe that the mayor kept a loaded revolver in her desk drawer, in spite of his best efforts to dissuade her. At one public meeting of the board she was raving at Tardif as usual. "Tardif, I don't know what to do with you." The devil made me say: "Don't shoot him." The mayor left the room, to return shortly with a toy pistol which she aimed at Tardif. "This is my gun," she asserted. An

---

[17] Claude Bennett tells me that, when he became a member of the Board of Control after Charlotte's defeat by Don Reid in 1964, Bob Gorman came back to his former post as Secretary of the Board.

[18] Charlotte suggested that the road to our sewage disposal plant be named "Tardif BULLevard."

alert photographer from the *Ottawa Journal* got a fine shot of the action which was printed the next day. Till his death, Tardif maintained that a real pistol was aimed at him, but I can confirm that it was a toy.

Years later, Charlotte's sister, Kay Ryan, invited me to review two chapters of a biography of Charlotte she was writing. While visiting at her home, she showed me a loaded pistol that had been passed on to her with Charlotte's effects. I advised her to take it to the nearest police station. Charlotte, it appears, had kept two pistols, one a toy to display if she were ever found out, and the other real.

It soon became clear from working with Charlotte that she was a loner, never a team player. In part she hated to share the limelight, and in part her work habits disrupted other people's lives. She had no hesitation in calling her staff, or officers of the city, or even for that matter members of the Board of Control, at any hour of the day or night. A call at two a.m. was not unusual.

Cartoonists found Ottawa Board of Control meetings a good target, 1960.

There was no denying her flashes of brilliance, however. While the new city hall was actually constructed during the term of George Nelms, the choice of Green Island in the Rideau River, just above the point where it empties into the Ottawa to make the curtain falls (hence the French name "rideau"), was clearly the result of Charlotte's persistence.

She should also be credited with the choice of Porter's Island as a senior care facility. During the First World War, it had been used as an isolation hospital with access by a very narrow bridge from St. Patrick Street. Indeed, first impressions were dismal. One bright summer's day, the mayor invited me to visit the island. Two acres in the middle of the city, with birds and trees in a natural environment, presented an incomparable site. Frank Ayers, the city engineer, assured us a new bridge and improved access could be constructed quite inexpensively. We were faced with howls of protest about abandoning our seniors in a desolate place, but when the work was completed, everyone wanted to take credit for the brilliant location.

Among the boards that I shared with the mayor and aldermen, was the Ottawa Civic Hospital. On one occasion, we were reviewing the budget. Alderman Charles St. Germain spoke up. "I know why the costs are so high. I was in hospital myself, recently. It is what they do to you. They give you this test, they give you that test. They give you this drug, they give you that drug. It all costs money, Your Worship." Without blinking an eye, she looked at him. "But Charlie, there is so much wrong with you."

On another occasion she had really vexed Charlie, flustering him. While one of the most perfectly bilingual persons I have known, he had trouble with his words in either language when emotionally aroused. "I don't know what is the matter with you today, Your Worship. You must have got up on the wrong side of the—uh-uh—fence this morning." The suggestion that she was a barnyard animal just popped out.

Charlie's ward included a stretch of frontage along the Rideau River, with neighbouring homes belonging to above-average income families. He complained that the police did not sufficiently supervise this area, where some scandalous activities went on at night. One evening, as he and the mayor were leaving a function, she suggested they inspect the spot. They stopped their car and were about to get out to look around when a police car put a search beam on them. The story somehow made the press. Just what were the mayor and Alderman St. Germain doing in a parked car at that spot at that hour? My friends still laugh about it.

My hair has been white since shortly after my discharge from the RCAF in 1945. On one occasion, she taunted me. "Just what is your secret formula to keep your hair so white?" "It is very simple. I just have to attend meetings regularly with you," I replied.

On another occasion, I over-reacted to my detriment. We were busy approving public housing projects as a part of extensive schemes of urban renewal, which was the planning rage of the time. A few of us who knew something about the costs of housing felt that some of the new projects had expensive price tags. Later, I discussed it with Robert Campeau, who agreed. Campeau submitted a proposal of his own, at a substantially lower per unit cost.

When it came before the Board of Control, all four controllers supported it. The mayor was furious. Turning to me she asked: "Why have you not declared your interest? You own the adjacent property and this is just a scheme to get sewer and water services to your land."

I was staggered. Being in the subdivision business in Nepean, I had scrupulously avoided any action that could be remotely construed as a conflict of interest in the city of Ottawa. For this reason, I had declined to assume the chairmanship of the Planning Board. Why had she chosen to slander me? I retorted, "You are a liar. I do not own that land, or any lands near it. You are an irresponsible person, so irresponsible that you are not fit to be the mayor of this city."

Today I am older and wiser. I should have confined my remarks to a simple denial of ownership and then instructed my solicitors to prepare an action. You can imagine the headlines, and the resulting issue arising from my statement that the mayor was so irresponsible she was not fit to hold office. I engaged the services of a distinguished solicitor who told me how I should have behaved. However, sensing that I was not going to sue her (on my lawyer's advice), the mayor was jubilant.

Shortly afterwards, the commissioner of Welfare, Stewart Bishop, resigned. He had been one of our star recruitments to reorganize the Welfare Department, and had only been with us a few months. This particular department was my responsibility, so I was surprised to discover one day a strange group of people going through our records. Bishop said that they were acting under instructions of the mayor and no one was to tell me what they were doing. I was furious and discussed it with fellow members of the Board of Control. Bishop felt that he had been placed in an impossible position. The mayor called an in camera meeting to announce Bishop's resignation, stating that he had not intended to stay in Ottawa, but had treated it merely as a stopping post.

"Why do you not tell us the truth?" I asked.

"The last time I lied, you did not have the guts to sue me," she replied. What could you possibly do with a person like that?

While George Nelms had negotiated the agreement with the province for the Queensway, a major east-west artery built on an abandoned railway right-of-way, actual construction took place in Charlotte's second term of office. Her brother-in-law, Frank Ryan, had a plan for creating parking places under the Queensway in the central part of the city. Charlotte dubbed it "Queensway on Stilts" and for reasons that I never understood, opposed it. It seemed a good idea to me. The board invited Frank Ryan to make a presentation.

Frank was always thorough, and had prepared a series of illustrations and charts. He came early to the presentation room and set up his materials where he could see them clearly. Frank had cataracts as well as the beginnings of tunnel vision. However, when he began, Charlotte immediately demanded that everything be rearranged, in order that SHE might see everything better. Frank was devastated and unable to complete his presentation.

The story of the visit of the Lord Mayor of London to Ottawa has been told many times. The City of Ottawa held a formal dinner in his honour. Both mayors were formally attired with ceremonial robes and their respective chains of office. Charlotte, however, also wore a corsage consisting of a single red rose. Leaning over, the Lord Mayor of London asked: "Your Worship, if I were to smell your rose, would you blush?" Quick as a flash, she replied: "If I were to pull your chain, would you flush?"

Charlotte, however, could be baited on occasion. The Boy Scouts were holding a public reception in Lansdowne Park and she appeared in her robes of office complete with tricorn hat and mayor's chain. As she entered, Paul Blais, a dear friend but an imp if ever there was one, told her to sign the visitors' book. He looked at her signature, then announced that he could not read it, and asked who she was. She strode away on her high horse, spoke a few words of public greeting to the audience inside, then on her way out scowled at Paul, muttering: "NOW do you know who I am?"

Charlotte loved fires. She would go to one in her mayor's car, siren screaming, and tell the firemen how to do their job. Father Larose served as chaplain to the fire department, and asked for a siren for his car so that he could get through the crowd if he had to administer last rites. The mayor refused and a certain amount of animosity developed between them. When she was on a visit to Moscow, I was the acting mayor and prepared a formal minute for the Board of Control ordering Father Larose to install a siren in his car. To his delight, the item was approved unanimously. On her return, the mayor fumed but could do nothing about it.

Controller Wilbert Hamilton and I were opposites in nearly every way—in age, in politics and in associations—but we spent much time together on city business and became friends. He knew the *Municipal Act* backwards. He knew Charlotte well and distrusted her. On more than one occasion he cautioned me on how to present a difficult matter to council. At the official opening of the George Dunbar Bridge in 1960, he felt slighted because he had not been invited to sit in front on the official platform. He indulged in his drink of rye whisky in milk (the only person I knew with such an addiction).

A woman in the audience came over to me asking if a doctor was available. Why, I asked. "Something serious is happening to Controller

Hamilton. I have been watching him and you might think he was drunk. He can't be, because I can swear that he has only been drinking milk."

It would not be right to leave this period of the administration of the City of Ottawa without reference to Joe Paradis, a perennial gadfly who called himself the Civic Watchdog. Joe ran in every election, sometimes for Board of Control, sometimes for mayor, and never spent a cent on his campaigns. He explained that he was retired early from his trade as boilermaker because of an injury to his head and therefore had the time to follow the garbagemen, policemen and civic work crews around, and to talk to everybody. He discovered that Paul Tardif's water department had purchased meat for some obscure reason and taunted Paul at every election rally shouting: "What about the meat?"

Joe had a good voice, composure and a sense of humour and obviously enjoyed himself. Controller Hamilton remarked that the rest of us campaigned hard, spent money for advertising and took ourselves seriously. Joe was not crazy, we were.

One day when we were due to file our nomination papers, Joe invited myself and a journalist to accompany him to the office of the city solicitor, Gordon Medcalf, whom he proceeded to question. "To file to run for mayor, I have to say what I do. What are the rules about the kind of job you must have?" "There are no rules, Joe." "Me, I am the Civic Watchdog." "That is good enough," said Gordon Medcalf, humouring Joe.

Joe went downstairs and filed his nomination papers for mayor as Civic Watchdog. Mayor Charlotte Whitton, standing beside him, said it was illegal, since there was no such occupation. But Joe had an opinion from the city solicitor, given in the presence of witnesses, to the contrary.

Charlotte called the police department to say that there was a mad dog in the rotunda of city hall that should be impounded!

Joe did succeed, however, in filing his nomination papers against Mayor Whitton with his occupation listed as Civic Watchdog.

One of the perquisites of membership on city council was the opportunity to attend conventions. As an alderman, I attended the Good Roads convention in Niagara Falls, Ontario. We travelled by chartered bus together with representatives from Gloucester and Nepean, including the reeves. It was a good opportunity for us to get to know each other better. This particular convention had quite a reputation in some circles, as I understood when I observed how some of the delegates from other municipalities behaved. It only takes a few to give an organization a bad name. The sessions on road maintenance, different construction materials, and the use of asphalt as opposed to concrete for street curbs, for example, were most informative.

Conventions of the Parks and Recreation Association of Canada were fascinating. I remember meeting in the Niagara Peninsula and touring the impressive lands of the Niagara Parks Commission and its greenhouses. We listened to their (unsuccessful) programs to control Dutch elm disease and to preserve a few specimens of the American chestnut, which been destroyed by a blight circa 1920. A convention in Edmonton had many highlights, including a tour of the Alberta Game Farm. Our Ottawa commissioner of Recreation and his assistant were most considerate in making sure that we got the most from the program.

As deputy mayor, I attended a convention of the Canadian Federation of Mayors and Municipalities in Halifax in 1962. One session was devoted to budgeting and the difficulty of providing all the services people wanted. I struck up a conversation with three delegates who sat by themselves and did not seem to say much. Did they have a problem with urban renewal, I asked. Not really, if someone felt their house needed a new coat of paint, for example, they would have it done. Garbage removal? Yes, they did have a problem. People were complaining about the noise and they were going to have to cut it back from daily service to three times per week. Building new arenas? They had just completed one. I learned later that they represented a small community on the Island of Montreal with the oil refineries within their borders. In a sense they embodied the dream of every municipality: to have a huge assessment and small population—although not too many people would choose to live beside a refinery. It was no surprise to learn soon afterwards that the province corrected the situation by shifting the assessment to the municipality of Greater Montreal.

At the same convention the federal minister of Public Works, the Honourable David Walker, was scheduled to address a luncheon meeting of several hundred delegates and spouses. A tour of the harbour by boat had been arranged for after lunch and the schedule was tight. The mayor of St. John, Eric L. Teed, would introduce the minister. Teed opined that Upper Canadians were a singularly uninformed lot when it came to matters Maritime and he would take the opportunity to correct this flagrant gap in their learning. Did they know that St. John had been given its charter by royal proclamation of the king of England? He pulled a copy from his pocket and proceeded to read it. Did they know about the great shipbuilding industry that once existed on the St. John River? He pulled out another piece of paper and read out details of the construction of schooners, frigates, two-masted sailing vessels, etc., year by year for the 1870s, 1880s and 1890s. Did they know how New Brunswick and Nova Scotia had been robbed when they entered Confederation?

On and on he went, starting at twelve-forty-five. One o'clock came, then one-fifteen, one-thirty. As he approached one-forty-five, he observed that his audience was a restless lot. "I guess you want to hear Davie Walker. I don't have to introduce him. Everybody knows him. Davie, take it away."

With perfect composure, David Walker began: "They say that, with some people, if you put a good dinner into them, up will come a speech. With others, after a speech, up will come your dinner."

He then continued for some five minutes and sat down. Years later, when he was a senator and I an MP, I reminded him of the occasion. Davie averred that it had all been a Grit plot to embarrass him. To the best of my knowledge, Teed was a Conservative but what party would claim him?

In the fall of 1961, as I was completing my first term on the Board of Control, I began to have serious thoughts about just what I wanted to do in a political career. Experience on city council had taught me a good deal, as Bob McKeown had predicted it would. On the whole, it had confirmed my childhood ambitions, but should I continue at the municipal level and run for mayor, or look at something else? Working with Charlotte had been an enormous strain, and her irregular calls disrupted my family life, although Margery never complained. Could Charlotte be beaten in a contest? Or would she back out as she had done three years previously, rather than face George Nelms?

Any politician quickly learns that dealing successfully with the press is essential. However, municipal reporters from the newspapers, radio and television were a mixed bag, as they say. Naively, I had assumed at the beginning that they would all be of the calibre of Robert McKeown. Some indeed were, like Larry MacDonald of the CBC, Roger Appleton of the *Citizen* and Peter Jackman of the *Journal;* but many were not.

The mayor presided over meetings with four members of the Board of Control, but the five of us were usually outnumbered by at least ten representatives of the news media. It dawned on me after a while that each one of them had to produce a different version of what took place at our meetings, if only to prove to their bosses that they had been present on the job! This was known as investigative reporting. One morning, I received a telephone call at my home at seven-thirty. The reporter asked a number of questions to which I replied as best I could. The story that appeared in the newspaper later that day bore little resemblance to what I had said. When I spoke to him afterwards, he nonchalantly replied that I could not prove anything, it was just my word against his and his editor would back him up! Mayor Nelms's secretary warned me against one reporter who had come into her office one day and read the name of someone from her notepad who presumably had an appointment with the mayor. As a result, a malicious speculative story appeared. From that point, whenever that reporter came into her office, she covered everything on her desk.[19]

As a member of city council, I quickly learned how important it was to check out every public complaint. One evening, we were leaving our house to go to the Ottawa Exhibition. The telephone rang and a female voice told me that I should check the canal sidewalk near Lansdowne Park

---

[19] I have since read with interest Conrad Black's comments on journalists and must agree with him that many suffer from lack of professional supervision.

because the wall and sidewalk had collapsed into the canal. How could this be? The National Capital Commission, who was responsible, had high maintenance standards. My instincts, however, insisted I stop the car at a dimly lit spot to look. What the woman had told me was absolutely true. I raced to city maintenance staff to have barricades erected. Fortunately, no stray pedestrian had been injured.

On another occasion, after I had assumed the portfolio of Social Welfare on the Board of Control, I received a call from a well-known complainer and malingerer, who maintained that there was an error in his welfare cheque, and he should have been receiving an extra $10 a month. He had checked the regulations. Staff at first refused to bother with him, but I insisted that they investigate. Sure enough, there was an error and the man was entitled to an extra $10. You really have to check out all complaints.

On the other hand, any elected representative has to learn to deal with that small minority of impossible constituents. They say that two percent of the general population is psychotic and a politician will probably meet them all. Our family usually went to our Big Rideau cottage on summer weekends. One Saturday evening as I fished quietly for bass, a fellow came over by boat, anchored beside me, and berated me for a full hour on a

Presenting plaques to west end Babe Ruth League, 1962
(PHOTO BY TED GRANT)

municipal matter. On another occasion the telephone rang as I arrived home one Sunday evening and I had to listen to a man complain that I had not been available all weekend!

Two controversial issues while I was a member of the city council resulted in repercussions later in my career. The University of Ottawa had decided to expand in its central location, rather than move to vacant land in the suburbs. For this purpose, it needed powers of expropriation to acquire adjacent and frequently older run-down houses. Many private owners fought the expropriation and persuaded the two local aldermen to support them. The council stood divided, but I felt that the university was doing us a service in redeveloping and improving the area, and could not do it without expropriation powers. Eventually, council agreed and the motion passed requesting the province to amend the university's charter accordingly. Members of the administration of the university thanked me for supporting them.

The second issue related to a proposal from a Roman Catholic order, the Little Order Of Mary, to establish a hospital in Ottawa. For this purpose, they applied for a civic grant. Again, I saw no problem. The Little Order had the backing of a group of Ottawa doctors, and the net cost to the taxpayers would be less than if the city had been obliged to build a new hospital, which was needed. The council divided again, largely on religious lines, and the Little Order of Mary withdrew its offer.

These two issues earned me a number of friends who supported me in my later political career. While members of the Irish Catholic community are generally Liberal, they supported me, an English Protestant, with unswerving loyalty. Alderman Jimmie McAuley from Centretown was one such individual. Volunteers from the University of Ottawa also helped in our campaigns. In the press, I was credited as a member of council who took the larger view of things.

On the whole, however, I was not enjoying as good a press as I had on the eve of the Board of Control election. The squabbles with Charlotte did not help, but they had not really done that much harm; any new incumbent passes through a honeymoon period. Moreover, I was a little wiser from my baptism of fire in politics. At this point, Keith Davey, the national organizer for the Liberal Party, sought me out with the suggestion that I should run for the Liberals in the federal riding of Carleton against the sitting Conservative, Dick Bell.

At this stage of my life I chose to identify myself as a Liberal, largely from my experience in the Department of National Health and Welfare. More than any other party, the Liberals were responsible for creating Canada's social security programs and I had an enormous regard for Paul Martin, Senior.

A popular saying of my youth maintained that if one was not a socialist before the age of thirty, one had no heart. If one continued after thirty, one had no head. As a teenager, I had repudiated my parents' Conservative views. After the Second World War, I had repudiated Marxism. In 1960, at the age of forty, I joined the Liberal Party.

I responded to Keith Davey's persuasion. Looking back, it was probably foolhardy to take on a riding as Conservative as Carleton, but who could have possibly anticipated the effects of a new Liberal government's language policies? As they say in poker, it was the luck of the draw.

Part 2

THE FEDERAL CAMPAIGN OF 1962

CARLETON HAD BEEN CONSERVATIVE since Confederation. The only break in this record occurred in 1922, when the United Farmers of Ontario won the provincial seat. When the leader of the Conservative Party needed a seat, he looked to the safe riding of Carleton. Sir John A. Macdonald won it in 1882, Sir Robert Borden in 1908, and George Drew in 1949. Dick Bell had won the seat in 1958 with 19,000 more votes than his Liberal opponent. For a Liberal to win it, would be a major coup.

Carleton, however, was changing. New Ottawa suburbs were spilling over into Nepean Township, including Lynwood Village, with which I had been associated. Carleton's population was more than twice that of either Ottawa Centre or Ottawa East, two Liberal strongholds. There was good reason to believe that the new residents would not follow traditional voting patterns, and it might be possible to overcome the huge Tory majorities in the rural townships.

Carleton, however, presented challenges to any political candidate. Geographically, it included not only the Glebe and Ottawa South in the City of Ottawa, substantial in themselves, but also a huge rural area, as far as the outskirts of Arnprior to the north, the Rideau River to the south, and the Township of Osgoode to the southeast. In the election of 1962, Carleton's 442 polls with 89,318 voters dwarfed Ottawa Centre's 177 polls with 35,635 voters and Ottawa East's 133 polls with 29,289 voters. Indeed, in the entire province of Ontario, only York Scarborough, York Centre and York West had more eligible voters than Carleton and their voters were concentrated in urban areas.

On my birthday, March 19, 1962, I was officially acclaimed as the Liberal candidate. Mitchell Sharp spoke at our nomination meeting, which was well attended. We had a good press. Frank Marchington, a fellow member of the Carlingwood Kiwanis, agreed to act as my campaign manager. However, when I approached well-known Liberals in Carleton, lawyers, accountants and others, many replied that they were committed to George McIlraith in Ottawa Centre. My good friend, Gordon Blair, for example, was the president of the Ottawa Centre Liberal Association, although he lived in Carleton. These Liberals did not believe I stood a proverbial snowball's chance in hell against Bell, and were going to work for George, some of them hoping that if their party won, they could get patronage from him. This was a shocker. I really needed their help.

As nearly as I could determine, no leader of the Liberal Party had ever made a public appearance in Carleton. Would getting Mike Pearson out to a rally help sway some of these faint of heart? At the very least, it would have demonstrated that my candidacy was fully supported at the top and not considered as some sort of quixotic venture. Keith Davey arranged for Paul Martin to come, but it surely was not difficult since I had worked for him as a public servant and he was more responsible for me joining the Liberals than anyone else.

Failure, however, to arrange an early appearance by Pearson in 1962 proved the first source of friction between Keith and myself. On the Saturday before the Monday election, Davey did arrange for the Liberal leader to appear in a motor parade going into Carlingwood, but organizing the parade detracted seriously from our preparations for election day and it was too late to influence those Liberals I had hoped to recruit to work in the campaign. The parade took a strange twist when Conservative candidate Dick Bell joined the motorcade, for reasons that I do not understand to this day.

All things considered, we ran a great campaign from our headquarters on the second floor of Carlingwood Shopping Centre. We attended Liberal Party campaign college for candidates and campaign managers. We had all of our committees in place—organization, publicity, finance and headquarters. Bob McKeown's help was beyond words. His wife, Vaida, told me on one occasion that Bob had secretly wanted to be a candidate himself, but did not have the resources to risk it, choosing instead to get some vicarious satisfaction from helping me. I will be forever indebted to him. Isobel Sparling converted from the Conservative Party in McKellar Park to join our organization committee. Ernie Murray, who had recently moved into the riding from Quebec, inspired the canvassers

Prime Minister Pearson in motorcade during 1963 election campaign

and Pauline Freeman, whose father had been an Alberta MP, worked in headquarters. Wes Nicol chaired a successful fundraising committee. Alf and Frances Gentile did our printing.

It would be an understatement to say that the Liberal Party organization in Carleton was weak. Ed and Elsie Hebert and a few others had kept the Liberal Association alive, with annual meetings. The Carleton Liberal Women's Club, however, met regularly, with frequent social events. When the time came for me to name election enumerators, the secretary of the Women's Club supplied the names.

It was tradition in Carleton for the returning officer, following the filing of nomination papers, to hire a hall and invite the official candidates to speak. This famous (or notorious, as you choose) "Confrontation Meeting" had for many years been held in the Village of Richmond, but was now in Hilson Avenue Public School in Ottawa. Each candidate had a nominator and seconder, with the speaking order determined by lot.

What happened was a total disaster for us. Tory supporters came in busloads from the rural areas. Dick Bell spoke first, in a booming voice, saying that the Liberals had nominated a man who would be lost ten rods off the Queen's highway and knew nothing about the real problems of Carleton. Every member of all seven rural township councils had signed his nomination papers. It did not matter that I had been born in Carleton, had attended a rural elementary school and had travelled many of the back roads delivering baby chicks from my father's hatchery. The crowd applauded every word from Dick's lips.

There was no microphone, since Dick did not need one. When it came the turn for my proposer, Herb Stevenson, a dignified professional engineer from the new Nepean subdivision of Manordale, to speak, he literally could not complete a single sentence. Nor could I, when my turn came. We were obliged to give up and leave, to the intense delight of the crowd. You can imagine the press—Liberal candidate booed off the stage! The *Ottawa Journal* ran a lead editorial in support of Carleton's own Dick Bell, whose family roots went back at least three generations.

The results from the rural polls were totally predictable. Elections often are not a matter of a rational choice between candidates or parties, but rather an occasion for solemn reaffirmation of ancient hostilities. In Carleton, every child at birth inherited his or her religion and politics, and did not change, either. Anglican descendents of the men who took up land grants after serving with Wellington at Waterloo were Tories. Irish immigrants who came as a result of the potato famine pledged allegiance to the Catholic Church and the Liberal Party. Early French Canadian arrivals frequently became assimilated and Tory, with the Bouchers pronouncing their name Bowcher, the Lafleures becoming Leafloor. Later French Canadians remained Catholic and Liberal. The only real question was the Scottish Presbyterians: Were they, or were they not, still voting for Alexander Mackenzie?

I had been baptised an Anglican, at my mother's insistence, but my father, while maintaining no religious affiliation, was a strong Tory. He had voted Conservative in every election with the exception of that of 1932 when he supported Stevens's short-lived Reconstruction Party. I replied to everyone who asked why I had become a Liberal, that I had chosen my party, not inherited it. I can still remember the vehemence with which one woman to whom I had just been introduced screamed at me: "I knew your father. You are a turncoat!" Shades of Northern Ireland!

For the record, neither my mother nor my father voted in the first two federal elections I contested. They could not vote against me and they could not vote Liberal, but they came around eventually.

Years later I sent a Christmas card to Senator Grattan O'Leary, whose sons had gone to Glebe with me, signed, "To the Senator from Carleton from the MP for Carleton," recognizing that he, as an Irish Roman Catholic Tory, was as much a renegade in the traditions of the Ottawa Valley as I, an English Protestant Liberal.

It was with some trepidation that I went to the strawberry social at St. Isidore Church in March Township. There was no need, for the parish priest, whom I did not know, met me at the entrance to the grounds, put his arms around me and introduced me to everyone present. Considering my background, the warm friendship that many Catholic priests over the years have offered me is something I can never forget.

At that strawberry social, I met Godfrey Armitage. He belonged to one of those old Huguenot Anglican families that had taken up their land grants after Waterloo, and were one of the six Protestant Liberal families in rural Carleton to whom alderman Howard Henry's father sent Christmas cards each year. Godfrey was a giant of a man, some six feet eight inches tall, and had been an unsuccessful provincial Liberal candidate. He regaled me with tales of elections past in Carleton, controversial meetings and the like. Although advanced in years, he retained all his faculties, including a sharp wit and memory.

Less than two years later, Godfrey died and I was then the victorious Liberal MP for Carleton. I called to pay my respects before the service in the chapel of Tubman's funeral home in Westboro. One of Godfrey's sons, Rolly, spoke to me.

"Mr. Francis, I am busting to tell a story, and you are just the man. Have you had a look in the chapel? Did you see Alex Wilson, the man second from the end in the fourth row? He was our neighbour on the farm on the fifth line. The last thing I intended was to eavesdrop on him, but he was talking to my father in his casket in a loud voice. He said something like this: 'Godfrey, this is the end. I have known you all my life. You were a good neighbour, you were a good farmer, you were a good father, you were a good man. But you sure were hard on the Conservatives!' With that, he walked away."

The NDP candidate, Bill Hanley, was a medical doctor and an old friend from the days of Campus Co-operative Residence at Toronto. The Social Credit candidate, Harry Splett, ran under the slogan, "Split the Debt with Splett," and attempted to illustrate his point with a series of amusing but totally incomprehensible charts. At a meeting in North Gower, he displayed his total ignorance of the rural county by repeatedly referring to "North Gowower," instead of the local pronunciation, "North Gore." No one corrected him.

I canvassed door-to-door in the old neighbourhoods of Mechanicsville and Hintonburgh, which had been annexed by the city of Ottawa about the turn of the century. Basically lower income, many of the families were still living in the houses built by their grandfathers. They voted solidly Liberal.

On one street, I approached a house that was clearly the home of a biker gang, with expensive motorcycles parked in front and by the side. My voters' list indicated that the adjacent residence was inhabited by a single woman, who came to the door. Yes, she would vote for me. Hesitatingly, I asked about her neighbours.

"Why do you ask? They are the nicest boys I have ever known. They shovel my walk in the winter, do my shopping for me, and every day someone comes over to see how I am. This neighbourhood used to scare me, with people who frightened me on the street. Now I do not see any of them and I feel perfectly safe on the street, day or night. True, their motorcycles make a lot of noise, but it no longer bothers me. Actually, I like to hear them."

The motorcycle gang had adopted an elderly neighbour who lived alone. Woe betide anyone who touched her. Such a person would likely end up in the nearby Ottawa River tied to a cement block! To cap it off, the gang told me that they were voting for me.

As expected, we made no change in the rural vote, or in the Ottawa districts of the Glebe and Ottawa South. These Ottawa polls had traditionally voted Conservative, and George McIlraith did not want them in Ottawa Centre. I was saddled with them for the elections of 1962, 1963 and 1965. We did much better in the new suburbs of West Ottawa and Nepean, but not well enough to win. The vote was as follows:

Bell (Conservative)	32,125
Francis (Liberal)	26,109
Hanley (NDP)	3,024
Splett (Social Credit)	922

We had reduced Bell's plurality in 1958 of 19,089 votes to 6,016, but were still far from winning the seat. I had not resigned my seat on the Board of Control and went back to Ottawa Council.

In the election of 1962, Conservative representation in the House of Commons decreased from 208 to 116. The Liberals won 99 seats, Social Credit 30, and the NDP 19.

John Diefenbaker's minority government lurched from one crisis to another. His refusal to permit American Bomarc missiles on Canadian soil led to the resignation of his minister of National Defence, Douglas Harkness. His cancellation of the Avro Arrow contracts and destruction of prototypes of this advanced achievement of Canadian engineering hurt local contractors in Nepean. Men like Dr. George Wilenius joined the Liberal Party in Carleton to work furiously for a new federal government. Other resignations from the federal cabinet followed, and the government was clearly in trouble.

Ottawa City Council at that time had a term of two years. There were few changes in the election of 1962, with Mayor Whitton being returned and myself confirmed again as deputy mayor by a few votes ahead of Don Reid.

THE FEDERAL ELECTION OF 1963

A federal election was called for April 8, 1963, only ten months after the previous one. Within a short period of two years, I had gone through two city-wide elections for the Board of Control and one federal election. That should have been enough for any normal person.

Elections, I discovered, were costly (and addictive)[20] but my wife never complained. We had put together a good team, and they were raring to go, with support pledged from many who had not participated in our campaign in 1962. Still, a plurality of over 6,000 votes would not be easily overcome and we all knew it.

In the end, I decided to go for it. Don Reid this time volunteered to sign my nomination papers, as did a few of the rural councillors. Plus, we had worked out a strategy for the "Confrontation Meeting" in Hilson School, thanks to a taunt from a well-known Conservative after the 1962 debacle: "We sure taught you Liberals a thing or two. Wasn't Dick Bell great? The only person with a voice as strong as his, is Frank Dunlap. Dick never needs a microphone."

Frank Dunlap, later a judge, readily agreed to be my proposer. Frank had been the Liberal candidate in 1958 and had a few scores to settle. The crowd tried to bait him, but he was more than equal to the occasion. In a stentorian voice, he pointed to an obnoxious heckler in the front row and declared that the last time he had seen a mouth like that, it had a hook in

[20] My old colleague Howard Henry told me at our first city council meeting: "If you run in one election and lose, you may get over it. If you run in two, you are in trouble. If you run in three, you have caught an incurable chronic disease that will never leave you."

it. Dick Bell had been parliamentary secretary to Donald Fleming, the minister of Finance in 1962, and Frank blamed the two of them, whom he dubbed the "Mutt and Jeff team" (referring to a well-known comic strip) for what had happened to Canada's economy.

Meanwhile, Dr. Jim Connolly had organized the crowd. When it came my turn to speak, he had unrolled a huge banner with the words FRANCIS—LIBERAL, which stretched from one side of the hall to the other. When the rural Tories tried to tear it down, Jim deployed a phalanx of Italian construction workers he had recruited to defend it. There were scuffles, but the banner stood.

One newspaper reporter, describing the event, said that the returning officer, Tom Davison, after calling the meeting to order, ran for his life. The papers were full of photos that suggested violence, but there were no reports of anyone being hurt. One thing was clear—we were not intimidated this time.

This was the last of the "Confrontation Meetings." Instead, we had a half dozen or so all-candidates meetings, usually sponsored by community associations or service clubs. Debate among the candidates was civilized and well covered by the press.

We again established our headquarters on the second floor of Carlingwood Shopping Centre with fellow Kiwanian Frank Marchington as campaign manager. Keith Davey was instrumental in directing two Liberals from other areas to help us. Dallas Taylor, of Winnipeg, was a superb organizer, and lived in our home with us for the campaign. Bill Pugsley, a professor of Business at McGill University, had contested a nomination against John Turner and later chose not to work in his constituency. Bill, whose grandfather had been premier of New Brunswick and a minister in Laurier's cabinet, later retired to Ottawa and remained a good friend until his death in 1994.

National headquarters of the Liberal Party supplied us with campaign manuals, opportunities to send key workers for training at campaign college, and tomes of briefing materials on party policy. These were most useful in preparing for the all-candidates meetings. I did a great deal of door-to-door canvassing and had to be ready for an enormous variety of questions. However, I could never be sure about the effect of Keith Davey's gimmicks, such as the comic books deriding our opponents, the "diefendollars" (worth only 92.5 cents US which sounds great today) that we handed out in great quantities, and the Truth Squads that dogged Conservative speakers to expose misstatements, but they certainly got press. On the whole, they probably helped.

Following the election of 1962, we left our house on Carling Avenue for a new, larger home we had built on Castle Hill Crescent in the Copeland Park subdivision. It could accommodate receptions of up to one hundred people on two levels and we used it well in eight federal elections. We had excellent neighbours and it was reassuring to live in a community that gave us good support politically.

An enthusiastic construction foreman looked after our polls in the new Minto subdivision of Parkwood Hills. His wife came from a well-known Conservative rural family and her widowed mother stayed with them. One night they were doing the dishes together.

> "Mother, you might as well know, I'm working for the Liberals."
> "Yes, dear."
> "Father would turn in his grave if he knew."
> "I was married to your father for forty years. I always cancelled his vote, but never told him."

In the rural areas, I usually addressed meetings with words like these: "I believe in a two-party system. Every hundred years the other party should be given a chance. Our turn is coming up soon, and maybe you could advance the date a little."

In the election of 1963, we made a little headway in the rural areas and did better in the traditionally hostile areas of the Glebe and Ottawa South. The new subdivisions of Ottawa West and Nepean Township turned the tide. The results were as follows:

Francis (Liberal)	32,325
Bell (Conservative)	31,168
Hanley (NDP)	3,144
Splett (Social Credit)	609

Lester Pearson formed a minority government with 129 seats out of 265. The Conservatives elected 95, Social Credit 24 and NDP 17.

What a celebration we had! I can still remember old Joe Purdy from Dwyer Hill with tears in his eyes and a glass in his hand telling the world that for the first time he had won his vote. For the very first time since Confederation, Carleton had elected a Liberal. Warm letters of congratulations came from across Canada.

We were told that, in one poll in the village of Carp, the Conservative organisers were furious because they could not account for the three extra Liberal votes. More turncoats!

THE 26TH PARLIAMENT OF CANADA, 1963-65

Every newly elected MP enters the House of Commons exhilarated, enthusiastic, determined to do more than, in Tennyson's words, leave "footprints in the sands of time." Few, however, are prepared to survive in the jungle that they experience in the backbenches of the government side, unless they are shielded from it by a senior minister.

Keith Davey had led me to believe that George McIlraith was not too well regarded by Pearson, and that I stood an excellent chance of getting a parliamentary assistant's post, if not a cabinet one. George, however, was a wily, experienced politician and not to be outdone. He had been parliamentary assistant to the minister of Reconstruction and Supply in 1945, to the minister of Trade and Commerce in 1948 and to the minister of Defence Production in 1951. In 1953 he had resigned as parliamentary assistant for some reason. Speculative stories appeared in the press that George would resign from Parliament if he were not named to the cabinet. He was made minister of Transport.

I was named to three of the least desirable committees of the House—Privileges and Elections, Miscellaneous Private Bills and Miscellaneous Estimates. If I had been named to committees dealing with the work of the Department of National Health and Welfare, or Municipal Affairs, or Finance, I could have made a much better contribution. Later, when I served as government whip, I discovered that whips rarely regard themselves as personnel officers trying to get MPs assigned to where they can do the best job. Assignments come as the result of pressure from many sources, mostly cabinet ministers. However, when it came time to set up a committee to review the Canada Pension Plan proposals, I did manage to secure a place, but I was not made chairman. After all, I had some claim to the post, since, as a public servant I had served on an inter-departmental committee on government annuities, and had some background in the pension field. Judy LaMarsh was the minister and she chose an innocuous Liberal from Toronto. Ministers do not help potential rivals.

It is essential to understand the role of a regional minister. Committee assignments, opportunities to speak on important occasions such as the budget and the speech from the throne, reports passed on about your performance to the prime minister, are all heavily influenced by him or her. Some, of course, lay on heavier hands than others. I had come into the House as a protege of Keith Davey, not George McIlraith, and paid a price for it.[21]

[21] I cannot help but contrast my experience with that of the Honourable James Jerome. Elected in a by-election in 1967, he was a protégé of Allan MacEachen, the Minister of National Health and Welfare, and who also chaired the Standing Committee on Procedure and Organization. Beginning in 1964, when Speaker Alan Macnaughton acted as chairman, the committee had made fundamental changes in Rules of the House, dealing with supply, establishing twenty-five Opposition days per session, and a modified form of closure. In 1968, when MacEachen became House Leader, Jerome was named as his parliamentary secretary and attended some cabinet meetings as an observer. After a period on the Justice Committee, he was elected Speaker in 1974. *Mr. Speaker James Jerome*, McClelland and Stewart, 1985, Chapter 1.
Jerome no doubt earned his promotions, and I must take part of the blame for my own slow progress. Frankly, I was too impatient and expressed my frustration when I should not have done so.

George McIlraith got away with many things that he could not have done today. While minister of Transport, he negotiated the sale of the Metcalfe Telephone Company, which he owned, to the Bell Telephone Company. During one Private Members' Hour, he persuaded Maurice Moreau, the MP for York-Scarborough, to help talk out an item affecting Bell's charter, and Moreau was furious when he learned of McIlraith's duplicity. As a federal minister, McIlraith owned a part of a small business bidding on construction of federal buildings, such as the post office in Bell's Corners. He ran a central committee collecting election contributions from companies doing business with the federal government, and decided how these funds would be distributed to federal candidates, both locally and in other provinces across Canada.

George McIlraith, however, had other talents. He could walk down Preston Street and call every merchant by his or her first name. His constituency was small enough for him to walk from one end to the other—which he did often, making him a constituency man par excellence. Charlotte Whitton discovered this when she failed to defeat him as the Conservative candidate in the Diefenbaker sweep of 1958. For a while, he was Government House Leader and could disarm the Opposition by his soft muffled responses. Then, when you read later in Hansard what he had actually said, it often came as a surprise.

The MP for Ottawa East, Jean Richard, told me that Prime Minister Mackenzie King had invited every backbencher to his office once a month while Parliament was in session. An alarm clock on the table was set for five minutes and the interview was over. In that time you were expected to report on your committees, participation in debates, and work in the constituency. It is a pity that subsequent prime ministers discontinued this practice.

Mike Pearson will no doubt be recognized in history as one of our great prime ministers. A distinguished diplomat, a Nobel Prize winner, the man responsible for our national flag, and whose regime enacted Medicare and the Canada Pension Plan, and lowered the age of eligibility for Old Age Security benefits, he merits his place. Ottawa, the nation's capital, owes the National Arts Centre to his personal initiative. Unfortunately for me, I had a difficult relationship with him and I cannot help but feel that George McIlraith, our local minister, had much to do with it.

Knowledge of his backbenchers was not one of Pearson's strong points. Once, a group from my constituency visited the House and I took the opportunity to introduce Mr. Pearson to them as he left the Government Lobby after Question Period. He was genial and spoke a few words to please me.

"Lloyd is a good, hard-working MP and looks after his constituents well. I don't need PhDs—just solid men like Lloyd."

Was it too much to expect my leader to know I had a PhD and had been employed for nine years in the public service as an economist? My friends knew. Why did he make his gratuitous remarks about PhDs? It certainly reflected on my relationship with him and on his with me.

The story circulated that Pearson, after the 1963 election, spoke to a newly elected MP in the hallway. Was he enjoying his work? Very much. Did he understand that there was really a bond among all MPs even though they belonged to different parties, and that he was always pleased to get to know Opposition MPs? "But sir, I belong to your party." Pearson did not recognize one of his own backbenchers.

During my time in the Twenty-sixth Parliament of Canada, I was never once in the office of the prime minister. Despite running as a candidate in three elections under his leadership, I was never once invited to a function at the prime minister's residence on Sussex Drive during the five years that the Pearsons occupied it. There were not, fortunately, too many backbenchers with experiences like mine. Many who reached the front benches or were made parliamentary secretaries had deeper loyalties to the party leader.

Backbenchers did have their happy hunting ground called Private Members Hour. MPs from all parties could present resolutions or private members' bills on any subject they chose. For years, priority on the Order Paper was based on the date of introduction, in later years by lot. The parliamentary counsel gave advice on the proper legal form. Douglas Fisher, now a member of the Parliamentary Press Bureau but then an NDP MP, specialised in long, florid titles that usually disguised the content of the bill. The deputy whip would line up enough government speakers to make sure that a vote did not come before the allotted time of one hour had expired. This was known as "talking it out."

On one occasion, Fisher was introducing his bill. Joe Greene, beside me, looked puzzled, then rose to ask a question. Did the honourable member not have his notes mixed up and was he not speaking to the wrong bill? There followed an awkward silence, then an embarrassed admission that Greene was right. Joe, of course, had reviewed the Hansard of previous Private Members Hours to discover that Fisher's bill had been talked out at least twice previously, and introduced each time by the same speech.[22]

Government backbenchers were supposed to talk out all private members' bills and resolutions. Sometimes there were not enough speakers, and a vote occasionally took place. The government usually ignored the result, but there were exceptions. Jean Chrétien's bill to change the name of Trans-Canada Air Lines to Air Canada was passed and

[22] The exchange between Greene and Fisher took place on October 9, 1964, pages 9867-68 of Hansard. Fisher was speaking to Bill No. C-56 to amend the *Criminal Code* (the Judas-Tree Amendment). Fisher had a similar Bill that he called the *King's Evil Amendment*.

implemented. Also, a number of resolutions dealing with consumer affairs and access to information eventually led to government legislation.

Joe Greene could really turn a phrase. In one speech, he described his feelings on the backbenches, where he could "feel the cold waters of the Ottawa River lapping at his backside." On another, he turned to me and said: "This is trench warfare. As they get knocked off down there in the front benches, we move up." In fact, that is not a bad description of what happens in a parliament.

If a member was not satisfied with an answer given during Question Period, or something arising out of House Proceedings, he or she could give notice to the Speaker. At five o'clock, three such notices were selected for the Adjournment Debate at ten o'clock, popularly known as the "Late Show." The MP had seven minutes in which to present his or her concern and the parliamentary secretary answering for the government a maximum of three minutes. (At present, the limits are reduced to six and two minutes, respectively, and up to five notices can be presented.) As a rule, this procedure was of more use to Opposition MPs who were given more opportunities to be recognized in the House than government backbenchers, but I did manage to make use of it on a number of occasions. My Liberal colleague from Halifax, Gerald Regan, made even better use of it than I did.

COMMONWEALTH PARLIAMENTARY ASSOCIATION—MALAYSIA VISIT

Backbenchers could also achieve some recognition in the parliamentary associations. In the fall of 1963, thanks to Jean Richard, MP for Ottawa East, who chaired the Canadian branch of the Commonwealth Parliamentary Association (CPA), I was named as a delegate to a conference in Kuala Lumpur, Malaysia. Originally founded in 1911 and renamed in 1948, the CPA was dedicated to the study of parliamentary practices in the Commonwealth, and provided a forum for MPs to share experiences. In addition to its general Commonwealth structure, the CPA is divided into eight regions of which Canada is one. Branches in all of the Canadian provinces and territories meet regularly and their conferences perform a function within Canada similar to the CPA's role in the Commonwealth.

The CPA suspends a branch if its parliament is not permitted to function freely, the only parliamentary association that does, to my knowledge. Nigeria, for example, was suspended in the late 1960s and later reinstated.

The trip to Malaysia was fabulous. Some five hundred delegates from every continent described how their own parliaments were evolving, and went on to discuss problems of the emerging democracies, human rights, and economic development.

One group of us visited a tuberculosis hospital on the outskirts. The climate was so benign that walls were scarcely required. The hospital, however, had four separate kitchens—one for Muslim Malays, one for the Chinese, one for Hindu Tamils, and one for Europeans. Providing food certainly must have been costly. I asked if they did surgery, and had blood banks. The answer was yes, they did do surgery, but had only one blood bank. People who would not share each other's food were willing to share each other's blood!

Our Malaysian guide offered us an explanation. Leaders of his country wanted to build a modern state but were impeded by ancient prejudices and prohibitions. Food was prominent in their everyday lives, but the sacred scriptures of their religions made no references to blood banks. Since there was no reference to them, it followed that they should be permitted!

Feeding such a large delegation involved logistics problems. Usually buffets were set up in tents, with different styles of food in each. At one meal, I was in conversation with Miss Shanta Vashisht, former minister of Welfare in the Lok Sabha, or parliament, of India. She had studied at the University of Chicago, and we had much in common. She kept referring deferentially to my white hair, but by a series of discreet questions I concluded that we were of the same age. We moved to the spicy Muslim food and I put a helping on my plate.

We sat down to eat, and I hungrily put some in my mouth and swallowed it. In my mouth it burned, in my stomach it exploded. Never had I been in such agony. Miss Vashisht noted my predicament, tasted the food, then announced that, even for her, it was hot. The only thing I could think of was to eat some bananas. Miss Vashisht summoned a waiter who was insulted that anyone should ask for such a common food as bananas in the presence of their cuisine. He brought a tray with a huge pile of bananas on it, while he and his cronies formed a discreet circle to laugh at me. But the bananas served their purpose.

The delegates were broken into small parties to tour the countryside. We visited a fish-freezing plant, built with Canadian aid funds, that was stocked full. Lack of refrigeration in the villages made it hard to establish retail distribution channels. In one hotel, armed guards barred us from climbing above the third story. Nailed to the wall of our room were the house rules, in at least five languages, to the effect that "The possession of contraband, gambling and prostitution are strictly forbidden. Guests are requested to conduct themselves to maintain their self respect." (I memorized the words.)

Five of us formed a small party in a small town near the Thai border—Lord Boyd (former colonial secretary in the UK), Patrick Holland of Malta, Capildeo of the Caribbean, an African delegate whose name I cannot recall, and myself. It was hot and we shared a few scotches, but Holland refused to join us. I tackled him afterwards.

"What the blazes is wrong with you, Holland? Why would you not join us for a drink, even with a soft drink if that is your concern?

"You would not understand."

"Try me. I am a big boy."

"Well, we have just got our independence in Malta. We had long confrontations, and Boyd was the colonial secretary who came to talk to us." He paused, then added with an embarrassed smile, "Guess who hit him squarely with a ripe tomato. Me."

Years later, I had a drink with Lord Boyd in his flat in London and told him the story. He recalled the incident, and laughed. It probably was not funny at the time.

We visited a native boat-building establishment at Trengganu on the East Coast, a large iron mining operation, and a barge recovering alluvial tin on a river with a posted schedule of the religious holidays for each of their ethnic groups. It must have been a major logistics exercise to make sure that a balanced work crew showed up every day. I will never forget seeing a native shadow play, with cut-out characters projected from behind on a screen. Bert Leboe, the Social Credit MP for Caribou, and I spent a whole day on a rubber plantation watching imported Tamil labourers tap the trees, collect and boil the sap and, finally, make sheets of raw rubber.

It is not possible to describe the benefit I derived from the trip. Malaysia at that time included Singapore, but the inter-racial problems were obvious. Singapore later became an independent state. Our problems with only two official languages paled beside theirs, with three or four official and several unofficial ones. I saw some of the results of Canada's international aid programs. These experiences, together with the opportunity to get to know parliamentarians from different countries and cultures, representing many stages of national development, could never be forgotten.

On the way back, at the suggestion of Miss Vashisht, I stopped off in New Delhi. The Canadian Embassy offered me a car and driver to go from my hotel to her place. Then, whom should I see walking in the street but Charles Lynch of Southam Press. I had the driver pull over to offer him a lift. Charles, a resident of Carleton, blinked. "What some politicians won't do to get votes," he muttered.

Miss Vashisht escorted me through the halls of the Lok Sabha in New Delhi where the lower house of the Parliament of India met. We visited a rural village in her constituency of more than two million people. I had my first introduction to an Indian slum, where thousands of people squatted outside the walls of Red Fort, built by the Mogul Emperors centuries ago.

THE WORK OF AN MP

The workload of an MP has steadily grown since World War II. Payment was traditionally by the session, with one in the spring and another in the fall. Gradually, sessions were extended in length to the point where in 1964, with the Flag Debate, Parliament sat through the whole summer.

As the number of sitting days grew, so did the need for MPs' staff. Prior to 1962, two MPs shared one secretary. By the time I was elected, I was entitled to one full-time secretary.[23]

Shirley Blackburn had worked for the Board of Control and we all distrusted her. Charlotte Whitton placed spies in as many places as she could at city hall and most were female, over thirty, and unmarried members of her church. Shirley fitted this description. I interviewed her anyway when she applied for the job as my secretary.

"Shirley, I know that you are competent, but this is the only position on my staff, and loyalty is critical." Quick as a flash, she replied: "You think I am a stooge. I most certainly am not. Oh yes, the mayor has put all kinds of pressure on me to repeat what I overhear from controllers and I can't take it any more."

Shirley was hired on the spot, and stayed with me through two parliaments. She was conscientious, hard working and discreet. Dick Bell had set a high standard of service for his constituents and a reliable secretary was essential.

I never did learn to balance time spent with constituents and time that should have gone to my MP's job as a legislator. It was important to get to the library and research the background of legislation, material for speeches and committees of the House and the like. But Dick Bell had spent an incredible amount of time seeing constituents who sought patronage employment, or contracts for government business, and farmers whose land had been expropriated for the Green Belt surrounding Ottawa (and wanted more money than the National Capital Commission was offering). In many cases, what was involved was personal counselling.

Recommendations for permanent employment included security guards, messengers, cleaning staff and elevator operators for the House of Commons. Seasonal employment, usually reserved for students, included the Experimental Farm in Ottawa, the National Parks (including canals), occasionally the National Capital Commission, and various government departments. Nothing remotely like this had applied to city council and I was ill-prepared to cope. Dick Bell's friends from rural Carleton, in key positions in the Central Experimental Farm, continued to hire Tories, which caused me no end of embarrassment. This situation was finally corrected by a direct appeal to the minister of Agriculture, Harry Hayes of Alberta, with whom I was on good terms.

---

[23] Douglas Fisher, who had served as a NDP MP from 1957 to 1965, described the struggle to improve services available to MPs and gave Pearson, as Leader of the Opposition, much of the credit for the results achieved.

Patronage was taken for granted by many people, especially in the rural areas. I nominated a man to the cleaning staff of the House of Commons, but not long afterwards he came to me, complaining that he had been fired. When I asked his supervisor why, the answer came that the man had been caught repeatedly sleeping on the job and had refused to change his habits. Needless to say, I did nothing for him. A few years later, when I returned to the House after losing an election in 1965, the same man came back to me, willing to overlook my transgressions and accept an appointment which he felt was rightfully due to him. When I refused, he swore at me, adding: "We had to defeat you and you ain't learned a thing." In his bitterness, he had worked against me, but had no scruples about coming back to me for favours.

One constituent came to Parliament Hill without an appointment and met me in the hall. He insisted that I stop and hear him on the spot. When I explained that I had urgent business before a parliamentary committee, he turned away in anger and from that moment bad-mouthed me to all and sundry.

One night I received a telephone call at two a.m., part of the price an MP pays for refusing to have an unlisted telephone number. A female voice asked if she was speaking to her MP. Yes, I answered. What was the problem?

"My boyfriend came down from the north and we went over to Hull to a night club."

"Well?"

"Mr. Francis, you do not understand. We had a few drinks and he got into an argument with the bartender. Now he is in jail and I can't leave him there. Can't you help me?"

"There is not much you or I can do at this hour. Why do you not just take a taxi home?"

"Surely you can do something."

"I can give you the telephone number of a lawyer who lives in Hull who can tell you what to do to get him out. You can call him."

"Mr. Francis, did you ever try to get a lawyer at two in the morning?"

To help cope with the mass of detail, I had only my secretary, Shirley Blackburn, who did her best. Some MPs declined to see constituents without appointment. Pauline Jewett, for example, was rigorous in this respect and nothing deterred her from her work plans. Russ Honey, from a constituency near her Ontario riding, complained to me that more than once he had been obliged to meet individuals and even delegations from Northumberland when she was not available.[24]

---

[24] When I was Deputy Speaker to Jeanne Sauvé, she criticized the time I spent on this kind of business, remarking that she "never interviewed constituents." That might work in Outrement but never in Ottawa!

THE FLAG DEBATE

It is not possible to leave the Twenty-sixth Parliament without some discussion of the Flag Debate. A fellow Liberal MP, John Matheson, had an interest in heraldry and chaired a committee of the House working out a design. He has written a book on the subject.[25] The debate dragged on and on, going right through the summer of 1964. The Social Crediter, Gilles Gregoire, had miniature hats that he placed on the desk of any MP who made the same speech three times, in an allusion to the "hat trick" of ice hockey. John Diefenbaker's obsessive opposition to the adoption of a distinctive national flag for Canada brought no credit to himself or to his party. Pearson's initial design had three maple leaves with the three colours of red, white and blue, like other countries bordering the Atlantic—Great Britain, France and the United States. The design of a single maple leaf with only two colours, red and white, was a last-minute compromise.

Eventually, a Conservative MP, Leon Balcer, broke with his party and suggested, in a question to a minister in the House, that closure be invoked. For the first time since the Pipeline Debate of 1956, closure was introduced to end a debate.

While I just wanted to get it over, the sooner the better, I am proud to have been a member of the parliament that adopted our flag.

Pearson unveiled the flag for the first time at a convention of the Royal Canadian Legion in Winnipeg, where he successfully stared down the initial criticism. Joe Greene told me that he was the one who had advised the prime minister that the Legion convention would be an appropriate time and place to launch it, but Pearson in his memoirs gave credit to Matheson for the suggestion.

The flag was the cause of an incident on the Big Rideau Lake where we had our summer place. Two families shared one of the points of land jutting some five hundred feet out, the Hambletons from Smiths Falls and the Jake Klassens from Ottawa. The elder Hambleton defiantly raised a Red Ensign flag on his part of the point. Jake, a friend of my brother, Jack, originally from Western Canada, promptly erected a bigger Maple Leaf flag and placed it nearer to the end of the point. Hambleton, of course, erected a still bigger flag on a taller flagpole. The two met and agreed on a truce, including the height of the poles, the size of the flags and their position.

One day I met a fuming Jake on the street in Ottawa. "The bastard broke our truce. I am going to build a pier out into the lake and put a steel flagpole on it," he bellowed.

Days later, while out trolling for fish, I noticed a spite fence over eight feet high and several hundred feet long, separating the two properties.

---

[25] *Canada's Flag: A Search For A Country*, by John Ross Matheson, Mika Publishing Company, Belleville, Ontario, 1986.

Hambleton came out in his boat to gloat. "Did you see my fence? It took ten gallons of paint to cover my side of it."

The fence still stands to this day.

BILINGUALISM AND THE PUBLIC SERVICE I

In the Twenty-sixth Parliament, an issue emerged that proved to be my nemesis. On July 22, 1963, the government announced the names of those who would serve on the Royal Commission on Bilingualism and Biculturalism. A series of meetings from coast to coast were widely publicised. On March 11, 1965, Mr. Pearson addressed the annual general meeting of the Professional Institute of the Public Service of Canada announcing that the government would introduce a policy of bilingualism in the public service.

"What we must contemplate is that the services of government should be available to citizens in their own language. We should also contemplate that ultimately it will be possible for any officer of the public service to deal with at least some of his superiors in his own language. . . . In working towards that objective we must guard against prejudicing the position of people already in the service. We must take great care that no injustice or injury is done to the prospects of advancement by people now in the public service who came here to provide the best service that they can to Canada, but who speak only one language. That is not the intention of this government and it will not be the result of the policies of this government."[26]

His words were interpreted as assurance that the futures of career unilingual public servants would not be adversely affected. For those wishing to learn the second language, training courses would be offered. This, together with Mr. Pearson's statement to the House of Commons on April 6, 1966, became known as the "Pearson Pledge."[27]

In the election campaign of 1965, I heard many complaints of discrimination and failure to observe the Pearson Pledge. Carleton had the highest proportion of English-speaking public servants in Canada and they were uneasy. I relied on Mr. Pearson's words to protect them. While

---

[26] Publication of the Professional Institute of the Public Service of Canada, *Professional Public Service*, May 1965, page 4. The Pearson Pledge was essentially repeated by Prime Minister Trudeau on page 1482 of Hansard of October 17, 1968.

[27] It is hard to reconcile the Pearson Pledge with Pearson's observations in Volume 1 of his memoirs. After the sudden death of the deputy minister of External Affairs, Dr. Skelton, in January of 1941, Pearson hoped to be named his successor. He noted that three French Canadians—Laurent Beaudry, Jean Desy and Pierre Dupuis—were being considered, and wrote on page 193: "These men were all fluently bilingual. I was not. I did not realize then as much as I did later what a grievous handicap this was to anyone who wished to make a career in the federal public service. It certainly did not prevent me from reaching the highest positions as it would now, and rightly . . ." *Mike, the Memoirs of the Rt. Hon. Lester B. Pearson*, Volume 1, University of Toronto Press, 1972, page 193.

bilingualism in the public service was frequently raised, I do not believe that it was the overriding issue in the campaign. While defending the bilingualism policy, I did my best to reassure career anglophone unilinguals that they would be protected but, in so doing, offended some francophones.

TWO WAR MEMORIALS?

For the record, I would like to describe a small item affecting the nation's capital on which I believe my views carried some weight.

In 1964, the minister of Veterans Affairs, Roger Teillet, who represented a Manitoba seat and had a distinguished war record, made a proposal for a second war memorial in Ottawa. His preferred location was Nepean Point, a splendid site overlooking the Rideau Canal and the Ottawa River.

I wrote a memo to Mr. Pearson, objecting strenuously to this suggestion. I could think of nothing more divisive than to have one memorial in Lower Town and another in the present location in Upper Town. Every November 11 we would have two ceremonies and there would be a grave danger of one being in English and a second, in another location, in French.

I heard no more about it.

THE 1965 ELECTION

In the fall of 1965, Walter Gordon and Keith Davey pressed for an early election. I still have campaign buttons that Davey made with the words, "I'm for a Liberal Majority." The slogan was popular with party strategists but no one else. We had been in office a little over two years. In 1963, we had campaigned on "Sixty Days of Decision" promising what great things a new Liberal government would do. Frankly, we had fallen a bit short of our promises. The debacle of the last days of Diefenbaker's government had been so total, however, that we still looked good.

I can still remember sitting in caucus beside Senator Dan Lang, an old friend from University of Toronto days, who had been named to the Senate in 1964. We were discussing whether or not an election should be called. I was solidly opposed. In two years, I had not really made my contribution to Parliament. On the committee dealing with the Canada Pension Plan I hoped to make a mark, but that committee had barely commenced its proceedings. My Conservative opponent Dick Bell was raring to go, telling everyone that he had been parliamentary secretary to the minister of Finance and that Carleton was now represented by an undistinguished backbencher. Surely I was not alone; other backbenchers must have been in the same kind of situation.[28]

[28] I cannot be sure whether it happened in 1965 or 1972, but after losing a plea to the caucus to avoid an election on the grounds offered to us, I faced the caucus with the words of the Roman gladiators in the arena: "We, who are about to die, salute you."

My arguments carried no weight with Dan. He eventually turned and said: "It is a good thing that decisions like this are made by professionals like us, not by MPs who are too close to the scene."

The election took place on November 8, 1965. By this time, Carleton had grown to 442 polls with 89,318 voters on the list, compared to 177 polls with 35,635 voters in George McIlraith's Ottawa West and 133 polls with 29,289 names in Ottawa East. It was a bitter, cold campaign. Everybody asked why we were having it. We had resolved finally the flag issue, got essential legislation passed, and we could hardly argue that the business of Parliament had come to a halt. We were a minority government. Why had we not just put our legislative program forward, and if we had been defeated on any item, the onus for the election would have fallen on the heads of those who had voted against us?

This time the NDP put forward a fresh candidate in Carleton, a United Church minister from Nepean, the Rev. Don Stirling, who had a sharp sense of humour as well as a good platform presence. He made jokes about Lucien Rivard, a convict who escaped from a Quebec prison using a hose on the excuse of watering a rink; and alleged scandals concerning furniture purchases by Maurice Lamontagne.[29] Dick Bell reported that wherever he travelled outside of Canada, everyone asked about Rivard, to Canada's shame. (He must have been meeting other people than I met, but everyone chooses their own companions.)

Between October 11 and 18 of 1965, we conducted a poll of urban Carleton with the following projection:

Bell	34%
Francis	30%
Stirling	9%
Don't Know	27%

In order to overcome the heavy rural Tory vote, I needed to do well in the urban polls, but these numbers were discouraging. Among decided voters, Bell had an edge of fifty-one per cent to forty per cent for myself. Among the undecided, I had an advantage of twenty per cent to seventeen per cent with fifty-three per cent refusing to say. The summary report presented to me merely stated that, "Bell is much stronger among civil

[29] Donald Stirling wowed the audience at one all-candidates meeting. Pearson's parliamentary secretary had resigned over an alleged impropriety involving a racetrack. Stirling quipped: "Liberals take their orders too literally. Pearson said he wanted a stable government and his parliamentary secretary promptly bought a stable." (Somehow, it does not sound as funny today.)
His good showing in the 1965 election raised Stirling's sights and he considered running for reeve of Nepean. In the opinion of several people, he might have succeeded, and Reeve Aubrey Moodie's friends held a council of war. They decided the best course was to persuade Stirling to run for mayor of Ottawa. He responded to the bait and ran in the 1966 election against Don Reid, failing to carry a single poll.

servants while non-civil servants are equally divided." Major issues overall were reported to be morality in government, national unity and majority government. With the civil service, the issues were national unity and bilingualism.[30]

The results were predictable to those of us in the firing lines. Prime Minister Pearson's Liberals elected 131 MPs, two more than they had in the previous House, and were still a minority in a House of 265. We had called an election asking for a Liberal majority and did not get it. The vote in Carleton was as follows:

Bell (Conservative)	32,456
Francis (Liberal)	31,523
Stirling (NDP)	9,953

My vote had decreased by 802 and Bell's had increased by 1,288. Stirling had increased the NDP vote by 6,809, largely at my expense. After the election, Senator Dan Lang wrote me a letter of apology.

FROM 1965 TO 1968—DEFEAT IS HARD TO TAKE

There is no way to describe the letdown after losing an election in which one has so much at stake. For the first time in my adult life, I did not have a job to go to in the morning. Plus, for nearly six years, I had not kept up with journals, or even former colleagues, from my previous profession as an economist.

After recovering from my depression, I accepted a series of part-time assignments. Each was interesting and in total they helped me get through a difficult financial crisis.

Walter Duffett, whose title at the time was Dominion Statistician, called me into his office for a chat. We had been acquainted since Professional Institute days. What were my plans? After three federal elections and one term in Parliament had I had enough? The issue of bilingualism in the public service did not render Carleton (and the new constituency of Ottawa West, created by redistribution in 1968) attractive for a Liberal candidate. Yet, at the age of forty-five, I still had two decades of working life ahead. Walter had a vacancy on his staff for director of the Census and my background as assistant director of the Research and Statistics Division of the Department of National Health and Welfare, as well as my PhD, qualified me for the job if I entered the competition under way for the position.

After careful reflection and discussion with Margery, I appeared before a selection board convened by the Public Service Commission. I had not met the chairman, Jacques Des Roches. When it came my time for an

[30] I suspect that my campaign manager, Earl Olmstead, held back the exact percentages of support in the public service to keep up my spirits for the rest of the campaign.

interview, he faced me with unconcealed hostility and said, "Do you think we will ever let a man like you back into the public service?"

Walter was as much taken aback as I, but told me later that he could no nothing about it. Des Roches later showed up as the chief commissioner of the Unemployment Insurance Commission. What his qualifications were for such a post was beyond my understanding. Together with Bryce Mackasey, the two fouled up the Unemployment Insurance Act, but more about that later. Des Roches' hostility had its roots in my attempts to defend the rights of unilingual anglophones in the public service. One thing I do owe to him—he made it easier for me to resolve to continue in politics!

THE OTTAWA TRANSPORTATION COMMISSION

Let me go back to city of Ottawa politics. In the campaign of 1964, Don Reid had easily defeated two rivals, Charlotte Whitton and her brother-in-law, Frank Ryan. Frank, a man respected by all who knew him, had delayed announcing his candidacy; so, when Don Reid entered the race, it was too late for Frank, despite recruiting the woman who had helped us so much in the 1963 campaign, Dallas Taylor from Winnipeg. Dallas died tragically of a heart attack soon afterwards, and we sorely missed her in the 1965 election.

Early in 1966, city council named me as a member of the Ottawa Transportation Commission,[31] along with Aime Arvisais, of the Separate School Board, and former mayor George Nelms, who acted as chairman.

The general manager was George Brady, a genial man who had spent his life in Public Transit and whom you could not help but like. We discussed minor problems: how to get the most value from bus advertising; whether we should run our own schedule for sightseeing buses in the summer, or contract out to a nationwide organizer of tourist sightseeing; representations to city council to improve the streets we wanted to use for buses; and the like.

We also had to do some hard thinking about maintaining our passenger loads in the face of competition from private automobiles. The fare box was not yielding enough revenue to meet our mounting expenses.

At one point, I suggested combining the parking authority—a money earner from parking metres and municipally owned parking lots— with the OTC. It seemed only logical that some of the revenues from parking metres, which were a device for renting out space on city streets, should go to the benefit of transit riders and that bus routes should be co-ordinated with the location of new parking lots in order to divert cars as much as possible from bus routes to other streets. But this did not fly with city council.

In 1966, members of the OTC Board attended a convention on public transit in San Francisco. It was a revelation. One session illustrated the effects of new throughway construction in a metro area, and how big

---

[31] Louis Rocque of *Le Droit* called the OTC a municipal Senate for old politicians.

dollars bought relief for short periods, five years or less, with the problem repeated at the end. We rode the newly constructed Bay Area Rapid Transit System and attended a session on alternating current versus direct current motors for transit. We listened to a heated discussion of the merits of steel wheels on steel tracks versus rubber wheels on steel tracks, the design adopted for the Paris underground system (and later Montreal). We rode the famous cable car, carefully preserved from earlier decades, and dined at Fishermen's Wharf.

Public transit is the efficient means to move people while private automobiles are the convenient means. As long as voters can force public authorities to give priority to the construction of new roads, public transit will suffer. When cars can no longer move, people will turn to transit. Priorities in a democratic society are difficult. The private automobile forces planners to build their cities around it with higher costs for street construction, traffic signals, even sewer and water mains, and leads to decay in the central core.

D.W. CARR & ASSOCIATES

For a period I joined a firm of private economic consultants, D.W. Carr & Associates. Bill Carr, with a PhD from Harvard, had spent some time in the public service before going out on his own. One project involved a review of royalty policy on mineral rights for Newfoundland which probably produced some useful results. Another comprised a review of an econometric model for a United States defence agency and I could make no sense whatever of it. For that matter, Wisconsin, when I was there, was not the place to study econometrics and I have never felt comfortable with econometric models that attempt to do long-term projections for resource use. The assumptions are often heroic, concealed, and wrong, as I believe they were in this case.

By far the most interesting assignment was a commission by the territorial government of the Yukon to survey its resources. Bill put together a team of specialists, including a remarkable man, "Slim" Monture, a retired federal deputy minister of Mines. Slim was a Mohawk, born on a reserve in Ontario, who had persevered to get a degree in mining engineering. Possessed of great dignity, subtle wit, infectious good humour, and excellent raconteur skills, he was a pleasure to have on the team.[32]

---

[32] I wrote a memo to Prime Minister Pearson suggesting that Monture should be named governor general. Clearly, he had the personal dignity, character and good judgement to perform well. The example of a First Canadian in this post would have been an inspiration to all Canadians, in my opinion. Pearson, instead, nominated Roland Mitchener, a former Speaker of the House of Commons. No one could fault this choice, but I still think Monture would have been a desirable break in what has become the practice of alternating between francophone and anglophone appointments.

We travelled to Whitehorse to get our final instructions. On one occasion, Bill, Slim and I walked to the outskirts and saw a number of Indians living in squalid conditions, putting it mildly. Slim stood still and tears slowly came to his eyes. What motivated you to get away from the reserve, I asked. The reply came carefully, deliberately: one teacher had called him a no-good Indian who would never amount to anything. From that point he had been determined to prove her wrong.

A RARE STONE IN YUKON

The day after my defeat in 1965, I came home to find that Margery had placed before my dinner plate a newspaper clipping about a night course in polishing stones for jewellery. I promptly enrolled in classes conducted by Ernie Eaton and his wife Marianne.

By mid-1966, I was enthusiastic about my new hobby (perhaps obsessed would be a better description). As Carr, Monture and I walked the track of the Whitepass and Yukon Railroad outside of Whitehorse, I picked up a shiny black pebble from the gravel.

"What is this, Slim?" I asked.

"A piece of bitumen."

I picked up a broken bottle and scratched it with my stone.

"Did you ever see bitumen that could scratch glass?"

"No, you have a point. It is probably chert."

In fairness to Slim, he specialised in metallic ores, not semi-precious stones, but I had already learned that geologists and mining engineers usually called anything chert that they could not identify. I kept this stone in my pocket, taking it out from time to time to rub in my hands.

As we stood on a corner of a main intersection in Whitehorse, an American watched me and came over.

"Can I see what you have in your hand?"

"Gladly, can you tell me what it is?"

He looked it over carefully, then answered, "Chloromelanite."

"What is that?"

"The family starts in the soft serpentines and goes all the way up to the hard jades, which is what this is. I am from Eureka, California, and we find small pieces of it. This one is worth fifty dollars. Where did you find it?"

I told him and he immediately rushed off. I went back and found a few more pieces, which I took back to Ottawa. The stone was indeed chloromelanite, a form of jadeite, which is very rare in Canada. One nice piece of it I polished into a stone that is part of the ring I still wear on my right hand.

To this day, I believe that chloromelanite is an untapped resource of the Yukon!

THE WAX MUSEUM

One day in 1965, Gerald Regan, the MP for Halifax, Joe Greene, MP for Renfrew South, and I were having coffee when "Gerry" suggested that a wax museum would do well in Ottawa. Thus began the worst business venture with which I have been associated.

We needed a local person to select a site and hopefully provide management, which we foolishly assumed would be routine. We chose a young man from a well-known Ottawa real estate family, and he recommended a site on the south side of Sparks Street in the Ottawa Electric Building. We hired a firm from the United States to produce the wax figures and scenes, on the theme of significant moments in the history of Canada, from the early explorers to the discovery of insulin by Banting and Best, and chose the name Confederation Wax Museum. Four of us shared equally the cost and our venture opened in the spring of 1966.

Initial reception was good, and the museum attracted a fair number of tourists who came to see the changing of the guard ceremony on Parliament Hill, little more than two blocks away. My wife, Margery, acted as manager, without salary, until we could select a permanent employee. In the fall, attendance fell sharply and during the winter approached zero. We barely serviced our bank loan and were disappointed in the performance of the manager whom we eventually chose. Things picked up again in the summer of 1967 but never approached the levels of the previous year. By the fall of 1967, we had to close shop. A remnant of the museum was moved by Gerry Regan to Atlantic Canada but I don't think it was terribly successful.

Our mistakes were many and nothing of the original capital was recovered. The site was not readily accessible to buses and I have noted that museums elsewhere derived considerable revenue from visiting groups. We did not change our scenes and there was little incentive for anyone to come back after one visit. We did not have a special section for children, nor any horror scenes, which seem necessary for a successful museum. Not least, visitors to Ottawa were spoiled, for there were so many attractions in the city not requiring any admission fee.

It never rains but it pours. The bank made immediate demands on me at a time when our son Paul was attending the University of Toronto. Plus, in exuberance at the success of our land development in Bell's Corners, now completed, I had made a commitment to participate in a further land assembly of six hundred acres in the south of Nepean Township, bordering the Jock River. This involved regular payments on land mortgages. I no longer had the salary of an MP and for the one and only time in my life came close to personal bankruptcy.

One venture, our one-third interest in Lynwood Shopping Centre, saved us. At the time it had opened in December 1959, I had joined with others in signing, with considerable trepidation, personal guarantees for over $1 million. After the first six months, it proved to be a solid investment. The decision over which I had agonized turned out well; the one that I had entered into enthusiastically turned out to be a disaster. Credit must be given, however, to my associate in the Lynwood ventures, Don Sim, whose business acumen was beyond question.

GENERAL ASSEMBLY OF THE UNITED NATIONS

In September 1967, Mr. Pearson named me to the Canadian delegation to the General Assembly of the United Nations in New York. The appointment did not involve any remuneration, other than my hotel room at The Barclay and an expense allowance of $10 a day, since it was assumed that delegates were on leave from their regular employment. It was simply too attractive an opportunity to decline, although it involved my full attention for three months at a stage of my life when I could ill afford it.

The Fifth Committee, which dealt with financial matters, was my assignment. We worked in close association with a body known familiarly as the ACABQ, which stood for the Advisory Committee on Administrative and Budgetary Questions. The head of the Canadian Permanent Mission to the United Nations was George Ignatieff, a distinguished diplomat whose family came from czarist Russia and who delighted in speaking his formal Russian with Soviet delegates.

George held a general meeting of the full delegation every week, so that we would all be informed of business in committees other than those on which we were serving. The delegation included some brilliant people, at least six of whom later became ambassadors, some to senior posts such as Washington and Tokyo. General Burns, former commander of a peacekeeping force in the Middle East, handled disarmament matters, which kept him busy, since Canada was serving a term on the Security Council.

My immediate advisers were two young officers of the Department of External Affairs. Meanwhile, Maxwell Henderson, Canada's auditor general, prepared a special report on audit procedures for the UN and I had the honour of reading it into the record. Somehow I found an excuse to invite everybody to Montreal for Expo '67.

Plenary sessions of the General Assembly were fascinating. Thanks to electronic procedures, votes took place by delegates pushing a button, taking no more than five minutes for the results. What a contrast with the time-consuming roll calls of the Canadian House of Commons! Simultaneous translations in five official languages provided an excellent opportunity for any student of English, French, Spanish, Russian, or Mandarin. At Glebe Collegiate, I had taken four years of Spanish and it was fascinating to listen to the differences in the Spanish spoken by delegates from Ecuador (very cultured), Argentina (half Italian) and Cuba (machine-gun staccato).

The delegate from Malta introduced a resolution on Law of the Sea, which George Ignatieff presciently observed would be far from the end of the matter. Indeed the subject formed the basis of many resolutions for decades to come, to say nothing of endless columns by Jeffrey Simpson of the *Globe and Mail.*

In the Fifth Committee, votes tended to follow bloc patterns. Despite ideological differences, representatives of the USSR, the UK, the USA and France presented a common front to control spending and establish firm procedures for audits. In general, representatives from the Third World liked to spend. Canada tended to vote with a group of smaller countries, such as Ireland, Belgium and Holland.

The cultural life of New York is of course legendary. Margery came down and we went to see *Fiddler on the Roof* and *Man from La Mancha*. The Metropolitan Museum has no equal. I can remember studying carefully ancient Chinese jade carvings, including yin and yang, noting that some were of jadeite and others of nephritic jade, the kind we have in British Columbia. The UN hosted concerts by artists from many countries and, on one occasion, a musician from India, Ravi Shankar, played the sitar with Yehudi Menuhin assisting. Bob McKeown came for a weekend and we discovered some fabulous (and not too expensive) restaurants.

I returned to Ottawa in time for Christmas. The alderman representing my old ward of Carleton resigned his seat to accept employment with a social agency in British Columbia, and I was appointed by resolution of council to serve the unexpired portion of his term.

There was no way of escaping federal politics. At this time, a retired executive of Canadian Industries Limited in Montreal, Leonard Hook, volunteered to go over our constituency records and to put them in order. Every day for several months he came to our house and prepared cards on every Liberal contact we knew in Carleton. Anyone who has been a candidate for public office will appreciate what such a service meant.

Both the Liberal and Conservative parties were in the process of changing leaders. Pearson had led the Liberals through four federal elections—1957, 1962, 1963 and 1965—without winning a majority and his troops were clearly restless. Dalton Camp masterminded a civil war in the Conservative Party to replace John Diefenbaker with Robert Stanfield.

The 1965 election, despite the gain of two seats, had weakened Liberal representation in Parliament. Losses included really able backbenchers such as John Mullally of PEI; John Stewart and Jack Lloyd of Nova Scotia; Bob Temple, Pauline Jewett, Maurice Moreau, Marvin Gelber and David Hahn from Ontario; and Margaret Konantz from Manitoba. Liberals now had no seats in PEI, Saskatchewan and Alberta and only one in each of Nova Scotia and Manitoba. Liberal numbers declined from twenty to fifteen in Atlantic Canada, from fifty-two to fifty-one in Ontario, from ten to eight in the four western provinces. In Quebec, they rose from forty-seven to fifty-six.

LIBERAL MINORITY GOVERNMENT 1965-68

The minority government of 1965-68 did have some outstanding achievements to its credit, however, including the Canada Pension Plan, Medicare and the Canada Assistance Plan. The formula of sharing costs with the provinces in such a manner as to give a better break to poorer provinces encouraged all provinces to participate in Medicare and the Canada Assistance Plan. Medicare involved a substantial commitment of resources, but the Canadian pattern based on comprehensive benefits, universal coverage, portability from one province to another, limited deterrent charges to patients and public as opposed to private administration has been a recognized model for others to follow. I had worked on Medicare background documents as an employee of the Department of National Health and Welfare from 1951 to 1960 and was pleased to see that what we had worked for was finally achieved.

Walter Gordon recognized that he had given bad advice on the timing of the 1965 election and offered to resign. His personal popularity, however, remained strong with rank-and-file Liberals, and he was re-appointed for a short time to the cabinet, but not as minister of Finance. His previous budget had been a fiasco, with punitive taxes on the takeover of Canadian businesses by foreigners and on dividends remitted abroad. It is my opinion that, prior to his second departure, he had a major role in persuading cabinet to make an even worse decision.

In 1950 Canada had pioneered a national scheme of universal pensions beginning at age seventy. The program was expensive but manageable, a cornerstone of our social security safety net. The Joint Committee of the Senate and House of Commons, in recommending the program, had called attention to the need to keep in mind the ratio of numbers in the labour force to the total population. In other words, no country could afford to shift too high a percentage of its population into retirement, leaving too heavy a burden on those still working. Walter Gordon was, I believe, responsible for persuading the government to commit itself to reducing the retirement age, one year at a time, until finally payment was made at sixty-five.

On April 24, 1997, I participated in a symposium in Ottawa celebrating the hundredth anniversary of Pearson's birth. Panellists rightly referred to the outstanding achievements of the minority government, including the Canada Pension Plan, Medicare and the Canada Assistance Plan, but none mentioned lowering the age for Old Age Security. I mentioned the enormous resources that this decision involved, more costly than Medicare, for example, and suggested that this decision had been made without adequate study. Demographic projections of future population would have revealed the increasing numbers of older people and the costs of providing pensions on a universal basis to them. Liberal strategist Tom Kent assured the audience that indeed the best of studies had been done, but unfortunately such studies had overestimated the growth of national income, had failed to anticipate the decline in birth rates and the consequent aging of the population, had underestimated unemployment rates and overestimated participation rates in the labour force. Some studies!

Having already made major commitments on the extension of social measures, the cabinet would have done well not to change the retirement age, leaving the Canada Assistance Plan to provide for needy persons between the ages of sixty-five and sixty-nine. Alternatively, they might have been content to lower the age by one year to sixty-nine, and not try to commit future budgets. Allan MacEachen, at the time the minister of National Health and Welfare, said it was not his decision. Mitchell Sharp, then minister of Finance, said he was not responsible (although the policy was implemented by a budget resolution). Since the ghost of Walter Gordon was not there to defend him, I can only conclude that Walter did it.

This decision was reckless and ultimately damaging to the good work the cabinet had done. It was taken as a blind act of faith, at a period when people were living longer and retiring earlier. Nobody thought to go back and read the 1950 Report of the Joint Committee of the Senate and House of Commons, which had cautioned about the dangers of having too many people on pensions, compared to those still in the labour force. Needless to say, however, the lower ages were immensely popular. Monique Begin told me that when she became minister of National Health and Welfare in 1972, the costs were already so high that she was facing a frontal attack on universality and she had no room to manoeuvre.

Beginning in the 1990s, budget deficits soared and the cost of the universal pension was an important element. It was simply not possible to bring budget deficits under control without the income tax "clawback," which was in effect a reversal of the 1967 decision, but late in the day after the damage was done. We have subsequently witnessed the slow, systematic erosion of universality, not only in the pension field, but throughout the social security net of which Canadians were so proud. We would have avoided so much trouble if cabinet in 1967 had not let itself get carried away.

THE 1968 NATIONAL LIBERAL LEADERSHIP CONVENTION

A feature of the 1965 election had been Pearson's recruitment of the Three Wise Men from Quebec—Pierre Trudeau, Jean Marchand and Gerard Pelletier—to run as Liberal candidates. They were offered as proof of the party's capacity to renew itself by bringing in new blood, and all three were elected handsomely.

It was a francophone's turn to lead the Liberals, and many looked to these three. Jean Marchand, a charismatic trade union leader, was the first choice of many but, for reasons of his own, he declined. Pierre Trudeau, former editor of *Cité Libre*, an influential intellectual publication in Quebec, and minister of Justice in Pearson's cabinet, soon emerged as a leading contender to succeed him.

Pearson announced his resignation on December 14, 1967, and a leadership convention was called for April 2-4, 1968, to be held in Ottawa. Notwithstanding the tradition of the Liberal Party in alternating between francophone and anglophone leaders, a number of anglophones entered the race—Bob Winters, Allan MacEachen, John Turner, Paul Hellyer and Joe Greene.

Greene, who was the minister of Agriculture and represented a constituency adjacent to Carleton in the Ottawa Valley, invited me to be his campaign manager. I accepted. To this day, I do not know whether or not he really expected to win, but a good showing would have certainly assured him a senior post in cabinet. At no time did we seek any support in Quebec, but we campaigned hard in the rest of the country. For my part, I was flattered at being asked and pleased to donate my services to help a friend.

Greene, a wartime pilot who had been awarded the Distinguished Flying Cross, practised law in the town of Arnprior. He had previously made an unsuccessful run for leadership of the Ontario Liberal Party, losing to Andrew Thompson, who had Metro Toronto support. Perhaps his greatest talent was that he was one of the most effective stump orators I have ever known; he was also an effective tactical politician.[33]

We drew support from fellow members of Joe's law class at Osgoode Hall in Toronto and from his contacts through the Department of Agriculture in western Canada. Compared to other candidates, our budgets were so small you could hardly notice them. We portrayed Joe as the Ottawa Valley's version of Abe Lincoln (whom in a way he resembled), a man with modest resources that you could trust to do the right thing. Joe's wife, Queenie, handled herself superbly at all times. We had good support in Ottawa, including most of the people who worked on my team, which proved valuable when it came time to get volunteers to do the necessary chores at a convention.

---

[33] In December 1965, after the November election that had been so disastrous for me, Greene had been made minister of Agriculture. As an easterner, he was received with some hostility in parts of the west. The farmers kept referring to him as "son," which Joe said he learned afterwards was an abbreviation for a well-known epithet! On one occasion, he rented a single-engine plane, which crashed on landing in a farmer's field. The farmer conceded that Joe, at least, could plough an unorthodox, but straight furrow!

On the Friday afternoon, the candidates were invited to speak to panels of two or three hundred delegates. It came as a shock to hear from more than one journalist that Joe had bombed, but they could not say why. I asked a CBC sound technician about it. He told me that the reason was that Joe had faced a fixed microphone. When he waved his arms with gestures and moved about on the stage, the sound carried by the microphone was occasionally so weak that no one could hear him and his punch lines were lost. What was the solution? Simple. Provide Joe with a hand-held microphone. He was happy to set one up for me.

When the time came for Joe's grand speech to the full assembly of delegates, Queenie and their five children all marched with him to the stage. As he got up from his seat, I told Joe to pick up the microphone on a stand to the right of the stage, and to use it. Joe followed instructions and the rest is history. He gave without question the most dramatic and moving speech of his life.

Paul Hellyer had preceded Joe and relied on a fixed microphone. Though a competent orator, Paul suffered in contrast to Joe and bombed.[34]

As successive ballots were counted, it became clear that the real contest was between Bob Winters and Pierre Trudeau. Joe had done well, edging ahead of Allan MacEachen, for example. After the fourth ballot, he withdrew in favour of Trudeau, whom he had been careful never to offend.

THE 1968 ELECTION CAMPAIGN

Sometimes everything goes as it should. Trudeau decided to call a general election for June 25, 1968, profiting from the favourable publicity coming out of the leadership convention. The Conservatives, meanwhile, had replaced John Diefenbaker with Robert Stanfield, who owed much of his success to Dalton Camp in a civil war that scarred their party.[35]

The campaign of 1968 was the easiest of my nine federal elections. Our nominating convention brought an acclamation, and Trudeaumania could be felt from the day of the election writ. Dick Bell and I faced each other for the fourth and last time.

By now, Bell was clearly feeling the heat from the government's bilingual policies. On February 1, 1966, the chairman of the Public

---

[34] Paul Hellyer's slogan was "Youth + Experience." I was standing beside him when a buxom young woman came on the stage with a sign stretching across her ample front bearing his slogan. It struck me as hilarious, and I burst out laughing. Paul asked why. I replied that one might say that on one side she was young and on the other side experienced. He did not think it was funny.

[35] Stanfield had been caught by a TV camera eating a banana during his convention, a shot that was carried nationally. Joe Greene kept munching apples, which he considered more appropriate for a Canadian and which he handed out profusely at the Liberal convention. Greene's TV shots with an apple never got the publicity that Stanfield did with a banana, however.

Service Commission, John Carson, while speaking to the Federal Institute of Management, announced a new policy that would award a bonus of ten per cent in points to any bilingual candidate for appointment in the national capital area. The staff associations protested that they had not been consulted, and Bell raised Carson's speech in Question Period on February 3 asking "upon what basis does the government or the commissioner countenance this wholesale departure from the merit system?" On March 8 Bell spoke, dealing, in his words, "briefly but explicitly with what has become a very highly sensitive, indeed, an explosive issue in the public service, namely the inept and improper handling by the government and the Civil Service Commission of the problem of bilingualism." When the *Civil Service Act* had been amended in 1961, the MP for Hull had moved an amendment to Section 47 of the Act to award a bonus of five per cent to bilingual applicants, but the amendment had been rejected by the Committee of the House examining the bill. Upon what legislative authority was John Carson now acting, Bell asked. How could he defy a specific decision of Parliament?[36] The problem was compounded when additional pay of ten per cent (the bilingual bonus) was later paid, in addition to the bonus points on initial appointment.

On April 6, 1966, Prime Minister Pearson made a formal statement to the House of Commons on the government's policy on bilingualism in the public service, from which I quote:

> " . . . the careers of civil servants who are not bilingual and who have devoted many years of their lives to the service of their country must not be prejudiced in any way by measures to develop bilingualism."

Reference to the Hansard index shows that Bell raised the problems of the public service repeatedly until the dissolution of parliament.

When the election call came in April 1968, we were ready. Our headquarters in a vacant retail store on the Richmond Road in Westboro were the best we ever had. Everybody loved Trudeau and the public service forgot about blaming me for bilingualism. Dick Bell as the incumbent received most of their criticism. We had no trouble securing our enumerators, always a good omen in an election campaign. Plus, a number of enthusiastic new workers joined us, such as Frank Padulo, recently retired from the public service. My NDP opponent, a former alderman on city council, fought a vigorous and nasty personal campaign, but fell 4,000 votes short of the number secured by the previous NDP candidate.

---

[36] See Hansard, 1966, pages 639, 1071 and especially Bell's speech reported on pages 2407 to 2410, inclusive.

The results of the election held on June 25, 1968, were as follows in Ottawa West,[37] the new riding created out of old Carleton by redistribution:

Francis (Liberal)	23,750
Bell (Conservative)	16,392
Sutherland (NDP)	5,003

In every election campaign, two critical decisions must be made, preferably by the candidate. The first relates to the choice of election headquarters. You need space that is immediately available and inexpensive. Sometimes a friendly landlord will donate the space for two months, but it is always desirable to have a lease. In one provincial election, Howard Henry in Ottawa West had the unforgettable experience of being locked out of his headquarters ten days before the election as the result of a little skulduggery by his opponents. You cannot refuse offers of help, but a lease protects everyone.

The second decision is more important: the choice of a campaign manager. The person chosen must be available on a full-time basis, know about elections and be able to work with the many kinds of people you meet in a campaign run largely by volunteers. My old (and still good) friend, Frank Marchington, who operated a service station, had ably handled my first two campaigns. My third was handled by a retired army officer, Earl Olmstead, who had all the required attributes, and did his very best.

For the 1968 campaign, we engaged a man who had been the Ottawa representative of a national industry association. Fluently bilingual, personable and meticulous in detail, he practically lived at headquarters for the campaign. We had the usual series of all-candidates meetings to debate the issues. This was the fourth time Bell and I had crossed swords on the hustings and we each had our own style of presentation. My manager demanded that I be more aggressive, and that I attack Bell, the incumbent, much more forcefully. I refused. After all, I was the candidate, and not exactly a neophyte; and could tell when things were going our way. He was furious with me more than once and countermanded my instructions on a number of matters, as I later discovered.

After our victory, I learned that he attended a reception at Liberal headquarters and met Mr. Trudeau. The prime minister congratulated him on the victory in Ottawa West, to which he replied: "I did my best but we would have done better with a better candidate." This after we had beaten Bell by a plurality of over 7,000 votes!

This man secured a job on the staff of the National Liberal Federation, where he lasted about a year. A member of the cabinet, Bud Drury,

[37] Only ten percent of the polls in new Ottawa West came from the old Ottawa West, which was renamed Ottawa Centre.

complained to me about him and I told Drury the above story. Drury nodded. He had been shocked to hear it also. I have since learned that, for all his polish, he has never held a position for long and, when last heard from, was unemployed and in difficult circumstances in Montreal.

You really have to check out the background of your campaign manager. Don't hire anyone out of the blue.[38]

I cannot leave this discussion without also referring to a candidate's choice of official agent, who will prepare the statement of election expenses. In one election, a professional man volunteered for the job, but he turned out to be much too busy. A candidate simply does not have the time to check out this kind of detail during the campaign, so the records were a mess.

In desperation, I turned to Vivien Dzau, a chartered accountant who had helped us. Vivien took a look at the files, then suggested that, if another chartered accountant could be found to assist, the two of them could prepare the best return they could and it would not likely be challenged. She felt that she should not do it alone. A fellow Kiwanian, Morris Agulnik, readily agreed and they jointly filed the documents. Neither of them has ever made any request of me at any time and I have been most grateful for the hours they donated to the task. Friends like these make politics worthwhile.

In my later campaigns, squadron leader Sam Hawkins, retired from the Royal Canadian Air Force, handled the task of official agent for me superbly.

THE TWENTY-EIGHTH PARLIAMENT, 1968-72

NATO PARLIAMENTARY VISIT TO USA, 1968

Days after the election, a delegation of members of the North Atlantic Treaty Association (NATO) was scheduled to make a visit to military installations in the United States. One of the delegates scheduled to go had been defeated and I was invited at the last minute to replace him. Marcel Lambert, the MP for Edmonton West, Perry Ryan, MP for Toronto Spadina, and I were the three Canadians in a delegation of some forty members of NATO parliaments.

We visited Cape Kennedy in Florida, the launching site for missiles in the US space program, where we met a number of Canadian scientists who

[38] Liberals shortly afterwards held a brainstorming session at Harrison Hot Springs, British Columbia, and this man was responsible for assigning delegates to rooms. A woman delegate, who had a masculine first name, was inadvertently placed in a double room with a male. When the man came down to breakfast the next morning, he was asked quietly if he had found his accommodation acceptable. He replied that it was just fine. When the woman came down later, she gave the same reply to the same question. It was decided to leave well enough alone.

had left our country when the Arrow program was cancelled. We visited the White Sands Proving Grounds, New Mexico, and one of the bases from which bombers carrying nuclear weapons were continuously in the air to counter any Russian attack. We toured a battleship in dock on the East Coast. I suspect that the tour was of greater value to our European allies, who were impressed with what we were shown but concerned with the lack of standardization of equipment and weapons with the various national forces of NATO.

I will never forget the four days we spent in Washington, the nation's capital. A week or so before, the city had been torn apart by incredible race riots. A wide swath surrounding the famous Capitol dome was burned and looted to resemble a battle zone.

All in the name of good planning, the authorities had maintained the old structures in the centre of the city and driven new office buildings and apartments to the suburbs. The owners of the old buildings, with no economic incentive (or even permission) to redevelop their holdings, had simply let them get run down. As a result, marginal economic groups from the south had moved in to take advantage of cheap rents.

Today, Washington is a city of sharp contrasts. It has some grand vistas and imposing monuments, befitting the capital of a great and powerful country. It also has slums that have to be seen to be believed. It is without question the most important black city in the world.

Whenever I hear people in Ottawa say that we must preserve the vista of Parliament Hill in the centre of Ottawa and not allow high buildings in the vicinity, I think of Washington. Whenever I hear them say that a freeze should be imposed on whole areas to preserve our heritage from the past, I think of Washington. Planners may be wise, but their judgment has to be balanced with that of down-to-earth practical politicians.

We also visited Arlington National Cemetery and John F. Kennedy's grave. It occurred to me that we might have something similar to Arlington in the Gatineau Hills, but when I made this suggestion, Prime Minister Trudeau rejected it. The little cemetery at Wakefield where Pearson is buried could have been expanded into an ideal location.

TRUDEAU, FULLERTON AND THE NATION'S CAPITAL

One of the earliest measures that the new cabinet implemented, under Prime Minister Trudeau's direction, concerned the national capital region. According to Section 16 of the *British North America Act*, Ottawa was designated as the nation's capital. The city of Hull had developed as a poor cousin on the other side of the Ottawa River. A few federal operations, including the government's printing bureau, had been transferred to Hull but not much else. Marchand and Trudeau were determined to change this.

Trudeau chaired the second meeting of the Federal-Provincial Constitutional Conference held in Ottawa, February 10-12, 1969.

Prior to the meeting, a draft resolution had been prepared by an exchange of correspondence with Ontario and Quebec, as follows:

1. The Constitutional Conference is agreed that the cities of Ottawa and Hull are the core of the Canadian capital area.
2. No changes be made to provincial boundaries or to the constitutional responsibilities of the governments concerned.
3. The boundaries of the Canadian capital area are to be established by agreement of the governments concerned.
4. In line with the aforementioned objectives, steps must be taken so that the two official languages and the cultural values common to all Canadians are recognized by all governments concerned in these two cities and in the capital region in general, so that all Canadians may have a feeling of pride and participation in, and attachment to, their capital.
5. That the Study Committee on the Canadian Capital continue its work giving particular importance to the following:
   (a) the definition of suburban areas that would eventually constitute, along with the cities of Ottawa and Hull, the Canadian capital regions;
   (b) a study of the administration and the financing of the tripartite organization.[39]

The resolution was adopted unanimously, with the agreement of all provincial premiers, including Jean-Jacques Bertrand of Quebec and John Robarts of Ontario.[40]

The federal government then proceeded to spend several hundreds of millions of dollars for the construction of new buildings in Hull that totally changed the appearance of that city. Several government departments were moved from Ottawa across the river.

The federal instrument to implement its policies in the National Capital Region is a crown corporation known as the National Capital Commission (whose name had been changed some years previously from the Federal

---

[39] Extract from the Official Proceedings of the Federal-Provincial Constitutional Conference, Ottawa, February 10-12, 1969.

[40] On December 16, 1996, I appeared before the Joint Committee of the Senate and House of Commons on Official Languages, citing the transcript of the February 1969 Constitutional Conference and the undertaking of Premier Bertrand to make the National Capital Region fully bilingual. Senator Louis Robichaud, who was premier of New Brunswick at the time, confirmed my report of the sessions. I suggested that the committee, in its report, should ask the province of Quebec to exempt that portion of the National Capital Region within its boundaries from the application of Quebec's language and access to minority education laws and that they might call Mr. Trudeau as a witness. The committee skated carefully around these problems in its report, which was tabled just prior to the election call on April 27, 1997.

District Commission). The NCC has grandiose responsibilities, according to the federal statute that created it, but must always walk on eggshells, deferring to the constitutional powers of Quebec and Ontario. It does, however, hold title for the federal government to large land holdings, including extensive parks systems in both provinces. It has also power to expropriate land or buildings and to undertake on its own initiative the construction of parkways, roads and bridges. It can make grants for a wide variety of purposes, from subsidizing public transit to sponsoring festivals, like the annual Winterlude in February.

Not least of the NCC's responsibilities is the continuing implementation of an overall plan for the National Capital Region. Following World War II, Prime Minister Mackenzie King engaged the distinguished French town planner, Jacques Greber, to prepare a grand design for the development of Canada's capital. The Greber Plan has been so modified in the light of developments as to be scarcely recognizable but one of its main features, the creation of a Green Belt surrounding the city of Ottawa, has given a unique and most desirable character to the area.

As his new chief of the NCC, Trudeau chose Douglas Fullerton, a man not without ability, but who at times could be blunt, aggressive and impulsive. He had earned a considerable reputation in the financial world and acted as financial adviser to Premier René Levesque when private utilities were expropriated to create Hydro Québec.

When it came to public relations, Fullerton proved that he had talents that few had suspected. He hired the president of the National Press Gallery, Dave MacIntosh, to make sure that no opportunities were missed. Although the Rideau Canal, which extended through the heart of the city, froze in winter, the experts all said that it was simply not feasible to plough it to create a skating rink. The City of Ottawa had tried but its bulldozers had broken through the ice. Fullerton proved the experts all wrong. With lighter equipment and a procedure to drill through the ice to flood and reinforce the surface, he created the "Longest Skating Rink in the World."

Fullerton became immensely popular and gave a warm human image to the federal government's operations. Summer garden plots were made available on NCC lands at nominal rents. Gatineau Park and the Green Belt were made accessible for cross-country skiing and snowmobilers.[41] To his credit, the list kept growing. Dave MacIntosh provided the press releases and Doug was always available for the cameras.

A new bridge across the Ottawa was essential to carry the traffic to the new federal buildings in Hull; however, a little more diplomatic skill on Fullerton's part might have produced better results. Portage Bridge, running from the Ottawa River Parkway to the city of Hull, was certainly

---

41 For example, see "NCC Developing 25 Miles of New Urban Ski Trails," *Ottawa Journal*, December 23, 1972, page 14.

in the right location and the federal government owned the right of way. The bridge, however, should have been directly accessible from Bronson Avenue in Ottawa, which would have made the route from Hull to the airport more direct and avoided the congestion and undesirable traffic patterns on Wellington Street. It is true that this access would have involved an expensive overpass for both Albert and Slater Streets, but I do not believe that cost was the problem. Fullerton ran out of patience, told off the city officials and simply proceeded to build the bridge without access to Bronson Avenue. This was most unfortunate. However, I understand that, to this day, the regional municipality retains title to the lands required to construct the proper access.

In his report commissioned for Prime Minister Trudeau, Fullerton gives his version of events:

> A number of meetings about the proposed Portage Bridge were held between the NCC and RMOC planners at the technical level in the early months of 1970, and intensive discussions were begun with the Quebec authorities to tie the new link directly into a widened Maisonneuve Boulevard in Hull; the costs for this latter were to be borne by Quebec. The $13 million project was approved in principle by Treasury Board in February 1970, but with the rider that, before it was announced, I (as NCC chairman) was to be given at least a month to consult with Ontario, in order to fill them in and to see if they could be persuaded to contribute to part of the cost. I made contact with the Ontario officials, a meeting was arranged, and then to my surprise I saw the next day in the papers that the Bridge project had been announced by the federal minister of Public Works, and belatedly confirmed several hours later by my equally surprised minister, the Hon. Jean Marchand.
>
> Ontario provincial politicians rose in their collective wrath, and denounced the bridge as going nowhere, as not having been subject to discussion, let alone negotiation, as costing local municipalities millions in developing proper approach roads, and as being a typical example of federal arrogance. The impression was also widely circulated that the chairman of the NCC had a good deal to learn about co-operation with other levels of government, an impression which lingered on to haunt me. As I write these words in February 1974, a newspaper report quotes a former area federal member of Parliament as considering "Mr. Fullerton's four years as NCC Chairman a disaster as far as over-all planning of the Region is concerned. The Portage Bridge debacle is cited as a prime example of the breakdown of consultation under Mr. Fullerton." Oddly

> enough, I had always thought that, in our system of government, it was ministers rather than officials who bore the responsibility when things went wrong.
>
> There is no doubt that the Portage Bridge, however urgently it was needed, did leave a legacy of distrust between the federal and Ontario governments, and made effective liaison more difficult. Opposition to the bridge would have arisen in any event (its purpose was definitely to meet federal, not municipal, priorities), but had there been time for adequate consultation in advance of the premature federal announcement, I am sure the criticism would have been muted. As it was, the release of the story turned the bridge into a *fait accompli*, made the proposed consultation a farce, and laid the federal government open to the charge of bad faith.[42]

Frankly, it is difficult to accept Fullerton's statement that a premature announcement by the Honourable Jean-Eudes Dubé destroyed all possibilities of further discussions. Certainly, by his own admission, discussions with the Regional Municipality of Ottawa-Carleton had been going on for months and the region was prepared to assume its share of the costs. My information maintains he was the one who stormed out of the meetings.

Prime Minister Trudeau wanted to integrate growth on both sides of the Ottawa River by creating two new planned satellite communities. One, on the Quebec side, would be largely English-speaking. The other, on the Ontario side would be predominantly French-speaking. While the concept itself was interesting, it would not really be feasible to direct the purchasers of homes to cluster themselves in this way, and it made no sense to me.

One day, a friend in the public service called to ask what would be my reaction if the federal government expropriated the land assembly south of the Jock River in which he knew I had an interest. I replied that we would not likely raise much objection. The lands had been assembled some seven years previously at a reasonable cost, not much over a thousand dollars an acre, and we would not expect much more than our cost.

My associates and I had been in the development business and our lands had been carefully chosen. The soils were free of leda clay, the curse of the Ontario side of the Ottawa River, and would support substantial structures. They could be serviced with sewer and water, but only in the course of time, not immediately. They were accessible to Highway 16, leading to 401, the major freeway to the south and to the United States. Our six hundred acres were contiguous, with few holdout parcels within their perimeter.[43]

---

[42] *The Capital of Canada: How It Should Be Governed*, published by Information Canada, Volume 1, 1974, pages 92-93.

It was with astonishment that we learned of an assembly of some nine thousand acres in the area of Carlsbad Springs to the east of Ottawa. A joint announcement by federal Urban Affairs minister Ron Basford, and Ontario Revenue minister Allan Grossman, on January 11, 1973, indicated that three levels of government would be involved. Ontario Housing Corporation would purchase some five thousand acres, with Central Mortgage and Housing Corporation putting up seventy-five per cent of the funds. The Township of Gloucester would play its normal municipal role of approving subdivision plans. In addition, the National Capital Commission would purchase a further four thousand adjoining acres. Basford indicated that a fund of $100 million per year for five years would be available for the land assembly. Over a period of twenty years, it would support a population of 100,000 persons. This was to be Mr. Trudeau's southeast community.

Local politicians reacted quickly. The reeve of Gloucester, Robert MacQuarrie, noted that the site was adjacent to an enormous bog, the Mer Bleue, and the "least suitable for development." There would be problems with the water table, drainage and the installation, as well as the maintenance of municipal services. He was happy for the local owners, however, who could now believe in Santa Claus. Councillors Fred Barrett and Mitchell Owens agreed. Reeve Andrew Haydon of the Township of Nepean, himself an engineer, thought the whole project might be a "can of worms" because of the enormous costs of servicing it. The entire area was basically a swamp with deep layers of jelly-like leda clay. It was not accessible to traffic arteries, although the bypass route constructed some years later, Highway 417, might have solved this problem, but at considerable cost. In other words, the land was cheap and worthless for development.[44] Even more astonishing, the province of Ontario, ever mindful of its prior constitutional responsibilities in the creation of urban municipalities, agreed to take over the Carlsbad land assembly through the Ontario Housing Corporation. The ministers responsible at the time certainly did not consult with their local colleague, Claude Bennett, who knew the area and tells me that he was appalled when he heard of the site chosen.

The director of Land Development for Ontario Housing Corporation, Walter Webb, told the press that competent engineering studies of the site had been conducted and that a long-term land bank would be available to

---

43 These lands are now being developed by the Monarch Development Corporation. Our company, Jockvale Realty, had joined in 1972 with Campeau Corporation, Urbandale Realty and Shenkman Properties in a proposal for a southern community of 4,300 acres that did not receive approval from the regional authorities.

44 See the articles in the *Ottawa Journal*, January 12, 1973, pages 1 and 4, and the *Ottawa Citizen* of the same date, pages 1 and 25, from which I am quoting. See also the *Ottawa Citizen*, January 27, 1979.

provide low-cost sites for private builders. OHC took some land under option at prices reported to be $900 per acre but many options expired before they could be exercised. Reeve MacQuarrie indicated that prices had escalated to $1,600 per acre when the ministers made their joint announcement. By my estimate, the five-thousand-acre assembly cost OHC $10 million. In addition, the NCC must have spent a similar amount for the four thousand adjoining acres.

The province, anxious to avoid expropriation procedures, paid too much for the land. When the NCC attempted to add to the core OHC assembly, they were obliged to expropriate and were faced with the high values established by the OHC.

Reeve MacQuarrie and his Gloucester council hired their own firm of soil consultants, the Casagrande brothers in Toronto, generally acknowledged to be the best in Eastern Canada. The Casagrandes confirmed what any casual driver through the area could see. Farmers had generally tried to locate their buildings on the firmest land, but there was not a corn silo to be seen that did not lean. MacQuarrie tells me that the Casagrandes assigned a density index of unity to most of the lands, which meant that if you stood on it long enough, you would sink. Deputy Reeve Mitchell Owens was quoted in *The Citizen* as follows:

> By the time the experts figure out a way to straighten the Tower of Pisa, they will have all sorts of work to do in Gloucester Township.

The chairman of the Regional Municipality, Denis Coolican, at first approved the idea of a land bank, but after reading the Casagrande report, changed his mind. He took me to lunch one day to ask what I knew about the development of this situation. I told him about the telephone call I had received concerning our own land assembly south of the Jock River. We agreed that it had to be Fullerton's doing. Fullerton had chosen the land because it was cheap (or so he thought; ultimately, it cost far too much), and persuaded or cajoled CMHC and the provincial officials to go along with him. He had not consulted the Gloucester Township people who knew their lands better than he did.

Needless to say, the federal and provincial governments lost close to $20 million on the deal. The lands were for the most part turned over to a nature reserve. Some were offered back at discounted rates to their former owners, but there were few takers. Fullerton had plunged into a land assembly without knowing what he was doing and without getting proper advice.

In the Regional Official Plan, a population target of 100,000 persons was included for the Carlsbad Assembly. The region, under the direction of its chief engineer, Frank Ayers, actually constructed a sewer partway to the lands, only to have it disappear in the swampy soil. The quota of 100,000 people was added to that of the adjacent Orleans development, to the delight of the developers concerned. Our assembly, in the south, was delayed by twenty years.

These two incidents, the approaches to the Portage Bridge and the Carlsbad Land Assembly, illustrate the enormous powers exercised by the chairman of the National Capital Commission. Members of the commission, a few appointed from the region but the majority appointed from across Canada, are simply not in a position to exercise any control over the chairman. From 1927 to 1958, the mayors of Ottawa and Hull sat on the NCC, but Charlotte Whitton's behaviour was so obstructive that the Act was amended to exclude them. This was unfortunate, because the present situation has led to many unfortunate consequences. Certainly, had the mayors been members of the NCC when the Portage Bridge was being built, they might have corrected the access by exposing the problem in the press. Douglas Fullerton quotes from an internal NCC memo to the effect that the mayors had been dropped because they took too parochial an interest in defending their own turf, and also talked to the press about the NCC agenda[45]. A reasonable solution would be to include the regional chairs of Ottawa-Carleton and the Outaouais, both of whom now have good backup staff to help them. As far as talking to the press is concerned, the NCC simply should not have so many of its meetings in camera.

Fullerton's flamboyant style clashed with that of his minister, Ron Basford, who was probably also unhappy with what he was now hearing about the Mer Bleue land assembly. Fullerton left his position as chairman of the NCC on January 30, 1973. A story in the *Ottawa Journal* on that date quoted him as saying that he "did not resign."[46]

After Fullerton left the NCC, Prime Minister Trudeau arranged for him to conduct the study (to which I have referred) on how the national capital of Canada should be governed, to include the whole of the National Capital Region in Ontario and Quebec. Understandably, the study reflected the prime minister's views. Fullerton repeated the undertaking at the Constitutional Conference of February 1969, by the premiers of Quebec and Ontario to make the entire National Capital Region fully bilingual. In support of Trudeau's concept of two satellite communities in Quebec and Ontario, one to be predominantly anglophone and the other francophone, Fullerton developed his "Limited Hiving Proposal," which perhaps others can understand better than I.

---

[45] Douglas H. Fullerton, op. cit., Volume 1, page 96. The issue of lack of elected representation on the NCC is raised as I write, concerning the decision of the NCC to widen the Champlain Bridge, in spite of opposition by residents on the Ottawa side of the river. Judge Francis Muldoon of the Federal Court denied the request for an injunction, but observed that it was unfortunate that Ottawa residents had no means of having their views reflected by elected representatives on the NCC. See the editorial entitled "Bridges and ballots," *Ottawa Citizen*, Sunday, August 10, 1997, page A12.

[46] *Ottawa Journal*, January 30, 1973, pages 1 and 4.

Fullerton relied heavily on academic studies on how other capitals of the world were organized, as well as language studies and public opinion polls. Most interesting, however, was his diary-like account of his own experience as chairman of the National Capital Commission, one of the rare opportunities the public has had to find out the views of the bureaucrats that were determining policy at the time.

In the early 1960s, as a member of the City of Ottawa's Board of Control, I had helped draft the by-law amending building heights, finally enacted as AZ-64. This permitted the piercing of the previous height limit from 110 feet to 150 feet above grade. In some cases, buildings could go even higher. The NCC opposed these changes vehemently. To quote Fullerton on page 110 of Volume 1 of his report:

> There is no single planning issue that has aroused more concern among residents, public officials and parliamentarians, all of whom fear the dwarfing of the Peace Tower as it is gradually fenced in by high-rise buildings.

The NCC even recommended that the Promenade Building on Wellington Street, which faced Parliament Hill, should have been kept below 110 feet. In my opinion, this would have destroyed any economic incentive for redevelopment of the property.

NCC planners were apparently aping the thinking that had produced Washington, a city that has preserved the vista of the Capitol dome, but at the terrible cost of no renovation of the adjacent areas and new construction confined to the suburbs.[47] Ottawa now has a vital core of new buildings, thanks to AZ-64. Washington, in contrast, has beautiful national monuments surrounded by slums.

At many points in Volume 1, Fullerton complains about excessive growth of the city of Ottawa. His recommendation #22 stated that the Government of Canada should "accept a policy of increased decentralization of its operations from the Capital, at least to the extent needed to bring a marked slowing in the Capital's rate of growth . . ."[48] His vision for the National Capital was that of a quiet company town.

In its early years, the NCC reported directly to the prime minister but was later assigned to other cabinet ministers. Fullerton did not approve and made his views clear.

> The proposal to have the NCC report directly to the prime minister is consistent with the difficulties faced by the NCC in carrying out its co-ordinating role in the Capital. These

---

[47] The NCC seems to be obsessed with the vista concept, which I call the Washington Syndrome. In late 1998, it proposed that seventeen blocks along Metcalfe Street be expropriated to construct a Grande Allée with a panoramic view of the Peace Tower from the south. The mayor of Ottawa and many of the general public opposed the proposal. See the story by Mohammed Adam, *Ottawa Citizen*, February 20, 1999.

[48] Op. cit., Volume 1, page 220.

> responsibilities cut across departmental boundaries, and to adjudicate the jurisdictional problems that inevitably arise, the NCC needs a minister with authority. The burden on the prime minister could be eased by assigning the supervisory authority to his parliamentary secretary.[49]

From my own experience, I can only conclude that the NCC simply wished to operate on its own with an absolute minimum of supervision by any elected officials. Rarely indeed could a parliamentary secretary exercise the degree of supervision required in this case.

Fullerton's reference to "jurisdictional problems" refers to conflicts with the Department of Public Works, which is also responsible for public properties in the National Capital Region, in particular those on the south side of Wellington Street expropriated to be part of the Parliament Hill complex. The NCC believed that it had superior talents in this respect,[50] and Fullerton went so far as to recommend[51] that the federal government "consider extending the work of the National Capital Commission to concentrations of federal property in major cities across Canada."

In summary, the picture of the NCC that emerges is not a pleasant one. This crown corporation, with no elected persons on its board of directors, exercises arbitrary power through its control of federal lands, its ability to expropriate and to make grants for a wide variety of purposes. Its vision of the nation's capital is focussed on the Washington Syndrome of national monuments without providing incentives for redevelopment of adjacent older buildings. In Fullerton's time, the NCC openly fought Ottawa's growth and recommended decentralization of federal government departments to other parts of Canada. At no time did it make efforts to diversify employment by attracting private industry.

In brief, the NCC wanted the nation's capital to be a single- employer town where it would play the role of big frog in a small puddle. It fought a running jurisdictional fight with the Department of Public Works and did its best to avoid having to report to an active, hands-on minister, such as Ron Basford. I simply cannot understand why the NCC has abandoned its bilingual policies in the Quebec part of the National Capital Region and completely ignored the undertaking given by Premier Jean-Jacques Bertrand in 1968.

Fullerton examined municipal structures on both the Ontario and Quebec sides of the National Capital Region, recognizing a number of deficiencies but acknowledging that the establishment of two regional governments had improved matters. He offered models for provincial and federal participation in two supra-regional councils for Ontario and Quebec respectively and even went so far as to suggest a Supra Council

[49] Op. cit., Volume 1, page 217.
[50] Op cit., Volume 1, page 109.
[51] Op cit., Volume 1, page 220.

combining both sides of the River. The problem with the last suggestion is political: Quebec would insist on half of the places on the Supra Council although the Ontario portion had by far the larger population and assessment. Ontarians would fear that Quebec would insist that half of the expenditures of such a council be spent in Quebec and would not likely accept the proposal.

By general agreement, the greatest deficiency in present arrangements is lack of co-ordination by the two regional municipalities in planning, constructing of traffic arteries and bridges, controlling pollution, etc. Fullerton recommended that a joint committee of the House of Commons and the Senate be convened to study his report and make more specific proposals on the restructuring of municipal governments. He further recommended that a standing committee of either the House of Commons or the Senate provide liaison between Parliament and the NCC.

To date, no action has been taken on his report and it has gathered dust on the shelf.

In 1969, following the adoption of the set of principles for the development of the national capital by the Federal-Provincial Constitutional Conference, I made some suggestions by way of private member's bills and a resolution. These were designed to overcome the lack of co-ordinated action by the municipal governments on two sides of the Ottawa River. Bill No. C-57, an *Act to Create a National Capital Region Planning Board*, received first reading on October 30. My Bill C-112, an *Act to create a National Capital Region Pollution Control Board*, received first reading on the same day. My private member's resolution to create a national capital transit authority was debated on March 6, 1970. Needless to say, all of these were (politely) talked out.

THE STANDING COMMITTEE ON VETERANS AFFAIRS

At the end of World War II, the Government of Canada put together a package of benefits for returning veterans known as the Veterans' Charter. I had taken advantage of the allowances to complete my Master of Arts degree at the University of Toronto and Doctor of Philosophy at Wisconsin. Canada treated its ex-servicemen as generously as any country had done.

Veterans' organizations, however, were increasingly frustrated with the work of the Canadian Pension Commission, which determined eligibility for pensions for a wide variety of service-connected disabilities. On September 8, 1965, a special committee chaired by Mr. Justice Mervin Woods of Saskatchewan, was established to investigate the complaints concerning the CPC. The report of the Woods Committee was tabled in the House of Commons on March 26, 1968. It made 148 separate recommendations whose sheer volume and complexity created a problem for the government.

The first response of the government was to prepare a white paper which met a number, but not all, of the recommendations of the Woods

Report. On October 29, 1969, an order of the House of Commons referred the white paper and the Woods Report to the Standing Committee on Veterans Affairs. At the same time, the minister of Veterans Affairs, the Hon. Jean-Eudes Dubé, asked me to chair the committee. Mr. P.E. Reynolds, director of legal services for the department, came on loan to the committee as director of research.

In its first phase, the committee held twenty-three meetings to hear evidence from the minister and his officials, the CPC, the Nationally Chartered Veterans Associations, the National Council of Veterans Associations, the War Amputations of Canada, the Hong Kong Veterans Association, the National Dieppe Prisoners of War Association, the Canadian Corps Association, the Canadian Paraplegic Association, the Sir Arthur Pearson Association for War Blinded, the War Pensioners of Canada, the Army, Navy and Air Force Veterans in Canada and the Royal Canadian Legion (Dominion Command).

In its second phase, the committee held sixteen meetings to sort out its recommendations. In addition to the minister and his officials, representatives from the Legion and other national veterans' associations were called back for further questioning. We recommended that the basic pension rate be that of an untrained labourer, with supplements for those severely disabled or with multiple disabilities. We rejected requests that a single member of the CPC could decide entitlement and that pensions be automatically increased with age. The most contentious item, however, involved appeal procedures. The veterans' associations were unanimous in requesting that an independent pension review board be created to review decisions of the CPC. The latter countered by offering to split itself into three divisions: entitlement, pensions and administration. After much soul-searching, the committee recommended the creation of a pensions review board, with its operation to be reviewed after five years.

The government accepted every item of our report, which was tabled on June 22, 1970. The veterans' associations were pleased, and Cliff Chadderton of the War Amps was particularly complimentary. As a former serviceman, it was an honour for me to chair the parliamentary committee that proposed the only revision of the Canadian Veterans Charter before it passed into history.[52]

SEMINAR ON PARLIAMENTARY PROCEDURE IN LONDON

In the Twenty-sixth Parliament, I had been an active member of the Commonwealth Parliamentary Association and attended its meetings in Malaysia in 1963. I was treasurer of the Canadian branch when plans were

---

52 See the fall 1970 issue of *The Fragment*, a quarterly publication of the War Amps of Canada, for Cliff Chadderton's article, "Veterans Affairs Committees—Past and Present."

made to host a general meeting in Ottawa in 1966, but my defeat in the election of 1965 precluded me from participating.

In July 1970, the Conservative MP for Lambton-Kent, "Mac" McCutcheon, and I were nominated to attend a seminar on parliamentary procedure in London, England. For one month, we listened to lectures on the origin of parliament, how rules and procedures had developed in different countries of the Commonwealth, and met with advisers to the Speaker of the House of Commons and to the Lord Chancellor in the House of Lords (who presides by sitting on what is called the "woolsack" and never utters a word but communicates by nodding his head).[53] We visited the parliament of Northern Ireland, then in session at Stormont in Belfast, and toured a number of counties in that country. We also met the fiery Unionist leader, the Rev. Iain Paisley. Our timing was fortunate, since conditions had not at that time deteriorated to the point of violence, which led to the suspension of the parliament at Stormont a year or two later.

We visited the island of Jersey in the English Channel, and met representatives of their elected parliament, which went back many centuries. "Mac" somehow arranged for us to visit a Jersey farmer who sold greenhouse tomatoes (to which he kept referring as "toms") in the UK market and raised cattle. During the German wartime occupation, he had been obliged, like other Jersey men, to give one animal per month to the military and naturally selected his culls. At that end of the war, he was left with a small but excellent herd, which became the basis of a profitable business for exporting breeding stock.

One evening I was seated at dinner beside the son of the prime minister of Northern Ireland during the Second World War. He told me that on one occasion Winston Churchill, with whom his father conferred regularly, offered a gift of one of his paintings. His father was taken to a windowless room with paintings covering every inch of the walls, and told to take his time to select one. After two hours Churchill came back to ask which he had selected. When his father pointed to one, Churchill flew into a rage, saying: "Dammit, you picked the only one in this room that I did not paint." His father never got his painting.

At the end of the seminar, Mac McCutcheon suggested that Margery and I join his wife, Pauline, and himself for a tour of Southern Ireland. Mac had planned the route carefully, beginning in Dublin down to the south coast, including Cork, north along the west coast including the Ring of Kerry, through Shannon and cross country back to Dublin. It was an unforgettable experience. Everywhere we went, the Irish were so hospitable and never took exception to our North American accents (probably assuming that we were Americans). In Shannon, Mac

[53] The Lord Chancellor may, however, leave the woolsack on occasion and participate in debate, a procedure not permitted in the Canadian Parliament.

discovered a distant relative practising law who had married a Frenchwoman during the war but was by then divorced and living alone. He painted a dismal picture of his plight, as a practising Protestant in the Irish Republic, in spite of the fact his ancestors had been there for two hundred years.

Every pub, it seemed, had a table carved from wood salvaged from a wrecked galleon of the Spanish Armada and more than a few displayed heads of an extinct elk with enormous horns found preserved in a bog. I will never forget how a friendly villager on the cliff of the Ring of Kerry pointed down to a sandbar, telling us that that was where the Danes had landed to pillage, as though it had happened a year or two ago.

My only regret during the trip was that Mac had booked us into Ryan Hotels for every night. The Ryan chain was well-run, but catered to North American tourists. We would have loved to stay at some of the bed-and-breakfast places we passed, many in castles and old buildings.

THE FLQ CRISIS

The fall of 1970 saw the culmination of terrorist activities by the Front de Libération du Québec (FLQ). Organized by cells, the FLQ had started with Molotov cocktails and mailbox bombings in 1963. They escalated their activities to bank robberies, thefts of dynamite from construction sites and major explosions. One explosion, at the Bourse de Montréal in February 1969, wounded twenty-seven persons, three seriously. They issued communiqués demanding correction of social injustices and independence for Quebec. Prime Minister Trudeau addressed the caucus, attempting to analyze whatever intelligence was behind the campaign—not an easy task.

In October 1970, the FLQ kidnapped the minister of Labour of Quebec, Pierre Laporte, and a British diplomat in Montreal, James Cross. Not long afterwards I was listening to the radio in the government lobby of the House of Commons and heard that the body of Pierre Laporte had been found in the trunk of a car. When I broke the news to Jean Marchand, he was overcome and broke into tears.

Trudeau's reaction was swift. At the request of the premier of Quebec, he invoked the *War Measures Act*. Hundreds of men and women were arrested and put into jail. Perhaps a hundred MPs, myself among them, were taken to Montreal for Laporte's funeral, where we marched for several blocks in the streets before entering the cathedral. Members of our armed forces lined the route, armed with machine guns, with lookouts on the top of every building. The Government of Canada was daring the FLQ to try something, but there were no further incidents.[54]

---

[54] The Honourable Gerard Pelletier has given a very personal interpretation of events in his book, *La Crise d'Octobre*, published by Editions du Jour, 1651 Rue Saint-Denis, Montreal, 1971. His appendix lists acts of FLQ violence in detail.

Eventually, James Cross was released and his kidnappers allowed to seek sanctuary in Cuba. Thanks to diligent police work, the back of the FLQ was broken. Those arrested under the *War Measures Act* were released and no doubt many of them were not participants in the FLQ terror. At the time, Trudeau was a national hero for putting an end to what was regarded as an attempted insurrection, however amateurish it was when we look back on it. Criticism of Trudeau for violating civil liberties came later, not at the time.

THE WHIP'S OFFICE

In October 1968, I had been named deputy government whip, a post which not everyone sought. Bernie Pilon, the MP for Chambly, had been whip since 1966. You could not help liking him. Genial, invariably good-humoured, tolerant, he was respected by everyone. Bernie had, however, an incredible capacity of finding out where MPs were at all times and kept it all in his head with a minimum of paperwork. Grant Deachman, the MP for Vancouver Quadra, called him Mr. Miracle Whip.

In December 1970, Bernie died suddenly from a heart attack while returning by car from Ottawa to Montreal. On December 17, I was named to succeed him.

Serving as deputy whip had not prevented me from chairing the Veterans Affairs Committee, or from going to St. Jean, Quebec, for French immersion courses held at Collège Militaire Royal. The technique of teaching a language by immersion of a week at a time in small groups is very effective and the instructors for the special school for MPs were excellent. My French improved to the level of reasonable fluency.

I cannot really say that I enjoyed the job of whip. Keeping track of the whereabouts of MPs when votes were called required some of those mystical skills that Pilon had but I lacked. In order to know just who was present in Ottawa, I undertook to check attendance daily in Question Period. The reporter for the *Windsor Star*, who could see what I was doing from his vantage point in the press gallery, decried the schoolmasterish approach of the new whip checking whether or not MPs were there every day. No doubt he had nothing better to write about that day.

I had good reason for what I did. One day six MPs were absent for reasons totally unknown to myself. On checking further, I found that two delegations had left for Europe and no one had informed the whip's office. I simply could not develop a close working relationship with the House Leader, Allan MacEachen, who was the only one really in a position to help me. The Speaker of the House, the Honourable Lucien Lamoureux, had taken the initiative in forming a new association of French language MPs and insisted on picking the delegates himself. Only after I complained bitterly did he give me notice of departure dates for delegations. To placate me, he offered me the opportunity to name one of the alternate delegates for one convention. (I ignored it, because I considered it insulting.)

When it came to staffing committees, I dug in my heels and had more success. Putting square pegs into square holes was not easy but at least I tried. What do you do when the chairman of a committee has a piece of legislation before him, but does not want to report back to the House promptly because he wants to call several witnesses for the sole purpose of getting publicity? How do you reward an MP who has done his or her best on a difficult committee? The whip must be able to use assignments on parliamentary delegations as rewards (and their denial as punishment). Gradually, I was able to influence a few assignments, such as having the MP for Victoria, David Groos, named to the Canadian delegation to the United Nations General Assembly. David had a distinguished war record in the navy, had served on the defence committee, and was later appointed parliamentary secretary to the minister of National Defence.

A whip simply must have a close working relationship with the prime minister and the House leader. Indeed, the whip should meet regularly with the prime minister if the latter really wants to follow the performance of MPs in the House. Unfortunately for myself, I only had the opportunity of meeting with him occasionally.

There were lighter moments. Prime Minister Trudeau's marriage to Margaret Sinclair was the highlight of the social pages. After their first boy was born on Christmas Day, 1971, the proud new father was handing out cigars in the Government Lobby. Being a non-smoker, I declined. Alastair Gillespie, the patrician MP from Toronto sitting beside me, accepted one gladly. He unwrapped it, licked it with loving care, and then frowned. Then he lit it, took two or three puffs and stamped it out.

"That damned cigar must be at least ten years old, if not more," he exclaimed. Trudeau, a non-smoker himself, had been saving them.

I never lost a vote.[55] One or two had been close, but as I had explained to the prime minister, our vote had been exactly as I had anticipated. That was not good enough for Allan MacEachen and, I suspect, the Speaker, Lucien Lamoureux, whose interventions with the parliamentary associations had not made my life easier.

PARLIAMENTARY SECRETARY TO VETERANS AFFAIRS

On September 30, 1971, I was named parliamentary secretary to the minister of Veterans Affairs, the Honourable Arthur Laing. Grant

---

[55] Votes in the early hours of the morning are rare in the Canadian House, but much more frequent in the UK experience. On one occasion, the British assistant whip was calling an MP's home at two a.m., to be greeted by a woman's voice. "Please tell your husband to come in for a vote."
He could hear a muffled conversation in the background. "It is the Whip's Office and they want you for a vote." "Tell them I am not here." The woman came to the telephone, saying: "My husband is not here."
The assistant whip responded: "In that case, tell the man with whom you are sleeping to come in. We need his vote."

Deachman, the MP for Vancouver Quadra, was named to replace me as whip.

Grant had a good sense of humour. Every MP receives letters written in the categorical imperative, telling you that the seal hunt MUST be stopped, or that housing on native reserves MUST be improved IMMEDIATELY, or that holes in the ozone layer MUST be corrected.

He received one from a woman who said that she had watched Cyrus Eaton, the well-known philanthropist, describe on television, following one of the famous conferences he sponsored at Pugwash, Nova Scotia, the enormous dangers of an atomic conflict that we faced. She demanded that Grant DO something. His reply was a classic.

"Dear Mrs.————-

"I have read your letter and re-read it. In the event that Mr. Eaton is right, I hereby wish you a FOND FAREWELL.

Yours truly,"

Art Laing had previously been the minister of Public Works and on one occasion asked Jean Richard and myself to do something for him. It was the policy to erect a statue to each former prime minister on Parliament Hill, and, at considerable expense, statues of Arthur Meighen and Mackenzie King had been cast. Would we go down to the warehouse and look at them?

The statue of Mackenzie King was conventional and posed no problem. The one of Arthur Meighen was grotesque, with his arms spread and his face turned to the sky as if he were contemplating Armageddon. The plight of a Liberal minister of Public Works was clear: If he caused the statue to be erected, there would be an outcry, but if he did not, he would be accused of slighting the memory of a distinguished Conservative prime minister.

Richard and I decided that we could not make a recommendation either, but suggested that he invite Liberal Senator Eugene Forsey and Conservative Senator Grattan O'Leary to advise him. Their reaction was predictable, and the minister of Public Works now had a recommendation from a bipartisan committee that it was in order to erect the King statue, but a new one had to be commissioned for Meighen. This seemed to me a valid function for senators, who did not have to be elected.[56]

Art Laing was one of the most considerate people I have ever met in politics. The Department of Veterans Affairs was past its most active phase, with rehabilitation programs for veterans over and the numbers receiving pensions decreasing slowly. I was included in regular weekly meetings with senior officials and kept informed of all developments.

---

[56] I recounted this anecdote in Private Members Hour, on November 1, 1974, Hansard, pages 992 and 993.

In this period I became active with the Canada-United States Inter-Parliamentary Association. We visited Washington and were recognized by the Senate Speaker, who was also the vice-president of the United States, Spiro Agnew. On St. Patrick's Day, we visited San Antonio, Texas, and toured the remains of the famous Alamo fortress, where a number of Americans had held out in one of the wars with Mexico. A return visit by our American friends to Ottawa was followed by a visit to Banff and Lake Louise in Alberta. The opportunity to get to know senators and congressmen socially and to discuss those trade irritants that never seem to end between our two countries could not help but improve relations between us.

In May 1972, on the thirtieth anniversary of the Dieppe Raid, a Canadian delegation participated in the ceremonies to mark the occasion. Larry MacDonald, my old CBC friend from City Hall days, had been badly injured in the Normandy campaign and joined our party. Marcel Lambert was one of those taken prisoner and he was able to point to the exact place where he had landed on the beach. General Churchill Mann had commanded the Canadian forces from a destroyer offshore and tears came to his eyes when I stood beside him on the high point from which German machine-gunners were able to direct a murderous fire on those landing on the beaches below them.

"To think that we sent men on those beaches without even aerial bombing to soften up the enemy first!" he exclaimed.

A local resident took us to a spot in the town, about three hundred yards from the beach, which a Canadian soldier had reached before being shot. She reported that she had watched from her window.

That evening, we joined the residents of Dieppe in the ceremony at the cemetery where Canadian and other Allied soldiers were buried. Marker after marker read: "Unknown Canadian Soldier." At dusk, we joined the residents in rows of perhaps twenty persons each. The row at the front bowed in silence for two minutes, then moved away to the side as the row behind moved up. There was no music and no spoken command, but everybody knew what to do. It was incredibly dignified and unforgettable.

We were told that this ceremony by local residents had taken place every year since the end of the war.

France also had a minister of veterans affairs and Art Laing joined him in Paris after the ceremony. Before leaving, he turned to me and said: "By the way, Lloyd, there is a little do at Runnymede in England that I will not be able to attend. Will you take my place?"

Needless to say, I was delighted. On the historic plains of Runnymede, where King John had signed the *Magna Carta*, was a huge monument to the thousands of airmen of the Commonwealth who had no known graves. I took the salute for the march past and made a brief speech in English and in French.

I checked the names engraved on the monument and found Lou Somers, a brother of Harold Somers, who had been my dean at the University of Buffalo. Lou was a brilliant student as well as a good athlete who had also graduated from Toronto in 1940. Beside his name was a star, which meant that there was additional information on his death. It seems that he had piloted a Lancaster bomber that had been shot down returning from a raid. While dredging the Zuiderzee, the Dutch found his aircraft with remains of the crew inside. Lou now has a known grave in Holland.

AMENDMENTS TO THE *UNEMPLOYMENT INSURANCE ACT*

My duties as parliamentary secretary to Veterans Affairs were not onerous and I decided to join the Standing Committee on Labour, Manpower and Immigration, whose chairman was the MP for Scarborough West, David Weatherhead. In 1970 The minister of Labour, Bryce Mackasey, had referred to the committee a white paper on amendments to the *Unemployment Insurance Act* and later the legislation that was eventually to be adopted by Parliament.

My interest dated back to my days in National Health and Welfare, where we had carefully examined all programs that were considered a part of Canada's social security network. The white paper proposed to add maternity benefits for women covered in the labour force, and sickness benefits for men and women similarly covered. It should be emphasized that both of these were limited benefits and really just extensions of the unemployment insurance concept. For example, they did not provide maternity benefits for women employed in the home.

Nevertheless, the private insurance industry made representations to have the sickness benefit deleted on the grounds that the job could be done more efficiently by private plans set up with employers, which they would administer. The companies made themselves targets for labour unions and also for many MPs, including Stanley Knowles, the NDP MP for Winnipeg North Centre, and myself. Testimony before the committee overwhelmingly supported the changes proposed in the white paper.

I have recently reviewed the transcript of the proceedings of the committee and cannot help but comment on how superficial they were. The white paper proposed extension of coverage to seasonal and part-time workers and, in so doing, changed the whole concept of the Act. I was, however, concerned about what would happen in a low-income family when a layoff occurred.[57] Under the Act, there would be a waiting period of two weeks and public welfare authorities would not likely provide any assistance until they could determine exactly what would be the benefit

---

[57] My intervention on November 11, 1970 is to be found on pages 35-36 of Issue No. 8 of the committee's proceedings.

eligibility under unemployment insurance. The low benefits for seasonal and part-time employees would certainly not be enough to support families. Were there any arrangements to co-ordinate with local welfare officials in such cases? No.

Representatives from Atlantic Canada (including the Honourable Jack Pickersgill) were ecstatic at the prospect of bringing fishermen under the Act, as were MPs with agricultural labourers among their voters. At no point were we given any reasonable estimates of the cost involved and I doubt that such studies had been done.

When the committee was about to report the amending bill back to the House, I received a memo from Cliff Murchison, a commissioner of the Unemployment Insurance Commission. We were good friends and the Murchison family had been long-time supporters in Ottawa West. He was totally opposed to the inclusion of seasonal workers, anticipating quite correctly that the costs would be enormous. These costs were in fact regional transfers that should be handled as part of regional assistance, or possibly public welfare; certainly not social insurance. They would ultimately be a subsidy to employers of seasonal labour and encourage too many people to stay in low-wage industries instead of shifting to other employment. Lastly, they would encourage a culture of persons who worked just enough time to qualify for benefits in a form of permanent underemployment.

Murchison's memo shocked me. The more I thought about it, the more disturbed I became. Des Roches, as chief commissioner, had given not the slightest inkling that there was such a difference of opinion among the commissioners. I discussed the matter with the committee chairman, David Weatherhead, who indicated that Bryce Mackasey was anxious to get the legislation out of committee and passed.

I was in a dilemma. Up to this point, I had been generally supportive of the changes, with reservations on the lack of mechanisms to co-ordinate with Social Welfare. Should I go back into committee and now oppose the bill? What were my grounds? What was my evidence? I could hardly cite the opinions of a UIC commissioner, who would have been obliged to resign if I had done so. (Actually, if Murchison had resigned and gone public with his reasons, it would have been much easier for me.) Weatherhead was not convinced that the criticisms were valid and suggested that I resign from the committee. Reluctantly, I did so.

It is now apparent that the 1972 amendments to the UIC legislation, combined with the reduction of the age for the national non-contributory pension from seventy to eventually sixty-five, were responsible for more than half the budgetary deficits of the 1990s. Economists comparing unemployment rates between Canada and the United States ascribe at least part of the reason why Canada's rates are higher to structural problems in our labour markets arising out of the 1972 amendments.

Clifford Murchison knew what he was doing, but Mackasey and Des Roches were in such a hurry to get their amendments passed, which would bring immediate praise from many circles, that they closed their minds to criticisms. Nor did they commission any fundamental studies to be placed before the parliamentary committee. Not until the time of Paul Martin, Junior, as minister of Finance in the 1990s were the necessary corrective amendments made.

Not going into the committee and fighting the amendments was probably a major mistake. Hindsight, as they say, is clearer than foresight. I would have had to oppose Stanley Knowles, all other Liberals on the committee, the minister and his staff. My reputation was already that of a maverick and I had some nagging doubts about Murchison's criticisms. Committee hearings were almost over and there was not really sufficient time to do the basic research needed to substantiate my change of position. Nevertheless, I should have tried.[58]

BILINGUALISM AND THE PUBLIC SERVICE II

From my constituents, I received a constant stream of complaints concerning the policy of the government on bilingualism in the public service. I had voted for the *Official Languages Act* in 1968 and truly believed that bilingualism was an essential measure to preserve the unity of Canada. Moreover, the public service was not as bilingual as it should have been. Many of my voters alleged that unqualified francophones were being promoted, that long term unilingual anglophones faced arbitrary caps in their careers and that discrimination was practised in many areas. I pointed to the Pearson Pledge and the free training courses available for those wishing to learn a second language, but this by no means satisfied them.

John Carson's policy of giving bonus points to any bilingual applicant for any position in the Ottawa area particularly infuriated them. Many believed that their unilingual sons and daughters would not be eligible for public service careers. The policy discouraged recruitment from many areas of Canada, such as the western provinces, where second language instruction in the schools had lagged.

An example will illustrate the point. If two candidates in a competition scored fifty-one and sixty points on professional competence, and the first received a bilingual bonus of ten points, the candidate with the inferior technical qualifications would be selected. If bilingualism was not a requirement of the position, the policy was seen as discriminatory.

---

[58] In the election campaign leading to the vote on October 30, 1972, the amendments to the *Unemployment Insurance Act* became a hot issue and Mackasey was sharply criticised. He was also responsible for immigration and attacked for allowing undesirables, who arrived on visitors' visas, to apply for permanent residence. On November 25, he announced his resignation from the cabinet to sit as a private member. He continued to defend his amendments to unemployment insurance as "the best in the world" and said all he did was to give money to poor people. He returned to the cabinet following the election of 1974.

In the October 1968 issue of *Professional Public Service*, the organ of the Professional Institute of the Public Service of Canada, an editorial by Leslie Barnes entitled "Bilingual Preference—Merit or Politics?" quoted from a study by Dr. R.A. Chapman as follows:

> As a result of the language bonus bilingual applicants with the merest pass standard in terms of academic and technical qualifications can rank ahead of unilingual applicants with decidedly higher professional qualifications. . . . The Professional Institute of the Public Service of Canada has taken a strong position that where a professional job calls for a knowledge of both languages, this should be reflected in both the requirements and the salary. Where no such requirement exists, a bonus in respect of a non-applicable qualification is contrary to the basic concepts of the merit system and potentially a serious permanent threat to professional standards.

Howard Henry, my old colleague from City Council, a retired public servant and a former Liberal provincial candidate from a family of lifelong Liberals, deserted me and the Liberal Party on this issue. A number of others publicly endorsed the Conservatives.

My response was twofold. First, it was proper to correct the lack of use of French and I defended the policy of official bilingualism. At the same time, I requested investigation of every reported case of discrimination, or violation of the Pearson Pledge, and sought clear, fair rules for everyone. I lost on both counts. The people who believed they were discriminated against turned against the Liberals and me as their representative. At the same time, many francophones regarded me as an enemy really fighting bilingualism, not defending it.

John Carson, chairman of the Public Service Commission, went further. In 1970, on a nationally televised program, he repudiated the Pearson Pledge, stating that he was guided by the law and not by the statements of two prime ministers. Instead of "no prejudice to careers," he substituted a policy of "no demotion or layoffs." On June 1, 1972, he spoke to a group of public personnel administrators in Ottawa without a prepared text. According to a reporter present, Carson stated that the public service was run by middle-aged WASP English language administrators whose day was over. These people had forgotten "what a thrill it was to do meaningful work and what a drag it was to fill in time." He called them "corruptible slobs." The reporter's version was confirmed by at least ten of those present to whom I spoke. You can imagine how public servants who had no means of appealing Carson's decisions felt. They were insulted.

The MP for Grenville-Carleton, Gordon Blair, made an excellent speech on the problems arising from the application of the bilingualism policy in the public service in the debate on the Speech from the Throne. He called it "the subject of the greatest controversy and concern" in his riding and went on to say:

> . . . the pledge which was given by two prime ministers, Mr. Pearson in 1966 and the present prime minister [Mr. Trudeau] in 1968, was not realized in fact. They said, in effect, that the career of any public servant who was not bilingual would not be prejudiced by reason of the application of this policy. Actually, this has not happened. The highest organ of the Public Service Commission has said that is not what the law says. They have said, further, that it does not matter whether Parliament was induced to pass this law by reason of the undertakings given by those prime ministers because they, the appellate organ of the Civil Service Commission, are not bound by these undertakings . . .[59]

Looking back, I cannot help but feel that the Pearson Pledge to protect the careers of long-term unilingual public servants was deceptive. Implementing a policy of bilingualism would of course have impaired the prospects of anglophone unilinguals, many of whom became bitter, believing that the government had lied to them. Others, relying on the Pearson Pledge, did not make the efforts to learn a second language that they might have done.

None of the francophone MPs were facing in their constituencies the kind of heat I felt from Ottawa West. Most of them had no sympathy and I got a bad name in the Quebec caucus.

It is almost impossible to explain to an outsider the immense power exerted by the Quebec caucus on the Liberal government. With over forty per cent of the members of the cabinet, strict discipline and tight lips, they frequently achieved their objectives before the rest of us even suspected what they were doing[60]. The Ontario caucus, in contrast, was disunited, dominated by MPs from Metro Toronto whose policies were frequently at variance with the needs of other regions of the province.

Word came to me from some friendly Quebec MPs that I was in deep trouble and should lie low on bilingualism. I really had few friends in Ontario to whom I could turn, and only two or three francophones from the Ottawa Valley understood my problem.

---

[59] Hansard, February 29, 1972, pages 385-388. Prime Minister Trudeau sealed Blair's fate during the election campaign by announcing to the press at a rally in Blair's headquarters that he had full confidence in John Carson.

[60] A good example of the influence of the Quebec caucus was the industrial milk subsidy. It was escalated beyond reason (with help from some MPs from other provinces) and the Quebec milk producers were able to hijack the bulk of it.

THE 1972 ELECTION

On returning to Ottawa from the visit to Dieppe and Runnymede, I received some upsetting news. Pauline Jewett had decided to leave the Liberal Party and to run against me as the NDP candidate in Ottawa West! Like myself, she had lost her seat in 1965 and had no desire to go back to the riding of Northumberland to face popular Conservative George Hees. She had spoken to the Ottawa West Women's Liberal Club and been in my home more than once. One evening, I did my best to persuade her to seek the Liberal nomination in the constituency of Grenville-Dundas, against the sitting Conservative MP, Mrs. Jean Wadds. She had declined, saying that she did not want to run against a sitting woman MP, regardless of party. Up to that point, I had always believed that our relations were friendly.

I never really understood why she decided to run against me. In part, her decision reflected some bitterness with the Liberals, since she had run for vice-president of the party at a national convention and been defeated. She was also quite unhappy with Mr. Pearson's leadership. The former Ottawa West NDP candidate who had done so badly in 1968, Ralph Sutherland, was anxious to even the score with me and offered to help her campaign. Andy Cohen, generally known as a Liberal, became her campaign manager.

An election was called for August 30, 1972. The first shock came when I tried to name enumerators, only to discover that more than twenty of those who had acted for me in 1968 were so infuriated over the bilingualism issue that they had deserted the Liberals, mostly turning to the Conservative Party. A number of professional women in the Ottawa area, some of whom had never previously been involved in politics, joined Pauline's team. Walter Gordon and Eric Kierans, the postmaster general, had promoted a campaign to advance Canadian nationalism and restrict foreign ownership of Canadian business, which Miss Jewett had endorsed. She flaunted at a public meeting a cheque for a campaign contribution from Walter Gordon, and Eric Kierans announced to the press that, if he had resided in Ottawa West, he would have voted for her.

If 1968 had been an easy ride, 1972 more than made up for it. One nasty surprise followed another. Gerard Pelletier's department had inaugurated a program of grants for community projects and the local MP was invited to comment on each proposal before the grant was made. I had objected to one grant in the Merivale Road area because I did not think it would serve a useful purpose. The local NDP organizer showed up at a public meeting with a copy of my confidential (or so I thought) letter to the minister, saying that I was the kind of MP who would deny his own voters funds!

On the weekend before the vote, I chanced to listen to a national CBC radio broadcast. Denis McVarish (I am guessing at the spelling of his name, because I never recall having met him) read an editorial to the effect that the voters of Ottawa West had a great opportunity. They could get rid of a useless sitting MP who had horns on his head and elect a fresh, brilliant academic who would grace parliament, Pauline Jewett. There was no possible way of replying to him. Private broadcasters, in my experience, would never do such a thing.

I have two quarrels with McVarish and the CBC on this incident. First, I believe it is improper for an editorial read over a national network to focus in a highly partisan way on one single constituency: a passing reference to a specific situation in a general context would be more acceptable. Secondly, such an editorial should not be read within forty-eight hours of an election. If it had been given at least a week before, there would have been some possibility of a reply on my part. Only a few CBC reporters are so unethical, but they leave a foul taste behind them. A backbencher stung this way could be excused for taking it out on CBC estimates when the time came.

My Conservative opponent, Peter Reilly, was a character. By profession a journalist, he was well known on private television. Peter had excellent stage presence, a good delivery and a keen sense of humour, but a reputation for imbibing a little. Confident of the hard core Conservative vote in the riding, all he had to do was to sit back and let Pauline tear me to pieces, which she did very effectively.

The national leader of the NDP, David Lewis, focussed his campaign on attacking national corporations that used write-offs permitted under the law to reduce their taxes, calling them corporate welfare bums. Pauline announced that, by eliminating the "corporate rip-off," it would be possible to increase the universal old age pension by $25 a month. In an all-candidates meeting in Laurentian High School, she hinted strongly that David Lewis, because of his age, might be retiring before long and she would be a good candidate to succeed him.

One of my neighbours, Al Johnson, who held many senior posts, including president of CBC, told me at the end of the campaign that, coming from Western Canada, he had been sympathetic to the NDP but after following Pauline's speeches at all-candidates meetings, he had decided to vote for me. His remark made my day.

The election results were as follow:

Reilly (Conservative)	22,169
Francis (Liberal)	18,423
Jewett (NDP)	13,498
Hamelin (Social Credit)	245

Compared to the results in 1968, the NDP vote had increased by 8,495, and the Conservative total by 5,777. My Liberal vote had decreased by 5,327. For all her efforts, Pauline had still run third and knocked me out in the process. I believe, however, that my defeat and those of Gordon Blair in Grenville-Carleton and Murray McBride in Lanark-Renfrew-Carleton were due to the government's bilingualism policy. The evidence is clear that the public service voted massively against the government.

Perhaps the most difficult moment came on election night. We had planned to meet in the hall of Our Lady of Fatima Church, hopefully to celebrate. As the results were known, the prime minister came on radio, to comment on how much he regretted his party's losses in the Ottawa area and mentioned each one, with the exception of Ottawa West.

OUT OF OFFICE AGAIN, 1972-74

This being my third defeat in federal elections, I was getting used to it. Fortunately, our shopping centre was doing well and I did not have a financial problem. Most encouraging, our core supporters stayed loyal. Bob Chiarelli, whose father had done business with my father a half century previously, became president of our local Liberal association and went on to act as campaign manager for my next four efforts. He later became an MPP at Queen's Park and, more recently, chair of the Regional Municipality of Ottawa-Carleton. Josephine Martin and many devoted members of our Women's Liberal Club, Joyce and Gerry Erskine, Ernie and Joan Murray, Glen Kealey, fellow members of Carlingwood Kiwanis, and numerous friends in the Italian, Greek, Ukrainian, Chinese, Jewish, Lebanese and other ethnic communities encouraged me to stay and continue the fight in Ottawa West.

After the election, Margery and I decided to take a holiday visiting an old friend in the Cayman Islands who had previously served as municipal engineer in Nepean. This has been to date my only visit to the Caribbean and we enjoyed it thoroughly. I did a little snorkelling and we visited a turtle farm. The beaches were fabulous and laden with pink conch shells, which we collected. It was easy to understand how a tropical relaxed way of life could grow on you, but I was by no means prepared to give up on Canadian politics.

Pauline did not continue to build the team she had created. Not living in the riding, she made little effort to keep in touch. Realizing that their efforts had helped to elect Peter Reilly, some of the professional women who had helped her, but were only lukewarm NDP supporters, came back to the Liberals.

Meanwhile, Peter Reilly's conduct as an MP in the House of Commons left much to be desired. On one occasion, having imbibed a bit too much, he publicly attacked John Diefenbaker, who responded by calling him a "Johnny one-timer." Conservative friends meeting me in the street told me that they would not vote if Reilly were the candidate in another election. A political opponent not voting is better than one voting! On January 10, 1973, in a nasty exchange in the House of Commons with Prime Minister

Prime Minister Trudeau speaking to Ottawa West Liberal Association, 1973

Trudeau, he credited his victory in Ottawa West to the way the Liberals had implemented the bilingual policy in the public service.[61]

In this period, I ran three articles in the *Ottawa Citizen*,[62] which no doubt made me enemies in high Liberal circles, but helped to re-establish credibility with my voters. In the first, after analyzing the results in Ottawa Valley ridings and comparing voting trends between 1968 and 1972, I concluded that Liberals were losing support in English-speaking ridings but gaining in the French-speaking ones. Three ridings on the Ontario side of the National Capital Region had been lost due to the anger of the public service. I suggested a number of changes in language policy and in hiring in the public service to help correct the situation.

In my second article, I reviewed John Carson's shenanigans—how he had publicly repudiated the Pearson Pledge given by two prime ministers and grossly insulted senior anglophone public servants.

In my third article, I cited a report leaked ten days before the election by Claude Lemelin of *Le Droit*. A study by a francophone group concluded that the attempt to teach anglophones French was a colossal waste of money. They alleged the cost to be $29,000 per person with dropout rates of ninety per cent. My Conservative opponent, Peter Reilly, charged that at this rate it would take $5 billion and 250 years to make the public service bilingual! John Carson had already taken away half of the Pearson Pledge, namely that the careers of long-term unilinguals would not be prejudiced. Now the other half of the pledge, that they would be able to learn French with courses paid for by the government, would possibly be denied them.

No one undertook to answer publicly my serious charges. Gordon Blair, with a forced smile, announced his resignation from politics.[63] Actually, I seriously considered resigning from the Liberal Party but did not want to quit politics and could not bring myself to join the Conservatives.

Liberals had suffered serious losses in the 1972 election and were reduced to a minority government. Their numbers had declined from 155 to 109, and Conservatives increased from 72 to 107. The balance of power was held by the NDP with 31 MPs and Quebec Social Crediters with 15. From its first session onwards, it was clear that this parliament would have a short life. Early in 1974, the government was defeated on a measure that could have been technically construed as a confidence vote. Robert

---

[61] Erik Neilson passed a harsh judgment on Reilly. In the epilogue to his autobiography, describing his "golden rules of politics," he wrote: "Avoid the degenerative diseases of middle age. These are, of course, the bottle and the nineteen-year-old. . . . Consider the case of Peter Reilly, a brilliant hard-working politician who struck Ottawa with almost physical force in the early 1970s and was burned out and dead within a few years . . ." *The House Is Not a Home: An Autobiography*, published by Macmillan of Canada, 1989, page 273.

[62] *Citizen*, 1972, November 18, page 7; November 20, page 7; and November 21, page 7.

[63] The *Ottawa Journal*, March 13, 1974, page 3. Gordon subsequently told me that he had a serious health problem.

Stanfield, however, did not pursue the occasion as vigorously as Diefenbaker might have done and the minority Liberal government was able to survive.

One day in the spring of 1974, Doug Fullerton, chairman of the NCC, invited me to lunch. After coffee, he turned and said bluntly:

"Lloyd, why don't you pull out of the contest for the nomination in Ottawa West? You know that the French-Canadian ministers don't like you."

I stared back. "Doug, take a message back that they will have to carry me out, when there is no life left in my body." Doug smiled and I could not help feeling that he admired my spirit. We had clashed on more than one occasion, but there was no personal animosity between us.

THE 1974 ELECTION

My nomination in Ottawa West this time was challenged seriously from two directions. Dr. Byron Hyde, a general practitioner in the riding, was helped by Jean Marchand. Donald Mitchell, a young Ottawa lawyer, was backed by a disgruntled worker in my former campaigns, Mrs. Pat Nicol.

Byron Hyde was supplied with headquarters on the Richmond Road and the services of four women who came from the riding of a Montreal MP who had faced nomination difficulties, but had been rescued by the party bosses. One of them, a Mrs. Haldimand, told me how she had been paid to come to Ottawa to work in a nomination campaign. A fellow Kiwanian, Don Jesse, employed as an information officer in Jean Marchand's department, was called into the minister's office along with the Montreal MP mentioned. He was told that he was to prepare publicity to help Byron Hyde's campaign; he refused to do it. Not long afterwards, he resigned from the public service.

Ottawa West is not the kind of constituency that responds well to parachuted candidates. Without a strong local base, it is almost impossible to win the nomination for a major party. Dr. Hyde was not a local person and had only been practising medicine for a short time. He had not previously been a candidate for a school board or for city council. More than 1,500 delegates came out to vote and Hyde was eliminated on the first ballot.

I was enraged at the efforts to defeat me by a Quebec minister, and prepared a detailed memo that I sent to Keith Davey and to John Turner. In the 1968 election, Turner had shifted from his Montreal seat to Ottawa-Carleton and, when George McIlraith went to the Senate in 1972, he became the minister responsible for the Ottawa area. Neither Davey nor Turner responded to my memo in any way, and refused to discuss it with me. Their silence hurt me deeply. Was this my reward for being the first Liberal to win Carleton in nearly a century, for carrying the flag for the Liberals in four elections, for defending bilingualism in a constituency dominated by English language public servants? Obviously, my articles in the *Ottawa Citizen* had infuriated the Liberal brass, but I believe they were well received in Ottawa West by my voters. Indeed, I do not believe that I would have been able to make a comeback later had I not taken a hard stand.

A more serious threat came from the campaign plotted on behalf of Donald Mitchell by Pat Nicol, who had been a competent area organizer for me in the Belair Heights area in 1963, 1965 and 1968. She later entered municipal politics, running successfully for alderman and the Board of Control. Walter Ryan, also a good worker, had followed the same route and run against Pat for the board. The night he lost, I called at his headquarters to offer my condolences, but made the mistake of going to see him before going to congratulate Pat.

She heard about it and concluded, quite erroneously, that I had helped Walter and not her. From that day on, she has been an implacable enemy.[64]

Don Mitchell, a member of our Young Liberals Club, had helped in previous elections and had just been called to the bar. A native of Ottawa West, he had many friends in Irish Catholic circles. Pat Nicol's husband, a prosperous builder-developer, bankrolled Mitchell's campaign. They had access to the lists of election workers and solicited them furiously over a period of weeks.

A contested nomination is a civil war within a party, and things get said about the contestants that can never be unsaid. Some workers that I valued highly defected to Mitchell and never worked in any of my campaigns again. Others renewed their efforts in order to counteract the malicious rumours that were spread. One group of members of the Catholic Knights of Columbus showed their disgust at the suggestion that I was anti-Catholic (I am a Unitarian) by conspicuously turning out to work on my behalf. In such times you get to know your real friends.

The meeting was held in Highland Park High School on Broadview Avenue. Beside the school was a vacant lot, on which we had pitched a huge tent the day before to serve as our headquarters. Senator Richard Stanbury, president of the Liberal Federation of Canada, acted as chairman. The voting dragged on after midnight, but I won by over a hundred votes. In a monstrous error of judgement, the scrutineers unanimously decided to announce the final result without giving the precise count.

The next morning, Mitchell told a reporter that the difference had been about six votes and that there should have been a recount, in spite of the

---

[64] When I returned from Portugal in 1987, my wife was admitted to hospital and diagnosed with a fatal illness. As we were bringing her home and entering our house, the telephone rang. It was Pat Nicol, seeking my support in a contest for the Liberal nomination in Ottawa West. I was hardly in the mood to discuss the matter!

fact that his representatives had been present as well as Senator Stanbury, whose integrity was beyond question. Prime Minister Trudeau wrote to the president of the Liberal Party in Ontario, asking him to investigate the convention to see if there had been any irregularities. He did so and reported that there was no evidence of wrongdoing.

The electoral law has subsequently been amended to require the signature of the leader before a candidate can be accepted by the party. Had such a law been in place in 1974, there is a doubt in my mind whether Mr. Trudeau would have signed my papers, although we were later on the best of terms.

Peter Reilly did not have the same aplomb in the 1974 campaign, and the NDP nominated a much weaker candidate, Doris Shackleton, a newspaper columnist who lived in a rural district to the south of Ottawa. I taunted her, saying that she was a parachuted candidate with no knowledge or interest in local affairs. She replied that indeed she had a real interest in Ottawa West, citing as one piece of evidence that she had purchased a funeral plot in Pinecrest cemetery. I replied that the cemetery was in Nepean, not Ottawa West, and wondered if she had got her marching orders from her party mixed up and filed her papers in the wrong constituency.

At one of the all-candidates meetings, Doris Shackleton was sounding off about the corporate welfare bums. The NDP always claimed that they were so much holier than the rest of us and this was just too much. How ethical was it to ask for a corporate donation and, if it was refused, to name that corporation as a corporate welfare bum, I asked. Was this not a form of blackmail?

The next morning a reporter from the *Ottawa Citizen* came to my home to ask what was my authority for making my statement the night before. Fortunately for me, I was able to get Bert Loeb, the president of M. Loeb Ltd., on the telephone and he was glad to speak to the reporter. Yes, David Lewis had asked him personally for a contribution. When he refused the request, his company's name was added to the list of corporate welfare bums. Bert Loeb was furious and would talk to anyone about it.

The *Citizen* carried the story on the front page.

The results of the election on July 8, 1974, were as follow:

FRANCIS (Liberal)	23,604
REILLY (Conservative)	21,838
SHACKLETON (NDP)	6,480

Compared to the 1972 results, Reilly's vote had decreased by 331 but, more important, the NDP vote had gone down by 7,010, more than fifty per cent. My vote increased by 5,261. In spite of an increase in population in the constituency, over 3,000 fewer votes were cast.

This time Liberals elected a majority government with 141 MPs, an increase of 32. Conservatives declined by 12 to 95, the NDP declined by 15 to hold 16 seats and Quebec Social Crediters went from 15 down to 11.

In November 1974, I was badly injured in an automobile accident and spent over a month in intensive care in the Ottawa Civic Hospital. Nearly six months passed before I could fully resume my duties as an MP.

Part 3

THE 30TH PARLIAMENT, 1974-79

IN THE FALL OF 1974, I was named parliamentary secretary to Jean Chrétien, president of the Treasury Board. We had both been elected in 1963 and were on excellent personal terms. However, because of my automobile accident, it was some time before I assumed full duties.

On my return, I found to my dismay that I had to make changes in the staff of my office in the House of Commons. Joyce Erskine left our constituency office to become my secretary and Audrey Maloney took her place. In addition, I had to make some changes with my full-time assistant. The growth of an MP's staff since my election in 1963 meant that more time and attention were required for supervision.

In the spring of 1975, I joined a delegation attending a conference of the Inter-Parliamentary Union in Sri Lanka. The IPU has a long history, going back to 1889. It accepts membership from any country claiming to have a parliament, without asking too many questions on democratic election procedures. All of the Iron Curtain countries, for example, were members as well as Libya and North Korea. With headquarters in Geneva and an excellent staff, the IPU provided a forum for legislators of different backgrounds, cultures and parliamentary traditions to discuss common problems. African and Asian delegates were concerned with struggles for liberation from imperialist powers. Europeans were more concerned with

Lloyd with Jean Chrétien, 1974

human rights and economic development. Many of the Third World countries brought resolutions similar to those introduced at the United Nations for a New World Economic Order. The likeable and competent Italian secretary, Terrenzio, was married to an Armenian and sensitive to issues involving genocide, that abominable crime that humanity does not seem able to eradicate.

At that time in Sri Lanka, the differences between the Buddhist Sinhalese majority and the Tamil Hindu minority were simmering but had not escalated to the point of violence. We landed at an airport built with Canadian aid funds and the conference was held in a magnificent new building in Colombo constructed with the help of the Republic of China.

The prime minister, Mrs. Bandaranaike, was the widow of a previous prime minister who had been assassinated by a deranged Buddhist monk. Her welcoming address highlighted the need to unite against neo-imperialism, whatever that meant. The country had inherited at the time of liberation an infrastructure that included not only roads, bridges, hotels, financial institutions, hospitals and schools, but even more important, a trained public service capable of administering government departments. Tea plantations were prosperous, and the private sector of the economy was expanding.

Chantal and Dijen De Saram, Dhevan and Chiara, Sri Lanka

Every newly independent country has its growing pains, and Sri Lanka's early flirtation with leftist politics had left its mark. The country, however, has spectacular scenery and friendly people. Sinhalese nationalism led to the elimination of the teaching of English for a year or two, but this was soon reversed. We toured the interior to Kandy, the ancient capital, and visited the Buddhist Temple of the Tooth, which contained a tooth relic reputed to have come from the Lord Buddha himself. A garden in Kandy displayed the greatest variety of orchids that I have ever seen. We stopped at a spot by a river where elephants were bathing and I remember one of our group, John Rodriguez, the MP for Sudbury, riding one of them.

The minister of Health, Mrs. Siva Obeyesekere, wished to have her daughter, Chantal, study abroad, but no foreign exchange was available for the purpose. To make a long story short, Margery and I sponsored Chantal at the University of Ottawa, where she completed a Bachelor of Arts degree. She lived with us and we paid her tuition. Chantal has since returned to her native country, married a lawyer practising in Colombo, and is the proud mother of a son and a daughter. I visited with them when I was a member of the international team of election observers in 1993, in 1994, and again in 1999.

Over the years, I have followed events in Sri Lanka with sympathy and not a little sadness. The country has shifted its policies to encourage development, with considerable success. Meanwhile, relations with the Tamils deteriorated to the point of civil war and some of the Tamils (but by no means all of them) resorted to terrorism. To an outsider, a military solution does not seem possible and concessions to Tamil self-government will have to be made. Where the Tamils control a territory, as in the north around Jaffna, a separate state is possible, but in the rest of the country such a solution is not feasible.[65]

On the way back, the Canadian delegation spent a week in Pakistan, returning a visit to Canada by a group of Pakistani parliamentarians. Robert Stanbury, the brother of Senator Richard Stanbury, served as chairman. Prime Minister Ali Bhutto granted us an interview that lasted a full hour. Having done post-graduate studies in California, he spoke eloquently, with authority, on a wide variety of subjects, including not least his own country. I remember his references to the population problem in Pakistan and how difficult it was to institute programs to control births. It is impossible to imagine how his country could have hanged such a man, as was done following a coup d'etat some two years later.[66]

In Islamabad, the capital, we visited the Canadian High Commissioner and I remember his words in the briefing session referring to "this

---

[65] As I write, the Sinhalese Army has captured Jaffna, but as a result, the Tamil terror has escalated.

[66] In 1976, Prime Minister Bhutto visited Ottawa with in excess of 150 persons accompanying him. I attended, by invitation, a ceremony in Ottawa's first mosque on Northwestern Avenue. The mullah recited the valiant efforts of the small Muslim community to build the mosque, giving precise amounts of the aid they had received from Saudi Arabia, Kuwait, and the Gulf States, concluding that they were short by $200,000 and requesting the great Islamic nation of Pakistan to help them. Bhutto rose immediately to say that Pakistan would give them that amount.
I told Prime Minister Trudeau about it the next day. Trudeau swore, then added: "He comes here to ask us for development aid. He is accompanied by a monstrous delegation and then he spends his money like that."

turbulent land." He lived with all the other heads of missions in a diplomatic enclave protected by security at entrance points. With a military escort we entered the tribal lands leading to the Khyber Pass, an incredibly beautiful route, with its succession of hairpin turns. At spots, you could look back and see miles of the winding trails that we had ascended. Whatever trees had once existed had been long since cut down, but numerous spots were marked with ruins of places of worship. There are no Buddhists in the area now, but the remains of numerous small pagodas told their own stories from the past. Stone panels carved into the rock face recorded the tours of duty of countless British regiments.

At Peshawar, we stopped for refreshments at the Khyber Rifles mess. In the place of honour, at the end of a long table, was an autographed photograph of John Diefenbaker. Some officer while in Canada had no doubt secured it and brought it back to be placed as a friendly gesture to Canada.[67]

We proceeded to the border with Afghanistan, but did not cross it. Many of the local Pathan tribesmen had blue eyes that seemed incongruous with their dark hair and skin. Someone said that they owed this genetic trait to the armies of Alexander the Great that had crossed the Khyber Pass two thousand years ago. Some of the Pathans still carried Greek names.

Canada had a minor role in the construction of the huge Tarbela Dam on the Indus River. Not long before we arrived, a section had collapsed, releasing the water that had accumulated in the dam for over a year. Some time later, I learned that the dam had finally been completed and from all reports now functions well. It was certainly a most impressive sight.

We visited the great port of Karachi and toured the Kanup nuclear reactor, which Canada had sold to Pakistan, using our natural uranium technology. In a small boat of the Pakistan Navy, we were taken around the harbour. It was hot, and I leaped at the offer of a cool beer, only to discover too late that it had an ice cube in it. This brought on a terrible attack of dysentery that made my return journey home sheer misery.

BACK TO OTTAWA

Meanwhile, the Thirtieth Parliament of Canada had been sitting. It came as a rude shock to me that Hugh Faulkner, secretary of state, had named as his executive assistant Andy Cohen, who had acted as campaign manager for Pauline Jewett against me in 1972. Faulkner's department administered a series of grants and I was understandably uneasy about them. Perhaps by coincidence, some prominent NDP supporters, including the woman who had been the president of the Ottawa West NDP Association, found places in government employment.

[67] When I came back to Ottawa, I told John Diefenbaker about it. He clearly did not believe me and thought I was putting him on, in spite of my best efforts.

REVISION OF THE *PUBLIC SERVICE SUPERANNUATION ACT*

Being parliamentary secretary to the president of Treasury Board had its challenges and its problems. Jean Chretien delegated two assignments to me that I thoroughly enjoyed. I know he was pleased with my efforts.

The first involved a revision to the legislation governing public service superannuation. In large part, the amendments simply brought many sections up to date and had the full support of the staff associations. As an MP for Ottawa and a former national president of one of them, I made it a policy of keeping in touch, assuring them that I considered it to be my job to represent their interests in parliament.

First reading of a government bill is a formality; debate comes at second reading, followed by referral to committee. I led off in debate and steered the bill through the committee stage.

One problem emerged that I had not anticipated. Under the existing legislation, a public servant was penalised financially by retiring during the year, which had the result of bunching retirements on December 31 of each year. You can imagine how this disrupted normal departmental operations. The draft legislation, prepared largely by Hart Clark in the Department of Finance, a man whom I had known and respected from my days at National Health and Welfare, would have permitted anyone to retire without financial penalty at any date.

Someone in the Prime Minister's Office, reviewing the bill, decided that conferring this privilege on public servants was giving them something they should not enjoy and issued instructions to have it deleted. This was my first indication of the abuse of power in the PMO. When I was in the public service, such a thing could not have happened. The minister would have conferred with his deputy and listened to the reasons why the section had been inserted in the first place. Expansion of staff in the PMO comes at the expense of the traditional relationship of a minister with his deputy. There was no appeal from a PMO decision, at least not in my experience. Some two years later, the Act was again amended to reinstate the provision we had been ordered to delete.

LOTO CANADA FRANCHISES

The second assignment related to the award of franchises for Loto Canada. The provinces, notably Ontario, had discovered that publicly run lotteries were great money-makers. The federal government, however, was not willing to concede jurisdiction to the provinces and set up its own national lottery. Advertisements inviting applications for franchises were placed in major dailies across the country and the replies screened. Names on the short list were then checked by a national credit agency.

Jean Chrétien told me to select from the list the successful applicants for nine provinces, but I was not to touch anything in the province of Quebec.

I was permitted to hire an assistant and chose Rod Rooney, a chartered accountant in Ottawa who had acted as treasurer for the Ottawa West Liberal Association and was one of the most trustworthy persons I have ever known. Needless to say, we were under pressure from local MPs who wanted awards to take place on patronage grounds.

Jean had also cautioned me that it was essential that good agents be named, or else the federal lottery would be discredited. In every case, local MPs were consulted before decisions were made. Sometimes they were quite helpful. In one case, we denied a franchise to an otherwise qualified applicant, because he had been convicted for netting fish illegally in the St. Lawrence River. In cases where applicants were equally qualified and it was hard to decide, the local MP's recommendation was considered.

The Metro Toronto area was particularly difficult. Loto Ontario franchises had been profitable and competition was keen. Every MP had his own favourite candidate, but there were not enough franchises to please everybody and we wanted to avoid having the subject raised in caucus.

The first award we made was to a well-known Conservative who had successfully run a Loto Ontario franchise. Then we did our best to please the Liberal MPs. Many were disappointed, but we met with them and explained how we had arrived at our decisions. When the list of successful applicants was announced, the *Toronto Star* assigned a reporter to interview me, asking bluntly if our choices were made on the basis of patronage. I explained the selection process, starting with the newspaper advertisements and the credit checks. He recognised the first name on the Toronto area list, laughed, and left my office without writing a story.

To the best of my knowledge, no story appeared in the press across Canada criticising the selection of Loto Canada agents and the matter was not raised in the Liberal caucus. It was unfortunate for those who made the final list that, in 1979, the federal government decided to abandon lotteries to the provinces and disbanded Loto Canada. Many of them had gone to considerable effort to get their franchises. [68]

---

[68] In the summer of 1975, my father died. His was a classic case of Alzheimer's, which was not as clearly diagnosed at that time as it is today. For the last two years of his life, he did not know me. I can still remember the last time he recognised me. The light came to his eyes, he smiled but could not speak. Two minutes later all recognition was gone and his face went blank. We had never been close, except for some moments fishing together in the Big Rideau Lake. Throughout my adult life, he had sought to dominate me, telling me what I had to do and criticising my business decisions, although we never knew how much money he himself had lost in get-rich-quick ventures with questionable associates.

Within a month, my very good friend Bob McKeown also died. He suffered from a form of intestinal cancer, I believe, but his mind was clear to the end. In his early sixties, he left a widow and two sons. One son, Robert Junior, has had a distinguished career in the same field as his father and is now in the United States.

CAPITAL PUNISHMENT

This parliament adopted a law to abolish capital punishment, one of the issues on which individual MPs are free to vote according to their own consciences and are not obliged to follow a party line.

Using my additional staff, we sent out quarterly reports to voters and occasionally included questionnaires on matters before the House. For some years I had considered myself to be an abolitionist, and was shocked to learn from responses to our questionnaire that fully seventy per cent of the voters in my constituency supported retention of the death penalty.

During a parliamentary break Margery and I went to Florida, living in an efficiency unit by the sea for a week. One day we listened to public television featuring a man who had spent his life as a professional psychologist in the prison system. He explained that he had been an abolitionist from his youth, but found that the prison system simply could not cope with a small number of hard men who had committed many murders. Unless watched constantly, they would kill in prison, refusing to modify their habits in any way. A handful of such persons in one institution made it almost impossible to manage, and corrupted everyone—fellow inmates, guards, anyone with whom they came in touch. Reluctantly, he had come to the conclusion that capital punishment was the best solution for such persons. Television is a powerful medium and this interview made an enormous impression on me.

There are two schools of thought on the function of an MP: do you lead your constituents, or represent them? In practice, sometimes you do one, and sometimes the other. Emotions were running high as a result of the trial in Western Canada of an inmate who had killed the child of one of the guards in his prison while on a weekend leave. Not long afterwards came the horrible case of Clifford Olson, who murdered eleven teenagers. Was I prepared to vote to prevent men like this receiving the death penalty? When the time came, the measure presented to us abolished the death penalty, but increased prison terms for a variety of offences in a crude sort of trade-off. I voted against it.

DECENTRALIZING THE PUBLIC SERVICE

In this period, the Liberal Party became enthusiastic for the decentralization of the public service, moving sections and entire departments across the country. Douglas Fullerton, in his 1974 report on how the national capital should be governed, had made this suggestion [69]. Local MPs rushed to the trough to grab everything they could for their own constituencies. [70]

---

[69] Op. cit., page 220.

[70] Mr. Speaker Jerome, for example, was pleased to be able to bring a taxation data centre to Sudbury in 1976. *Mr. Speaker James Jerome*, McClelland and Stewart, Toronto, 1985, page 140.

Treasury Board directed the operation and the issue affected my constituency of Ottawa West intimately. My minister, Jean Chretien, no doubt influenced by Fullerton's comments, was surprised that I did not support the policy. It was quite understandable that employees were reluctant to leave their homes in Ottawa and take their families with them to remote parts of the country. The Tourist Bureau moved to Nova Scotia, the government cheque-clearing unit to Matane, Quebec, the Mint to Winnipeg and the entire Department of Veterans Affairs to Prince Edward Island. Every region got something and strong cabinet ministers got more.

The theory was that it brought government closer to the people and cemented national unity. The reality was patronage and jobs for your own backyard. The disruption to staff morale was incalculable. Certainly some of the moves were costly and wasteful. I can remember appealing to caucus to bring some sense to the process, but my words fell on deaf ears. One minister, Alastair Gillespie from Toronto, supported me, no doubt at cost to himself by attracting criticism from his colleagues.

The proposal to move the Surveys and Mapping Branch of what was then the Department of Energy, Mines and Resources to Sherbrooke, Quebec, was just too much. The union of employees involved, under its able president, Marcel Longtin, fought the move and I decided to fight with them. An expensive new building was required, costing an estimated $40 million. Quebec's language laws would require the sons and daughters of the federal employees to attend French language schools. I went to Prime Minister Trudeau twice on this issue and he and Jean Chretien agreed that, without some exemption by the province from its language laws, the move should be delayed.

The member for Sherbrooke, Mr. Gerard Pelletier, received an evasive answer when he asked the prime minister about the move in the House on December 19, 1977. [71] He did not fare any better when he asked Jean Chrétien on March 22, 1978, [72] whether or not the federal government would accept Quebec's offer of permitting the children of English-speaking public servants to attend English schools for six years, as a solution to the problem.

Gerard Pelletier and I had a series of sharp exchanges in Hansard. On December 4, 1978, [73] I pointed out that the policy was costly, not achieving its stated objectives and had an undue impact on Ottawa. Pelletier bragged to his constituents: [74]

> The federal government is determined to relocate that service in Sherbrooke, in accordance with the commitment given to

[71] Hansard, page 1987.
[72] Hansard, page 4022.
[73] Hansard, page 1783.
[74] Hansard, page 1447.

> the public servants and all the provinces in the House in 1974. Let us think about it: it concerns 750 employees, plus spouses and children, a total of about 2,000 people. It means creation of at least 1,500 direct and indirect jobs, total annual wages of over $15 million, and capital investments in the range of $40 million.

The MP for Sherbrooke went on to make another point that was particularly offensive to many of my constituents. Referring to the proposed move of the Surveys and Mapping Branch, he reported as follows: [75]

> I see, Mr. Speaker, that the government's decision provided that between 750 and 1,000 jobs would be decentralized. It means that nearly 1,000 public servants now in Ottawa, of which 75 per cent are English-speaking and 25 per cent French-speaking, would move into our region. But within a decade or a dozen years, the linguistic breakdown of that decentralization would nearly reflect the breakdown we now find in the region and which is the opposite of what it will be at the beginning, that is about 25 per cent English-speaking and about 75 per cent French-speaking.

In short, he was suggesting that half of the English-speaking employees of the Surveys and Mapping Branch would be replaced within a decade or so. Many of these were skilled technicians in specialized fields, such as mapmaking, for whom there was really no alternative employment.

A part of the branch was later moved to Sherbrooke, but most of it stayed in Ottawa. I cannot help but observe that no language guarantees were given to public servants moved to Matane and I believe that my interventions with the prime minister and Mr. Chrétien had some effect. [76]

Treasury Board was not the place for me at that time and I was relieved when my term ended in 1975. My opposition to decentralization certainly contributed to my reputation as a maverick

RESIGNATION OF JOHN TURNER

After four years as minister of Finance, the Honourable John Turner resigned as a minister and as a member of Parliament on February 12, 1976. The full story of his disagreement with Prime Minister Trudeau has

[75] Hansard, November 29, 1977, page 1390.

[76] My dire predictions for the city of Ottawa did not anticipate the growth of employment from the high technology sector that fortunately offset the losses caused by decentralization. While total employment did not fall, many of the public servants affected did not move to the new positions and suffered because their skills did not match the requirements of the new high-technology companies.

never been made public. Turner had been the cabinet minister for the Ottawa area and his departure understandably raised hopes that one of the area MPs would be promoted. You can imagine our disappointment when Bud Cullen, the minister of National Revenue who represented Sarnia, was named by the prime minister to be the Ottawa area cabinet minister. It was a brutal, unprecedented slap in the face for all of the local MPs.

When a by-election was held on October 18, 1976, for John Turner's seat, the results were as follows:

Piggott (Conservative)	34,447
Rocque (Liberal)	18,796
Langdon (NDP)	12,777
Crawford (Ind.)	716
LeBer (Ind.)	602

Two years previously, John Turner had won with over fifty-three per cent of the votes cast. The by-election results were a clear indication of how the voters felt.

UNOFFICIAL VISITS ABROAD

Members of parliament often receive invitations to visit foreign countries, sometimes individually, sometimes as part of an unofficial delegation. In most cases, it is a judgement call whether to accept or refuse.

The move to Sherbrooke defeated, July 8, 1982 (Rusins, *Ottawa Citizen*)

I was tempted to visit Taiwan, but declined on the advice of Mitchell Sharp, the minister of External Affairs. In 1976 I joined a delegation to Israel and in 1982 attended an international development conference in Sanaa, North Yemen.

For those of us raised in the Judeo-Christian tradition, a trip to the Holy Land touches deep emotional roots. We landed near Tel-Aviv, a thriving modern city on the Mediterranean coast, and passed through enormous orange groves as we climbed the hills toward Jerusalem. We stayed in the King David Hotel, visited the Wailing Wall and the site of King Solomon's Temple, and walked the streets.

Words fail to describe Masada. Two thousand years ago, on this barren plateau in the desert not far from the Dead Sea, a Jewish group had withstood siege by a Roman army for perhaps two years. You could look down and still see the remains of the Roman camps below. Rather than be taken prisoners, those besieged committed mass suicide.

We swam in the Dead Sea, spent a night in a kibbutz on the Sea of Galilee, and visited Canadians forming part of the international peacekeeping force separating Syrian and Israeli troops on the Golan Heights.

The Israelis have created a modern, dynamic state making the best use of lands that had lain barren for centuries. We could never forget what we had seen.

THE PUBLIC ACCOUNTS COMMITTEE

On my return to Ottawa, I decided to join the Public Accounts Committee. Its chief function was to review the annual reports of the auditor general, one of a group of public servants that did not report to a minister, but to Parliament itself. The chairman, since Prime Minister Diefenbaker's time, was chosen from the Official Opposition, and in my initial period on the committee was Ron Huntington, the MP for Capilano, British Columbia. He was succeeded by the Conservative MP for Northumberland-Durham, Allan Lawrence, a former Ontario cabinet minister who had failed to become leader of his party (and premier) by only forty-four votes. Both Allan and Ron were able and experienced, and you could work with them. The auditor general, James MacDonnell, was breaking new ground in his office, going beyond examining where money had been spent, to working out systems that would give value for money. For the balance of the Twenty-eighth Parliament, I served as the senior Liberal on the committee.

The annual release of the Auditor General's Report used to cause a frenzy in the Press Gallery. Today, he issues a number of reports every year and their news value has diminished. In an operation as large as that of the Government of Canada, there are numerous instances of waste, misappropriation of funds, empty buildings whose rents are still being paid out of public funds, wharves built but not used, and so on. Each case, if properly dressed up, is good for a headline. The ones you cannot use today will be good for tomorrow.

The task of the public accounts committee is to make sure that such situations are corrected and do not recur. This is not always an easy task, because you have to understand what happened in the first place, which involves public hearings and calling witnesses. From my experience, there is less political partisanship on this committee than on most, although when it came to making specific recommendations and assigning blame, party differences did arise. Seldom was the auditor general himself criticized, although the expansion of his staff did raise questions later.

Anyone wishing to understand how our government operated in the 1960s and 1970s should examine the testimony given by the former president of Atomic Energy of Canada Limited, Lorne Gray. [77] Three basic issues are involved. Firstly, how did Atomic Energy secure in excess of a billion dollars of public money for a project that does not seem to have had any parliamentary scrutiny? Secondly, how was it possible to do this with a bare minimum of approval by cabinet ministers? Thirdly, what were the ethical considerations involved in selling nuclear reactors to South Korea and Argentina by bribery?

Every Canadian has reason to be proud of our country's achievements in developing nuclear technology. Canada and the United States were the only two countries that developed nuclear reactors for export. Canadian sales to Taiwan and to India proceeded without problems. The industry, including back-up suppliers and contractors, was geared up to a demand greater than the Canadian domestic market could offer.

Efforts to sell reactors in Mexico, Australia and Romania, however, failed. Competition from United States suppliers, especially General Electric and Westinghouse, was intense. It seems that, in some instances, local agents were given large sums of money to be passed on to unknown parties; this procedure helped sales.

When the prospect of a sale to Argentina arose in 1971, AECL was, in Lorne Gray's words, "gun-shy" and engaged the services of an Italian agent, Italimpianti, on the recommendation of "knowledgeable people." At Italimpianti's direction, the sum of $2.5 million was paid into a numbered Swiss bank account. When asked about it, Mr. Gray replied: [78]

> The ultimate beneficiary of the remittance of $2.5 million was neither a Canadian citizen nor a company or body subject to Canadian law. Furthermore, the above-mentioned beneficiary

---

[77] See the transcript of the Public Accounts Committee, issues 1-14, beginning on January 25,1977.

[78] See Issue 10 of the transcript of the Public Accounts Committee, January 27, 1977, page 34.

> was neither the company Italimpianti nor a company or other body controlled by the same.

Subsequently, Atomic Energy of Canada successfully negotiated a sale for what became known as the Cordoba nuclear reactor in Argentina.

The story in South Korea was similar. In this case, an agent based in Israel was used and payments directed to numbered bank accounts in Europe. The ultimate beneficiaries of these accounts could not be traced. Again, AECL was successful in negotiating a contract.

Mr. Gray was frank in describing his operating procedures to get approval from the Canadian bureaucracy for what he wanted to do, with an absolute minimum of involvement by cabinet ministers. His remarks on January 2, 1977, are reported in Issue No. 11 of the committee's proceedings. Briefly, he arranged lunches in his office, with his secretary doing the cooking, and invited such senior officials as the clerk of the Privy Council, the secretary of Treasury Board, the deputy minister of Finance, the undersecretary of External Affairs, the deputy minister of Industry Trade and Commerce and the deputy minister of Energy, Mines and Resources. After these people were briefed, memos requesting funds for his projects had clear sailing. The knowledgeable MP for Don Valley, James Gillies, remarked that it was, in his words, "extraordinary, absolutely incredible," that ministers were not consulted in the critical stages of developing policy.

When I heard the above testimony before the committee, I could hardly believe my ears. It received a minimum of attention in the press, and as far as I know, not much in academic circles. It certainly did not reflect well on the cabinet of the day. One could well ask: Were the bureaucrats the ones responsible for the decision to sell atomic reactors by bribery?

The ethical issue came up again when the committee examined the operations of the Department of External Affairs. I have not researched the proceedings, but recall that the committee discovered that part of the rent for premises occupied by our staff in Belgrade and Warsaw was paid by transfers to numbered bank accounts in Switzerland. The committee ordered that such payments cease and as a result our embassy was obliged, in at least one city, to operate out of hotel rooms for a couple of years.

Alan Gottlieb testified on this matter to a closed session of the Public Accounts Committee. I cannot cite the date but others present at the time confirm it.

One of the satisfactions of working with the Public Accounts Committee was the opportunity to get to know the auditor general, James MacDonnell. He was trying to go beyond examining where money had been spent, and whether or not there was legislative approval for expenditures, to the basic question of how the government could get value for money spent. This required that systems be in place to ensure, as far as possible, economy and efficiency. He caused a bill to be drafted, redefining the functions of his office, and creating a new office of controller general. It was a pleasure to support his efforts, but I am not sure that the results he expected have been achieved.

On March 9, 1979, James MacDonnell presented me with a Certificate of Appreciation "in recognition of DISTINGUISHED SERVICE to the Office of the Auditor General of Canada." The citation reads as follows:

> Cyril Lloyd Francis, true son of Ottawa, has flowered in its principal institutions including Glebe Collegiate, City Hall and the House of Commons. Doctor of Economics, airman, teacher, public servant and labour leader-turned-politician, he has earned the wary respect of his colleagues in and out of his own party as a constructive maverick.
>
> This former Deputy Mayor and later Chief Government Whip, mellowed by experience, has, as Vice-Chairman of the Public Accounts Committee, been a key influence in bringing about this Committee's present stature as the most effective and influential of the House of Commons.
>
> This Certificate of Appreciation is presented to Cyril Lloyd Francis in recognition of the esteem in which he is held by the Office of the Auditor General of Canada.

CERTIFICATE OF APPRECIATION

presented to

CERTIFICAT DE MÉRITE

présenté à

Cyril Lloyd Francis

in recognition of DISTINGUISHED SERVICE to the Office of the Auditor General of Canada.

en reconnaissance de SERVICES INSIGNES au Bureau du vérificateur général du Canada.

AUDITOR GENERAL OF CANADA
VÉRIFICATEUR GÉNÉRAL DU CANADA

OTTAWA, CANADA

MARCH 9, 1979

Certificate of Appreciation presented by Auditor General of Canada J.J. Macdonell

PRESIDENT OF THE CANADIAN BRANCH OF THE IPU

For some years, I had served on the executive of the Canadian branch of the Commonwealth Parliamentary Association. In 1976, a new executive was to be elected and, according to the usual procedures, it was my turn to serve as president. I assumed that everything was in order but got a rude shock at the very last moment.

A fellow Liberal MP decided to contest the election and systematically canvassed senators and MPs. My first inkling of trouble came when the deputy whip, Crawford Douglas, the MP for Bruce-Grey, started calling Liberal MPs to make sure they would turn out to vote. Why? Well, it seemed the Conservative MP for Edmonton West, the Honourable Marcel Lambert, a veteran who had served a short term as Speaker, was a candidate. I was not worried about him because Liberals, by far more numerous in the Senate and House combined, would not support him on party grounds. Crawford broke the news that another Liberal was running and the whip's office was afraid that the split Liberal vote would elect Lambert.

The whip's office need not have worried. I lost by an overwhelming majority of votes cast. Perhaps more than any other MP, I knew the Senators and had many friends among them. One after another, they apologised because they did not know that I was running and my opponent, of course, never told them. As a holder of elected office, I have never committed myself to supporting any candidate without knowing who else was in the race and have had to make difficult choices many times among candidates for school boards, or city council. To think that the professional politicians in the Parliament of Canada would commit themselves as they did to a candidate shook my faith in democracy.

I was hurt, because I felt that I had earned that spot. Shortly afterwards, the post of president of the Canadian branch of the Inter-Parliamentary Union became vacant. The MP in line to succeed had been elected for the first time just two years previously. I took a leaf out of my CPA opponent's book and campaigned for the position, winning it handily. As they say, what goes around, comes around.

The IPU holds spring and fall meetings and its executive council is based in Geneva. Two delegates from each parliamentary group form the Inter-Parliamentary Council and give general direction. Gordon Fairweather, MP for Fundy-Royal, had been Canada's representative on the executive council for some time. When he resigned on August 31, 1977 to become our Commissioner of Human Rights, I was elected at the fall meeting in Bulgaria to take his place.

A group of western nations called the Eleven-Plus met prior to the regular meetings to discuss the agenda and to be prepared against any unpleasant surprises from the Iron Curtain bloc. It took me a little while to get used to the internal politics of the organization, but Canada had a good name and many smaller countries trusted us, often seeking guidance.

Prior to proceeding to Sofia, the Canadian delegation split in two. One group, including myself, went to Budapest to return a previous visit to Canada by Hungarian parliamentarians. The other group spent a few days in Belgrade, Yugoslavia.

Budapest is really two cities, Buda and Pesta, on the two banks of the Danube. We stayed in a new hotel, the Hilton, which had all the amenities. Views from the bridges crossing the Danube were unforgettable, as were the magnificent palaces from the days of the Austro-Hungarian Empire when Budapest and Vienna alternated as the capital. However, we were surprised to discover that Attila the Hun, thoroughly reviled in our history books, was revered as the founder of the nation. The main square is named after him.

We visited the building where the parliament sat in the days of the old empire. A bullet was clearly visible, lodged in one of the arms of the Speaker's chair. We learned that the Speaker of the day had so infuriated one of the deputies that he had tried to assassinate him. The bullet that passed through his arm was left in place to remind future Speakers to exercise more discretion.

We had a congenial interview with the Speaker of their parliament and a group of deputies. To make conversation, I asked how many sessions they had per year. The answer came, three. How many sessions per year did we hold in Canada? Two at the most and in the year of the flag debate, only one. How long did their sessions last? Three days each. How long did ours last? In excess of 150 days per year. The Speaker paused, then asked the interpreter for a repeat of the question. Incredulously, he turned to me and asked: "Can't you arrange your business better than that?"

One afternoon we were taken for a boat ride on Lake Balaton, which covers a large surface area but is shallow. We were supposed to see the historic castles bordering the lake, but there was one problem. It rained furiously during the whole trip and no one could stand being on deck. Our Hungarian hosts brought out case after case of their good wines, which the group promptly emptied. The Hungarian governor was a big, burly man with a capacity for emptying his glass before you could turn around. Whether he had some secret way of disposing of his wine or not, I cannot say. I became increasingly worried about our own delegation, especially one or two elderly senators.

It was a relief when we docked and everyone safely negotiated the gangplank to shore. Our host promptly announced that we would be taken on a tour of a winery! We watched the processes from pressing the raw grapes to fermentation and bottling. Then followed a ten-course banquet, with toasts following every course. At the end of the evening when I could hardly stand, our host announced that he had a special present for the leader of the Canadian delegation and handed me four magnums of wine nicely packed with six gold-tinted glasses. I could not refuse, but it was an effort to carry them.

The next morning, we were to fly to Sofia, Bulgaria, in a small chartered plane. At the hour scheduled for departure from the hotel, one of our delegation was not there. I went to his room, to have him answer the door without a stitch of clothing on, to the embarrassment of his young wife. Our Hungarian hosts accepted the delay in departure with smiles.

Sofia was hosting a full conference of the IPU in September 1977 with more than a thousand delegates. One day, the entire group was taken by bus to Bulgaria's second city, Plovdiv, some three hundred kilometres distant. The countryside was rich with vineyards, orchards, nut groves and grain fields. Unfortunately, there were no rest facilities and the buses had to stop from time to time for the call of nature, which everyone accepted with good grace. Our guide explained that Bulgaria had few old churches, because they had been destroyed during the Turkish occupation, which had lasted for centuries. We had lunch in a seniors' home and toured the city, with its brick walls built by the Romans two thousand years ago still in good condition.

For dessert, we were served fruit. I found peaches, fully ripe, but firm as an apple, which no doubt would have interested Canadian geneticists. In my enthusiasm, I ate two of them.

A full plenary session was on the agenda for the next morning and, to my extreme consternation, I woke up with a dreadful case of cramps and diarrhea. I did not feel that I could leave the plenary because I was concerned about what a Social Credit member of our delegation might say. In our private group meetings, he had espoused some wild ideas. Tommy Douglas, a former premier of Saskatchewan, came to my rescue, volunteering to follow this man around and, if he made an inappropriate intervention, Tommy would immediately follow to correct it. Tommy was, without question, one of the most considerate MPs who ever served on a delegation.

As my plight got worse, Senator Bud Olson, a former minister of Agriculture and, as I write, lieutenant-governor of Alberta, got firm with me. "Lloyd, you must go to the infirmary. My wife had the same thing and they gave her pills. They worked."

Off I went to a room with some eight people sitting around in it. One thing I have learned is that you should never place yourself in the hands of a group of people looking for work to do. To start off, we had a communications problem, since my knowledge of Bulgarian is understandably limited. The senior officer, a sixtyish, huge, unsmiling and dominating ogress, had two words in her English vocabulary: "Belly? Hospital."

One of the junior doctors present spoke French. I protested that I had had no medical examination and no one had even checked my temperature. He merely raised his eyebrows, saying that she was the boss.

I got out of the room as soon as I could, but not before someone had checked my badge. From my hotel room, I telephoned a member of the

British delegation who had been dean of a medical school. He promised to come right over.

Someone knocked at our hotel room door. A charming young French-speaking translator, accompanied by two men who looked as though their occupation was putting straitjackets on mental patients, explained that I had no choice. Orders for my hospitalization were signed by a senior officer. An ambulance was waiting outside. I hastily said goodbye to my wife and surrendered.

The ambulance did not have too many springs and Sofia's streets had numerous potholes. We came to an ancient brick building, with iron gates that opened to admit us and then closed behind us. After a short wait, I was examined by a thoroughly competent medical doctor who spoke excellent French. She had been born in Spain and evacuated to France when the Loyalist side collapsed at the end of the civil war. In France she had studied medicine and married a Bulgarian. She agreed that I had no temperature and probably suffered from an intestinal upset. But the ogress had signed an official hospital admission document.

After careful reflection, she said she would prescribe a medication and made me promise faithfully that I would take it. The next morning at seven-thirty the young French-speaking translator appeared at my hotel room door. Fortunately, I was able to assure her that my symptoms had passed and that I was indeed well.

My British friend explained the probable cause for the ogress's action. Bulgaria was on the trade route from Turkey to Europe and typhoid was endemic in Turkey. He had heard rumours that one or two cases had shown up among the delegates and the Bulgarian health authorities were alarmed. In my case, they were being extra careful. They had caught up with one member of the British delegation, who, he assured me between chuckles, was a known hypochondriac.

At the end of the conference, Steve Paproski, the MP for Edmonton Centre, had a birthday. We had a party in the hotel and I offered to bring the wine. The Hungarian magnum bottle had impressive seals on it and I pulled the cork, offering the first glass to Steve. He sipped it once, then again.

"Francis, taste this." It was water, as were the contents of the other three magnums. Someone had stolen the wine as it was being bottled and substituted water. "Francis, you have a bad talent. You can turn wine into water," Steve jibed.

There were a number of members of our delegation and the story circulated around Ottawa. The minister of Agriculture, Gene Whelan, not known for subtlety, was entertaining the Hungarian ambassador and told him what had happened. The next morning, six bottles of fine Hungarian wine were delivered to my house!

Sofia was an interesting old city, with new features. The body of the national communist hero, Dimitroff, was mummified and preserved in a special structure, as had been done in Moscow with Lenin. Underneath Red Square was a magnificent shopping area. Margery discovered a leather goods shop with some fine products on display at good prices. We were encouraged to spend our Canadian currency shopping and Margery could hardly wait to do so. Unfortunately, it was closed and remained closed every time we went there. Someone explained that the shop received its merchandise once per month, sold out in two days and was closed for the rest of the time. We purchased a number of small household items (including a can-opener) of excellent design and for inexpensive prices.

The fall meeting in Sofia was followed by one in the spring of 1978 in Lisbon, Portugal. Scarcely four years previously, the Portuguese Army, tired of being bled white trying to suppress rebellions in Angola and Mozambique, had removed the dictatorship that had ruled for nearly half a century. General Ramalho Eanes, who had commanded the critical army division in Lisbon, was elected president. Representatives of newly established political parties welcomed the IPU delegates and were anxious that the rest of the world should know about their efforts to build a modern democracy. Are there many countries in the world where the fires of democratic convictions emerged from the military? That was certainly the case in Portugal.

Sessions were held in the Gulbenkian Foundation Museum, a magnificent structure donated to Portugal by an Armenian who had amassed a fortune pioneering oil concessions in the Persian Gulf, on each of which he received a commission of five per cent. He had originally intended to establish his foundation in France, but had been unable to come to an agreement with the French authorities. The Gulbenkian was the centre of intellectual and artistic life in Lisbon, as I came to know later when I served as Canadian ambassador.

Lisbon, with its magnificent central Avenida da Liberdade leading down to the harbour with its carefully sited quadrangles of government buildings, was an early example of city planning. Our ambassador, Dan Molgat, brother of Senator Gil Molgat, received us in his residence in Restello, an old quarter built on one of Lisbon's many hills. We were taken on a bus tour west along the Marginal running on the north shore of the harbour entrance, to the historic Mountain of Sintra, then farther west to Cabo da Roca, the most westerly point of continental Europe.

Following the plenary sessions, I was obliged to stay in Lisbon for the meetings of the Inter-Parliamentary Council, envying those who were free to rent cars for visits to the Algarve in the south, to the Alentejo in the east, or north to a host of fascinating older places. (Fortunately, I more than made up for it later.) The council debated, among other things, the implications of a new weapon, allegedly developed by the United States. The neutron bomb, we were told, could leave buildings intact while killing their occupants. Looking back, I doubt that such a weapon was ever successfully developed.

The council had many distinguished members. I recall the Iranian representative, a cultured multilingual dean of a medical school who was later liquidated in one of the purges in his country. The Yugoslav general who was reported to be the liberator of Belgrade was respected, and I formed a personal friendship with the old Bulgarian revolutionary whose youthful fires were burning out, but had an endless supply of anecdotes and spoke excellent French.

The fall meetings were held in Bonn, capital of the Federal Republic of Germany, preceded by two days of meetings of the Eleven-Plus group in Copenhagen, Denmark. Agenda for the Eleven Plus was how to work out a strategy to counter initiatives from the Iron Curtain and Non-Aligned blocs. We held our meetings in the building where the Bundestag met and got to know deputies from different parties.

The German electoral system was so different from ours! Members of the Lower House were elected on a combination of proportional representation, which produced deputies from a slate of names, and also from single member constituencies similar to ours. Members of the Upper House were selected by the states, but that body could in no way be compared to our Senate.

On a beautiful, sunny day the delegates were taken for a Rhine cruise on one of the large boats specially built for this purpose. Castles appeared as we turned every bend in the river and we stopped to visit one or two of them. Terraced vineyards stretched as far as the eye could see. All kinds of river traffic passed us on the way up and later back down. We passed under countless bridges, while an orchestra played on deck for those who cared to listen.

The Federal Republic was clearly prosperous and there were no visible signs of wartime damage. Our ambassador, John Halstead, and his wife Jean gave us excellent briefings at a reception in their residence. Spouses enjoyed a trip to Cologne and other nearby places. A number of delegates were taken to see Berlin, then surrounded by communist East Germany, but I was obliged to stay in Bonn for meetings of the Inter-Parliamentary Council.

My two-year term as president of the Canadian section of the IPU expired in 1978 and Senator Gil Molgat succeeded me. I continued as the Canadian representative on the executive council until defeated in the general election of 1979.

LAST DAYS OF THE THIRTIETH PARLIAMENT

The mood of the voters in Ottawa West was anything but pleasant and we were beginning the fifth year of our parliamentary term. Prime Minister Trudeau's personal popularity, which tended to ebb and flow, now entered a low phase. As a result of television, however, the image of a national leader was carrying more and more weight with the voters, frequently at the expense of local candidates. My Conservative opponents, sensing blood, held a spirited nominating convention, contested by three men. A City of Ottawa alderman whom I had assisted in his campaigns was the first eliminated. The reeve of Nepean, generally presumed to be a Liberal up to this point, was the second. The successful candidate turned out to be Ken Binks, a local lawyer who had previously failed to defeat Liberal Paul Tardif, my old colleague from City Hall days, in Ottawa-Carleton.

In January 1979, the minister of National Defence, the Hon. Barney Danson, invited Margery and myself to join him in an inspection of the Canadian Peacekeepers in Cyprus. We flew by Hercules transport aircraft to a British airport base in the southeast of the Greek sector and proceeded to the capital, Nicosia. Peacekeepers were stationed in the no man's land separating the Greek and Turkish troops throughout the city. Barney and I, with a small military escort, walked the demarcation line. Canadians told us that they had witnessed the public flogging of Turkish troops. At one point there was mounted a good telescope at an observation post. Why? Well it seemed that there was a house of ill repute on the Turkish side and the girls from time to time put on a show! I can also remember an automobile showroom situated at an unfortunate point in the demarcation line, with its never-used cars still there over ten years later, it not having been possible to reach an agreement to remove them.

We borrowed a car with a United Nations flag, and passed through the Turkish lines to reach Kyrenia on the northern coast. Some seventy miles away was the Turkish mainland, from which Turkish aircraft had flown to attack Greek points in Cyprus. At a high point in Kyrenia Castle, our military driver pointed to the twisted remains of what had been a mounting for a machine gun, still there although the gun had been removed. Presumably the Greek gunner had died at his post before the bullets of the attacking Turkish aircraft. By digging in the dirt, we found some empty shell casings, clearly stamped Springfield, Massachusetts, USA. Were the shells fired by Turkish guns manufactured in the same place?

Before leaving Cyprus, we toured the southern coast, passing through lush banana plantations as far as Paphos, where St. Paul had landed on the beach. Inlays on the floor of a Greek temple of St. Paul's time were still in excellent condition. Amateur scuba divers from the occupying British troops had carefully mapped locations of underwater archaeological sites that they hoped someone, some time, might explore.

Was Cyprus the original Garden of Eden? It certainly could have been. The countryside was rich with olive groves, fruit plantations, harvests in the fields; the climate was idyllic. Why should such a country be inhabited by Greeks and Turks who wanted to kill each other?

THE 1979 ELECTION

The less I say about the election of May 22, 1979, the better. Bob Chiarelli, our campaign manager, did his best with our troops, who remained loyal with few exceptions. The national tide, as well as local issues involving the public service, such as decentralization and bilingualism, were against us and the reputation of being a maverick really hurts. [79] The word starts with the employees of ministers' offices, through officials of the National Liberal Federation, to employees on the Hill and to representatives of the press. Francis is a complainer, a whiner, a critic of the party and, along with other local MPs, has been passed over for the cabinet. The machinery to silence independent voices is difficult to counter.

The official results of the election were as follows:

BINKS (Conservative)	24,981
FRANCIS (Liberal)	22,985
POLLONETSKY (NDP)	7,051
TURMEL (Ind.)	193

Prime Minister Trudeau's Liberal Party was reduced from 141 to 114 seats. Joe Clark's Conservatives improved from 95 to 136 and formed a minority government. Although Social Credit were reduced from 11 to 6 seats, their support was still enough to give the Conservatives a bare majority in a House of 282 MPs. Meanwhile, the NDP were delighted to have their numbers go to 26 from their previous 16.

MARKING TIME, 1979-80

Well, we were getting used to losing elections. At least, I was. The 1979 defeat weighed heavily on Margery and she entered a period of severe depression. Looking back, I think we pushed her a bit too hard. She had always been a good campaigner, going from door to door, working in headquarters and helping in every way she could. Candidates' wives should probably not do door-to-door canvassing, because, while you meet some wonderful people, you also meet some who are rude and insulting. For a sensitive person as she was, insults are hard to take. Jean-Luc Pepin, who had just taken the seat of Ottawa-Carleton away from Jean Piggott, offered me a job on his staff that I was pleased to accept, as it gave me something to do. I did not realize what was going on at home, however, until I came home one night to learn that my wife had come near to suicide that day. Years later, the Sri Lankan student living with us, Chantal Obeyesekere, gave me further details of what went on during this period. Chantal, fortunately, knew enough to stay close to her.

---

[79] James Jerome has a good description of the difficult role of a maverick MP on pages 71-72 of his book, *Mr. Speaker James Jerome*, McClelland and Stewart, Toronto, 1985.

In the summer of 1979, we took ten days to attend, at the invitation of Henry Smith, a former US congressman from upper New York State, a meeting of former members of Congress in Milwaukee, Wisconsin. Smith and a number of his friends were anxious to see a similar Canadian association formed. Seed money for their association had been provided by the Johnson Foundation (established by the company that had marketed a brand of floor waxes) and now they were receiving a grant from Congress. My interest in working with a Canadian group was suspended when I was re-elected, but more about that later.

Following the sessions in Milwaukee, we visited the campus at Madison, Wisconsin. We dined with old friends from graduate student days—Ed and Phyllis Young (Ed having retired from his post as chancellor of the university), Bob and Jo-Ann Lampman (Bob had served on the President's Council of Economic Advisers and was generally credited as the inspiration for President Johnson's War on Poverty), and the family who had been our landlords years before at Marshall, Wisconsin.

Joe Clark's government lasted nine months, to go down when the Socreds failed to support Finance Minister Crosbie's budget promising short-term pain for long-term gain. Thanks to my position with Jean-Luc Pepin, I was able to observe question period every day in the House of Commons and was determined to have at least one more kick at the can.

Lloyd with Jean-Luc Pepin, 1982

THE 1980 ELECTION

Mr. Trudeau had announced his intention to resign as leader of the Liberal Party and Donald Macdonald, who had resigned as MP in February 1978, made plans to contest the proposed leadership convention. The unexpected defeat of the Clark government persuaded Trudeau to consult his shadow cabinet on what he should do. A majority suggested that he continue and fight the election, since there was hardly time to run a leadership convention. Gossip had it that one or two who offered advice to the contrary did not fare well when Trudeau chose his new cabinet later.

As Ottawa West had looked good to the Conservatives in 1979, it now looked good to aspiring Liberals. The national director of the federal Liberal Party, Blair Williams, decided to challenge me for the nomination. He had previously sponsored, along with a few others, a conference in Winnipeg that had raised eyebrows in top Liberal circles. Was he aiming to replace Trudeau as party leader?

Another Liberal emerged from underneath the rocks. Murray McBride had taken on Joe Greene's old riding of Lanark-Renfrew in 1968 after Joe had abandoned it for Judy Lamarsh's safe seat in Niagara Falls, and won it. He had been defeated by Conservative Paul Dick in the election of 1972 but, though anxious to make a comeback, did not choose to run against Paul Dick again. From his patronage post on the Egg Marketing Board, he found excuses to issue one press release after another to get his name in the headlines before finally resigning. Murray nearly won a nomination in one of the Toronto ridings and, failing that, took on Ottawa West. Originally a minister of the United Church of Canada (he reminded me of the Rev. Donald Stirling in 1965), Murray mustered some support in church groups and announced to the world that he was prepared to play a major role on the Liberal scene.[80]

McBride certainly had a good opinion of himself. In the Trudeaumania sweep of 1968 he had defeated the Conservative candidate Jim Baskin by a vote of 13,160 to 12,736. When the reporter for the *Ottawa Citizen*, Joe Quinn, asked whether Trudeaumania had helped him, he replied emphatically, no. Quinn quotes McBride as saying: "On the contrary, in the early stages of my campaign I had to knock down the Trudeau 'swinger' image, particularly in the rural sections. I had to convince people Mr. Trudeau was a serious-minded, dedicated leader with plenty to offer to this country."[81]

This time, to my pleasant surprise, people at the top of the Liberal Party were cheering for me. Blair Williams spent a pot of money seeking the

---

[80] In the *Ottawa Journal* of Friday, January 4, 1980, page 8, reporter Jim Withers, in summarising the campaigns of the contestants for the nomination, wrote: "McBride's campaign pamphlet indicated that the former United Church minister plans to be a candidate for the Liberal leadership whenever Pierre Trudeau steps down."

[81] *Ottawa Citizen*, June 26, 1968.

Nomination meeting at Woodroffe High School, 1979

nomination, campaigning from door to door and, we suspected, paying membership dues for newly recruited members of the Ottawa West Liberal Association. He succeeded in attracting one of our talented young Liberals, Rick Anderson, who had actually worked on my staff at one time. (I later discovered that Anderson was engaged to Williams' daughter. He later became a strategist for Preston Manning and the Reform Party.)

My old friends were totally loyal and this time we had recruited a few extra, such as the relatives of employees of the Surveys and Mapping Branch. From calling the lists, I knew we were in good shape. Members of the Italian, Greek, Lebanese, Ukrainian, Chinese, German and other ethnic communities came out solidly. When Mr. Frangione told me that he would bring out ten votes (and we did not have to pay their memberships) I knew I could count on him all the way. Blair Williams could not count on his instant recruits from door-to-door canvass.

Keith Davey called me with some concern asking how the campaign was going. I assured him it would take only one ballot, but that ballot would take some time to count. Fortunately, we had hundreds of hand-held signs left over from the campaign of nine months previously and gave them to our friends as they came in. The centre of the Woodroffe High School auditorium where the meeting was held was a solid mass of FRANCIS signs and how intimidating they must have been to our opponents! Veteran supporters like Josephine Martin, Joyce and Gerry Erskine, Ernie and Joan Murray, and Glen Kealey had a field day, as the results were at no time in doubt.

The election of February 18, 1980, was fought in bitter cold winter weather. In Canada, when a government has a choice of election date, winter is generally avoided. In this campaign, our workers were more strongly motivated than our opponents, who really never understood what had happened on Parliament Hill to bring on the election.

The February 18, 1980 results were as follows:

FRANCIS (Liberal)	22,460
BINKS (Conservative)	21,940
POLLONETSKY (NDP)	5,995

While our vote had dropped by 500, the Conservative vote had dropped by 3,000 and the NDP by over 1,000. It was a sweet victory and this time I was congratulated in a warm letter from Mr. Trudeau.

After Blair Williams's sally into Ottawa West, I was very leery of our local Liberal association's relationship with the National Liberal Federation. The names, addresses and telephone numbers of our membership had been provided to them routinely, but not for some time after the 1979 convention. As a matter of policy, the Liberal Party should place restrictions on any member of its staff using access to membership lists in order to get a head start in a contested nomination.

DEPUTY SPEAKER

Shortly after the 1980 election, Pierre Trudeau named Jeanne Sauvé as the first woman Speaker in the history of Canada, a post that was not her first choice, as she was alleged to have preferred a senior cabinet spot. She was also the first Speaker in the history of Canada never to have served in the backbenches.[82] The post of deputy speaker was offered to John Reid, who had been dropped from the cabinet for advising Mr. Trudeau to proceed with his resignation. Reid issued a press release, declining what had been offered to him.[83] The position of deputy speaker was then offered to me.

For some time I had been concerned about irregularities in the administration of the House of Commons and welcomed the opportunity to help correct the situation. I accepted, thinking I could improve the administration. As it turned out, Jeanne cleaned up the working conditions on Parliament Hill and I made my reputation as a presiding officer.

In April 1980, Margery and I took our grandsons, Andrew and Casey, then just turned four years old, on a trip to Disney World in Florida. These identical twins, born to our daughter Elaine and deserted by their

82 Charlotte Gray, in an article entitled "The Education of Madame Speaker," published in *Saturday Night*, May 1983, states: "But in 1980 Trudeau did not want Sauvé back in his cabinet; she had been seen as a John Turner supporter in the brief leadership race that had begun the previous December, shortly before the Clark government fell. Trudeau, however, couldn't demote her to the backbenches. The speakership must have seemed the perfect slot for Sauvé, whose brains, style and stability he had always respected. He would get Jeanne Sauvé out of his hair and at the same time be praised for appointing the first woman speaker." Note: Charlotte Gray's reference to John Turner should have been to Donald Macdonald.

83 John Reid must have been disappointed at being offered the post of deputy speaker. He is now the Commissioner for Access to Information.

father when they were eighteen months old, were Margery's second family. She helped to raise them, as they lived with us for the next five years. We enjoyed every minute of the trip, which was a welcome and necessary diversion for both of us.

CORRUPT ADMINISTRATION OF THE HOUSE OF COMMONS

Back to Ottawa and to my new job. Three incidents in particular had disturbed me greatly in 1978 and 1979. A woman on the staff of the House of Commons came to me to complain that her last three years' merit increases had been taken away. No reason or explanation was given to her. How could merit increases be taken away retroactively? She had filed her income tax returns based on them. I wrote to Mr. Speaker Jerome and received a totally meaningless reply.

The second incident related to a young woman working for one of the committees as a clerk. From talking to her, I found out that she had been placed there by one of the employment agencies who, two years later, were still taking twenty-five per cent of her earnings. Again, how could this be? Canada was a subscriber to a convention of the International Labour Organization limiting to six months the period for which an agency could charge. How could the House of Commons, of all the employers in Canada, violate this undertaking by the Government of Canada?

Again I wrote to Mr. Speaker Jerome and received no reply. The young woman avoided me. Sensing that something was wrong, I cornered her to ask what had happened. She broke into tears, telling me that her supervisor had threatened to have her fired if she ever spoke to me again.

I met the supervisor in the corridor and gave him, as they say, a piece of my mind. "You son-of-a-bitch. If you fire that girl, threaten her again or in any way harm her, I will rise in my place in the House, and name you and the employment agency. I will call to the attention of the Speaker that the House is violating an ILO convention, that you have threatened her with dismissal for speaking to me, and ask the Speaker to investigate any possible kickback arrangements between you and the agency."

I meant every word of what I said. Nothing happened to her and the agency ceased to receive any further part of her earnings. Actually, I seriously considered doing just what I had threatened, but had two concerns. First, would the Speaker cut me off after my first few words and not allow me to complete my statement? More than likely, he would have done so. Secondly, Mr. Speaker Jerome enjoyed an excellent press, thanks to his skill as a presiding officer and his receptions and poker parties. It was doubtful, to say the least, that my charges would receive any publicity.

The third incident was so unbelievable that I did not know whether to laugh or cry about it. I received a message to call a woman who worked in the Privy Council Office (in a clerical capacity, as I discovered later.) What was the problem? It seems her husband worked on the cleaning staff and had just been transferred from the night shift to the day shift. Was she not pleased, I asked. The answer was incredible. "You do not understand, Mr. Francis. My husband is not capable of working and he does not have to do anything on the night shift. On the day shift, he will be expected to. Mr. Francis, you must have him transferred back to the night shift immediately."

She assumed that I would have no trouble complying with her request. How could a backbench MP do this? I was aware that initial appointments to the cleaning staff were patronage (and had named a few myself), but surely there was a limit to how far an MP could interfere, especially for so unworthy a reason.

At this point, I was not dealing with the complaints I received of sexual harassment. More than one person working on the Hill named a woman who was alleged to have no other duties than to attend social functions outside of office hours. Whether or not it was true, they believed that she was available for immoral purposes. Others alleged that they were threatened with loss of their jobs if they did not attend these events.

In early 1985, when I had ceased to be Speaker, the parliamentary librarian, Erik Spicer, invited me to record some tapes of my experiences on the Hill, similar to the 150 that had been collected from others over time. I was assured that they would be kept confidential for an agreed period but available eventually for future historians in the National Archives.

A CBC journalist, Tom Earle, was assigned to interview me. As I recounted a number of spicy episodes, Earle remarked that they would certainly be of great interest to newsmen. My reply was that, as long as they were kept secret until after the turn of the century, I would not worry about them.

Imagine my chagrin when, shortly after my arrival in Portugal, the CBC played long extracts from the tapes; they caused quite a stir across the country. Tom Earle had sent the tapes to the archives with no time restriction. He has never apologised for this serious omission. Actually, there was very little I said in the tapes that had not been previously reported. In 1978, I had in fact mentioned to one journalist a complaint of sexual harassment. Douglas Fisher published a sensitive and thoughtful article on the subject in the *Ottawa Citizen* of May 14, 1980.

Similarly, stories about eavesdropping by House employees were carried by the Canadian Press, for example in the *Ottawa Citizen* of November 13, 1980. The criticisms of the auditor general on the substandard administration of the House were leaked repeatedly, as were reports that senior officials of the House of Commons had been released as a result. Georges St. Jacques, director of administration and personnel, sent copies to MPs of an angry letter to Speaker Jeanne Sauvé stating that he was quitting because he was asked to pursue his career elsewhere, not because of anything the auditor general had said.

Clearly, I was dealing with the tip of an iceberg. The administration of the House of Commons was inefficient, incompetent and corrupt. Senior officers of the House reinforced their positions by giving patronage to some MPs, favours to others and solidly opposing any attempts at reform. The sergeant-at-arms was in an especially favourable position. MPs' offices were assigned by him in consultation with the whips and he controlled the budget (such as it was) for furnishings.[84] Mr. Speaker Jerome had inherited a system going back to the days of Sir John A. Macdonald, but which he now realized was clearly out of control. Over objections from the Management and Members Services Committee, he called on the auditor general to investigate.

I consider it to be a serious indictment of the Press Gallery during this period that only one of its members, Stevie Cameron, did any in-depth investigation of what had become an incredibly corrupt administration. Jason Moscovitz of CBC Radio and John Burke of Global Television did make critical observations as did Douglas Fisher in his columns, but no one else as far as I am aware. The auditor general of Canada, James MacDonnell, later told me that it was the worst he had ever encountered. The Press Gallery itself, and for all I know, possibly individual members of the Gallery, received services and favours that came from the budget of Parliament. In that respect, they were treated by the permanent staff of the House in the same way that the staff treated (and influenced) MPs.[85] It is to the credit of Mr. Speaker Jerome that he finally did something about it, but only after five years in office.

Today I have a much better perspective on the origins of the mess. In 1979, I resolved to document my case and seek a common front with other MPs. You had to be careful, because you could never be sure who was a friend and who was an enemy on matters like this.

The administration of the House of Commons is governed by the *Parliament of Canada Act* (Revised Statutes of Canada, 1985, Chapter P 1), as well as the House's Standing Orders. Section 50(1) establishes a board whose function provides a mechanism for reviewing and controlling the House's own expenditures, without reference to the executive branch of government. Ultimately, the estimates are referred to the minister of Finance. The board's composition was amended in 1985 to include the Speaker, deputy Speaker, two privy councillors who

---

[84] Auditor General: "House of Commons: Comprehensive Audit Report, April 1980," page 40 and paragraph 7.5.

[85] Stevie Cameron has commented on a number of occasions on the old boys' network that existed on Parliament Hill and its corrupting influence. See Chapter 5 of her book *Ottawa Inside Out: Power, Prestige and Scandal in the Nation's Capital*, published by Key Porter Books, 1989.

are also MPs, the leader of the Opposition or someone designated by him or her, two MPs from the government caucus and two from opposition parties.

Apart from the amendments to the composition of what was called the Board of Internal Economy, little of the framework has changed from Sir John A. Macdonald's time. A good description of the effects of patronage in these years is given by Professor Norman Ward:

> The use of patronage for manning the lower echelons of the House of Commons staff resulted in the employment of some people of remarkable incapacity. . . . As long as the legislative staff was not under any civil service rules, citizens who were too old for the regular departments, or otherwise incapacitated, sought employment in the House of Commons. . . . It was for years a common practice for newspapers which could not afford to maintain a man at Ottawa to seek sessional clerkships for their parliamentary correspondents; the government frequently employed journalists in this way, thus gaining the support of the press by subsidizing newspapers . . .[86]

In 1908 the Laurier government introduced a bill[87] to place employees of the House of Commons under the Civil Service Commission, with regard to appointment, classification, salaries and promotions. The bill was amended to relate to a small number of permanent employees, and to exclude sessional appointments, which continued to be made on the same basis as before.

The application of the merit principle was resisted bitterly by senior officers of the House. One argument alleged that interference by an outside body violated the privileges of Parliament. It was further maintained that the House was unique and for this reason had to run its own affairs. Dr. Arthur Beauchesne, as Clerk, and Dr. Maurice Ollivier, parliamentary counsel, waged a constant struggle against the commission.[88]

By 1961, half of the employees of the House were permanent and subject to the procedures of the Civil Service Commission. The government of the day undertook to revise the *Civil Service Act*, and during the ensuing consultations all employees of the House and Senate were removed from the jurisdiction of the commission. At the same time, no alternative machinery for selection, classification, promotion and salaries

---

[86] Norman Ward, "The Formative Years of the House of Commons, 1867-91," *Canadian Journal of Economics and Political Science*, November, 1952, pages 439-444.

[87] *Civil Service Amendment Act*, Statutes of Canada, 1907-8, Chapter 15, s 3(2).

[88] See the paper by Gary Levy, of the Library of Parliament, "Arthur Beauchesne: A Case Study in Legislator-Staff Relations," 1979, prepared for the Conference on Legislative Studies in Canada, Simon Fraser University, February, 1979.

was created and the House of Commons reverted to the situation of Macdonald's time, with one major change. In 1867, all employees, including the sergeant-at-arms, had reported to the Clerk. By 1961, the sergeant-at-arms reported directly to the Speaker and was responsible for security, pages, messengers, maintenance, food and other services and, not least, purchasing.[89]

Dr. Maurice Ollivier, the veteran parliamentary counsel, later testified on November 6, 1966, before the Special Joint Committee of the Senate and House of Commons on Employer-Employee Relations in the Public Service (page 818) as follows:

> The amendment was introduced by the Member for Carleton, Mr. Richard Bell, and seconded by the Member for West Ottawa, Mr. George McIlraith, and was approved unanimously by the Committee studying the new legislation. I might mention here that I had something to do with it. I fought pretty hard so that our staff would not come under the Civil Service Act.

In 1963, Mr. Speaker Macnaughton requested the Organization Division of the Civil Service Commission to undertake a complete survey of the services of the House. Its recommendations are summarized in the Sixth Report of the Special Committee on Procedure and Organization, May 20, 1964. Some 170 specific problems in the administration of the House of Commons services were described. The increase in the number of sittings per year, improvements to MPs' services, increasing demands due to the influx of tourists, and the need to service MPs' offices in other buildings—all had added to the complexities and difficulties of administration. The report concluded:

> Taken together, all the foregoing changes in the volume and complexity of House of Commons services demand a radical re-arrangement of the organization structure. What is clearly needed is a revised structure which includes positions for administrators who have the time, the skill and the authority to deal effectively with administrative and personnel problems.[90]

On June 30, 1964, the Speaker announced changes that superficially looked attractive but failed to deal with fundamental problems. The House of Commons was structured as a government department, with the Clerk as the deputy minister. He was given new staff to assist him: a director of

---

[89] The amendments were introduced during committee hearings by Mr. Richard Bell, MP for Carleton and parliamentary secretary to the minister of Finance, on June 9, 1961. See Minutes of Proceedings and Evidence, Special Committee on the Civil Service Act (Bill C-71) 1960-61, page 475.

[90] Sixth Report of the Special Committee, page 333.

administration, a director of legislative services, a secretary general for parliamentary associations, a second deputy sergeant-at-arms and an executive assistant to the Speaker.

What developed in the next fifteen years was an almost complete breakdown in the administration of the House. The number of sitting days per year increased from 50 in Macdonald's time to 139 in the period 1956-65, to an average of 165 days per year between 1975 and 1981 (excluding the election years of 1979 and 1980).[91] Between 1961 and 1979, the staff multiplied by a factor of three and the budget by a factor of ten. The Clerk, of necessity, spent his time on procedural matters, delegating administration to officers of the House. The Personnel Office was grossly understaffed and the auditor general in 1980 estimated that Personnel was not informed of decisions to hire, establish pay scales or to promote in eighty per cent of the cases until after decisions were made.[92]

In brief, individual managers were free to deal with employment agencies, make retroactive adjustments to staff pay, promote, establish pay scales and to hire. There was little or no consistency from one section to another. The auditor general noted an instance of a House employee two grades below the Clerk being paid more than the Clerk and one study revealed that "House employees [were] paid one level above their public service counterparts."[93] Needless to say, this led to a great deal of discontent. The Ottawa newspaper *Le Droit* ran a series of six detailed articles on January 31, February 1, 2, 3, 13 and 22, 1973, on the problems of security guards on the Hill, alleging a general climate of fear, and that promotions were arbitrary, based on favouritism with no right of appeal. They further alleged discrimination on the basis of language. The *Ottawa Journal* on June 20, 1978, carried an article saying that the 2,500 employees on the Hill were looking to the Speaker to improve the way pay increases and complaints over working conditions were handled.

Matters came to a head before the Standing Committee on Management and Members Services and I quote the words of Mr. Speaker Jerome:

> During the summer of 1978, the prime minister announced that he was committed to some two billion dollars in spending cuts and was directing each of his ministers to prepare the necessary Proposals. . . . I saw it as my responsibility to ensure that if the Members decided to address the question of whether we could achieve similar economies, the information should be available to them. I therefore asked the team of senior officials

---

[91] John B. Stewart, The Canadian House of Commons and Reform, Montreal, McGill-Queens University Press, 1977, page 203.

[92] Auditor General's Report, 1980, page 64.

[93] Auditor General, op. cit., page 66.

> responsible for the preparation of the annual spending estimates to do a preliminary set, so we could put them before the Standing Committee on Management and Members' Services. ... After several meetings ... [they] ... indicated ... that they were deeply dissatisfied with the quality of responses during the hearings and therefore very concerned about management skills in the most senior positions.[94]

REPORT OF THE AUDITOR GENERAL

The chairman of the Standing Committee on Management and Members' Services, Mr. Robert Coates, MP for Cumberland-Colchester, suggested that an outside independent group be hired to conduct a "complete review of the structure and administrative practices of the House of Commons ..." and that the auditor general be invited to suggest names of consulting firms.[95] Instead, the Speaker invited the auditor general to do the job, the first time in the history of Canada that the auditor general had been invited to review the House.

In spite of the change in government on May 22, 1979, the work continued. Mr. MacDonnell presented his interim report to the Speaker on October 4, 1979. In addition to repeating nearly all of the 170 recommendations of the 1964 report, the auditor general stressed the need to separate administrative and procedural functions. In his words, "the quality of general and financial administration [of the House of Commons] was significantly below a minimum acceptable standard," with an absence of clearly defined administrative mandates, organizational relationships and delegations of authority. Financial and personnel control systems were almost non-existent. In the words of Mr. Speaker Jerome, grievance procedures "were woefully inadequate and would have been considered laughable by any Human Rights organization ..."[96]

Mr. Rheal Châtelain, senior deputy auditor general of Canada, was seconded to the House on an interim basis as administrator on November 19, 1979. He would report directly to the Speaker, along with the Clerk, Dr. C.B. Koester, who had been appointed only three months earlier, and the sergeant-at-arms, Major General M.G. Cloutier, who had been appointed eighteen months previously. The Government House leader, the Honourable Walter Baker, gave a clear endorsement to the Speaker's actions.[97]

Rheal Châtelain had a most difficult time for eight months, after which he left to become auditor general of the Province of Quebec. In many ways

---

94 *Mr. Speaker James Jerome*, op cit., page 125.
95 Letter dated February 14, 1979, from Robert Coates, chairman of the Standing Committee on Management and Members' Services, to Mr. Speaker Jerome.
96 *Mr. Speaker James Jerome*, op. cit. page 124.
97 Hansard, November 1, 1979, page 843.

he was a victim of events. The House of Commons was dissolved on December 14, 1979, and an election held on February 18, 1980. Men like Walter Baker were not in the same position to assist and defend him. Walter, as a local area MP, must have been receiving the same kind of complaints as I was. The Speaker, the Honourable James Jerome, announced on December 19 that he would not seek re-election and on January 4, 1980, was appointed associate chief justice of the Federal Court of Canada. Mr. Châtelain was in effect deprived of the critical support of the Speaker until the election of the Honourable Jeanne Sauvé to that office on April 20. Indeed, the House was for a time in the most unusual state of having no Speaker, although, by law, a Speaker continues in office until a new one is appointed.[98] Lastly, the Clerk, although new in his office, was able to support Châtelain for only a short period before suffering a heart attack that sidelined him for some months.

Meanwhile, a solid wall of resistance built up accusing the administrator of all kinds of misdeeds. Those who had benefited from patronage appointments were concerned that they might lose them. Layoffs were taking place in the public service at this same time, creating an atmosphere that sparked their worst fears.[99]

Senior and middle-rank managers became very disturbed when, for the first time, they were asked to account in detail for their functions and performance. The position of administrator was seen as a direct challenge to the Office of the Sergeant-at-Arms and to that office's previously unquestioned rights in the areas of purchasing, accommodation, hiring, and personnel and financial management for the one thousand blue-collar workers under its direction.

One of the first acts of the new administrator was to match monthly cheques issued against the number of bodies that could be accounted for on the Hill. Some twenty more cheques were issued than the number of persons identified as working and the explanation was offered that the difference was due to sick leave. No records of medical certification for sick leave could be found.

REFORMS INITIATED BY SPEAKER SAUVÉ

I can recall meeting with the new Speaker in early May 1980. Elected first in 1972 to the House of Commons, she had been appointed immediately to the cabinet as minister of State for Science and Technology, then minister of the Environment and later minister of Communications. She had never served on the backbenches and could

---

[98] *The Parliament of Canada Act*, Section 45.

[99] According to the chairman of the Public Service Commission, Edgar Gallant, over 8,500 were released and contracts of a further 17,800 not renewed. "The Public Servant—a Relevant Canadian; Notes for an Address," presented to the Institute of Public Affairs, Halifax, October 18, 1983.

hardly believe what she was hearing about the administration of the House of Commons. Mr. MacDonnell's final report was presented to her in April and treated with the utmost secrecy. Each copy was numbered and every one of its 118 pages stamped, "Confidential for Discussion Purposes Only." Eventually, she distributed it to the MPs of the Management and Members Services Committee and insisted on its release as a public document.

At the same time, Madame Speaker was faced with having to make a ruling on a matter in the House. It is normal for a Speaker to take under advisement a complicated decision and I was with her when she received comments from those available to advise her. The Clerk had just undergone open-heart surgery and the next two assistants in line were consulted. Reading from handwritten notes on foolscap, they contradicted each other on every essential point. The Speaker gasped, thanked, and dismissed them.

Turning to me, she asked what was she to do with such incompetents. The best I could do was suggest that she invite the parliamentary counsel, Joseph Maingot, to assist, recognizing that this was not part of his regular duties. To his credit, Maingot came through with good advice. Later, we added Mr. Philip Laundy, director of Research of the Library of Parliament, who had written a book on Speakers of the Commonwealth and was an authority on the functions of a Speaker.[100]

It was clear that there was no training to develop advisers in the Clerk's department, nor career paths outlined. This was generally true in all sections of the House. In his first years, Jerome was able to rely on advice from Alistair Fraser,[101] an experienced Clerk, who gave good procedural advice but was a weak administrator. Fraser had retired the previous August. The new Speaker was made acutely aware of the need to strengthen the services backing up the Clerk, and I believe that this incident helped to crystallize her decision to implement the recommendations of the auditor general.

Madame Speaker persuaded Mr. Arthur Silverman, whom she had known in the Department of Communications, to accept the position of administrator on July 14, 1980, after approval by the commissioners of Internal Economy and later by the Standing Committee on Management and Members' Services. Thus began a wholesale review of personnel practices and procedures, financial controls—in short, the whole operation of the House.

---

[100] The manner of Laundy's appointment caused him some embarrassment. Madame Speaker Sauvé decided to appoint him while he was absent from Canada and told Chief Librarian Erik Spicer that he should advertise for a replacement for his director of research. Spicer assumed that Laundy had applied for the job without telling him.

[101] James Jerome, op. cit., page 11.

The consolidated opposition that had undermined Rheal Châtelain continued unabated. It focussed on two places—the sergeant-at-arms and the Standing Committee on Management and Members' Services, on which he had a strong influence. New offices, conveniently located, became available in the East Block, which had undergone renovations. I was furious to learn that they became occupied by MPs serving on the Management and Members' Services Committee. Moreover, they were each supplied with a small refrigerator, something not previously available to backbench MPs. In a rash moment, I called these MPs "monkeys, bribed by their own peanuts," which probably did not help the situation. This was typical of the way that permanent staff of the House influenced MPs in order to retain their privileges and to resist reform.

The press, which had been oblivious to problems of House of Commons administration previously, suddenly found the running battle between members of the Management and Members' Services Committee and Madame Speaker's administration, newsworthy.[102] Fortunately, the Clerk of the House, Dr. Koester, made a good recovery from his illness and became a key member of the Speaker's team, which met regularly to deal with one crisis after another.

EAVESDROPPING ON THE HILL

I do not wish to leave this period without mentioning a serious incident that gave no end of concern to Madame Speaker Sauvé. One day I had lunch with a friend who had a senior post with Bell Canada.

"Lloyd," she began, "I do not know how to say this. Our people in servicing Parliament Hill came across some very sophisticated eavesdropping devices."

I told Madame Sauvé, who reacted sharply. "The prime minister is terribly worried about caucus leaks. He tested the waters recently by using a special phrase that appeared in the press forty-eight hours later. He thinks an MP is responsible, but maybe it is someone else."

The RCMP were requested to investigate. Committee reports were routinely transcribed in the building on the south side of Wellington Street and all committee rooms were wired for this purpose. Only a simple modification was required to permit a group of senior staff people in one office to listen to any conversation in any committee room on the Hill. If any committee that dealt with many matters of interest to Hill staff, for example Management and Members' Services, decided it wanted to sit in camera, the staff simply retired to eavesdrop in their own sanctuary. Almost certainly, this listening centre was the source of leaks in party caucuses.

The modifications were removed but what to do about the people who created them? Should criminal charges be laid? How many people should

[102] Stevie Cameron gives a good account of what went on in this period, op. cit., Chapter 5.

be charged and what kind of evidence should be presented before a court? What would this do to the image of Parliament across the country?

Madame Sauvé in her wisdom summoned one senior administrator and told him that he was going to accept appointment for a prolonged period with one of Canada's foreign aid programs in central equatorial Africa. When he demurred, she threatened him with criminal charges. He accepted. I do not know whether or not she meted out punishments for others, but she probably did.

Erik Nielsen, MP for Yukon, describes how, in his words, "from late 1965 until well into 1966, we had a pipeline into the Liberal caucus." He alleges that, during a period of reconstruction of the West Block, communication wires were interconnected by error. Liberal and Conservative caucuses took place at the same time on Wednesday mornings, in different rooms. By using the earphones that were normally supplied for simultaneous translation, any one of ninety-seven Conservative MPs could hear what was being said in the Liberal caucus and use the information secured by this means to embarrass Liberal ministers during the question period of the House of Commons.[103]

This is Nielson's version. I can only add that some people who worked on the Hill at the time do not accept this explanation and do not understand how such an "error" could have occurred. They still believe that the eavesdropping operation was planned.

Procedures on the Hill were generally very lax and a number of instances of conversion of funds and even minor theft came to light. In part, MPs themselves were responsible. Two signatures were required for cheques of the parliamentary associations but MPs routinely signed a bunch of blank cheques to make the task of the staff officer assigned to them easier. Other MPs used clerks to do their banking for them. In order to put a stop to these doings, Madame Speaker made an example of one clerk, insisting that he be prosecuted. He received a sentence of six months, but much of the blame should have been placed on the MP involved.

POLITICAL CROSSFIRE

In this period, I made a determined political enemy. Reuben Baetz was the Conservative member of the provincial parliament for Ottawa West and a member of the provincial cabinet. In the election of March 1981, my assistant, George Anderson, decided to seek the Liberal nomination against him. I did my best to dissuade George, since I did not think that he had the personality to be a candidate and, moreover, he would be a sacrificial lamb. Reuben and the Tory machine in Ontario were running strong.

---

103 Erik Nielsen, *The House is Not a Home*, published by Macmillan of Canada, 1989, pages 152-154, inclusive.

In spite of my advice, George ran and I gave him time off from his job. My support was nominal, since I was more than busy on the Hill as deputy Speaker, but I did give him a modest financial contribution. Reuben defeated George by a vote of 17,418 to 9,112.

On election evening, after the results were known, Reuben told those assembled that I was responsible for the entire Liberal campaign and had coerced Anderson into running. I could not believe what the press reported. A reporter present had made a tape of Reuben's remarks and played them back for me. The press reports were bad but the verbatim tape was incredible. Baetz vowed revenge for what he believed I had done.

The pitfalls of politics! Perhaps I should have refused Anderson time off and made him resign, which would have infuriated many Liberal friends. Baetz, however, worked hard to defeat me in 1984. On reflection, I believe the story reflected more on him than on Anderson or myself.

MY EXPERIENCE IN THE CHAIR

In the time of Mr. Speaker Lamoureux, who had preceded Jerome, it was usual for the Speaker to preside over the House for a number of hours per week, in addition to question period and taking votes. Jerome had gradually reduced his presiding to question period, votes and special debates. As deputy Speaker, I was automatically chairman of the Committee of the Whole House, a less formal procedure adopted by unanimous consent to expedite passage of a bill. The deputy chairman of the Committee of the Whole was Mr. Denis Éthier, MP for Glengarry-Prescott-Russell, and the assistant deputy, Mr. Rod Blaker, MP for Lachine. Madame Sauvé followed Jerome's practice, and Éthier, Blaker and I were usually responsible for presiding about twenty-five hours per week.

For some time it had been the practice for the Speaker to meet four days per week in the morning (excluding Fridays, since the House commenced its sittings at eleven a.m. that day only), with the deputy Speaker and two assistants, the Clerk, and such other staff as seemed relevant, to discuss the business of the House, any Notices of Motions filed with the Clerk, and to anticipate other questions that might be raised. The sessions were most useful. Later, Éthier, Blaker and I had similar sessions to review the periods over which we would be presiding.

It was not long before I faced my first test in the Chair. The minister of Finance, the Honourable Allan MacEachen, was speaking in the debate on the speech from the throne, and introduced what was termed a mini-budget on April 21, 1980.[104] When he sat down, the MP for Carleton, Walter Baker, gave notice that he would be raising a question of privilege

---

[104] Hansard, page 248.

the following day. John Crosbie, MP for St. John's West, sought to be recognized, but it was the turn of an NDP member and I recognized the MP for Winnipeg-St. James, Mr. Cyril Keeper. Crosbie sputtered that it had been agreed among the whips that he would follow the minister of Finance. If so, no one had told the Chair, which was the normal thing to do in such circumstances.

Erik Nielsen, MP for Yukon, moved that "the honourable member for St. John's West be now heard," and the motion carried by a vote of 148 to 1. The member for Beauharnois-Salaberry, Gerald Laniel, alone voted against it. A challenge to a decision of the occupant of the Chair is embarrassing, but I stood my ground, and obliged the House to resolve the matter by resolution.

The press did not know what to make of this incident and the following morning, as I was driving to work, I heard Ed Broadbent, the NDP leader, being interviewed on the radio. He was asked what Francis had done wrong and replied that the deputy Speaker had behaved properly, recognizing an NDP MP in his due turn. If the party whips had agreed on changing the speaking order, the least they should have done was to inform the occupant of the Chair. Broadbent set the record straight.

Erik Nielsen, who later became House Leader for the official Opposition, adopted an extremely aggressive attitude towards the Chair, no matter which of the four of us was occupying it at the time.

One of my assistants in the Chair appeared in the press in a manner not to his liking. His story was that he answered the door of his office one evening to speak to a woman who wanted to come into his office. While trying to dissuade her, he stepped out into the hall. Somehow, the door behind him was closed and locked. There he was, naked except for a towel around his waist, and was promptly labelled the "deputy streaker." Rumour has it that the door was locked behind him by another young lady who did not want her presence disclosed, but you cannot always believe rumours. The security staff later opened the door for him.

THE ASSAULT ON THE CHAIR

On the evening of October 23, 1980, I was presiding over a debate on a motion to appoint a "Special Joint Committee of the Senate and the House to Consider a Proposed Resolution for a Joint Address to Her Majesty." The resolution contained a series of constitutional amendments sponsored by Prime Minister Trudeau and the Joint Committee was to report back to the House not later than December 9. Opposition MPs had wanted the committee to travel across the country, but the government had resisted. Deep emotional feelings were aroused and the debate became very partisan. The original closure rule, Section 33, adopted by the Conservative government of 1913, had been invoked and it was my duty to interrupt the debate and put the motion. The motion had been amended by the MP for Carleton-Charlotte, Fred McCain, seconded by Walter Baker, to extend the reporting date to February 12, 1981.

The member for Pembina, Peter Elzinga, rose on a question of privilege, on the grounds that he had not been recognized to speak in the debate. There was clearly no question of privilege and I so ruled. At this point the House was becoming unruly, with members standing beside their seats, speaking loudly and refusing to sit down when requested. As I endeavoured to read the motion, as amended, two members, Tom Cossitt, the MP for Leeds, and Robert Wenman, MP for Fraser Valley West, left their seats to stand in front of the Chair shouting that they were being deprived of their rights. They were later joined by four others, Peter Elzinga; Dave Nickerson, MP for Western Arctic; Scott Fennell, MP for the constituency of Ontario; and Douglas Neil, MP for Moose Jaw.

The actions of these members were a clear violation of Section 8 of our rules which states that no one should create a disturbance of any sort during a vote. They were totally unprecedented in the history of the Canadian House of Commons. Fortunately, the Clerk of the House, Bev Koester, was beside me to advise on the options available to the Chair. I could adjourn the House on the grounds that it was unruly. That would prevent a vote, which was clearly the object of the exercise. I could name the members, but that was cumbersome and time-consuming. The Rules of the House at the time (they have since been amended) would have required a separate resolution by the government House leader for each MP named. How many members would have to be named? Six? Likely many more than that before the night was over, and again it was doubtful that a vote would eventually take place.

One of the Table officers (not the Clerk) suggested that I sit down and reflect. That was bad advice as I would have lost control of the House at that point, and the audiovisual tape clearly records my reply: "I will not sit down."

The Liberal member for Gloucester, Herb Breau, approached the Chair with the suggestion that I should get the bells ringing. Koester and I had already come to that conclusion, but how could it be done? Eventually, after twenty minutes, I decided that I had to try it. In the loudest voice I could summon, I read the rather lengthy resolution, with the amendment, in English and French, and then asked the time-honoured question: "Is it the pleasure of the House to adopt the motion? Those in favour please say 'yea'."

Some voices shouted "yea," and then I said: "Will those opposed please say 'nay'." "In my opinion, the 'nays' have it."

I looked towards the government House leader, Yvon Pinard, who promptly rose to his feet to demand a recorded vote. I was then able to utter the words: "Call in the members."

The bells started ringing. Had Pinard not risen, it was not likely that the Opposition House leader would have called for a recorded vote. The Opposition strategy would then likely have been to challenge the vote itself, on the grounds that the noise and disruption were so great that no one knew what they were doing. Once the bells started to ring, however, there was nothing more that the six MPs standing before me could do. Some fifteen minutes later, Madame Speaker presided over formal votes to defeat the amendment and carry the motion.

I have a little story to tell as a sequel to the above. Shortly afterwards, the Speaker caused the chair to be made adjustable, rising up or down. Being small of stature herself, she wanted to be able to lower it. Rod Blaker, being tall and with a slight back problem, wanted to raise it. The new mechanism worked perfectly.

I later met Tom Cossitt at a reception. "I must warn you, Tom, that we have made some changes in the chair itself." "Yeah, I know, it gives you a lift." "Not only that, Tom. We have a new button. All I have to do is push it, and you will be in the Ottawa River." Tom grinned. "I deserve it." How could you stay angry with a man like that?

Six MPs do not spontaneously break the rules as these did. It had to be part of a predetermined strategy and had all the indications of Nielsen's fine hand. The incident has become known as The Assault on the Chair.[105]

Prime Minister Trudeau had been present and observed the proceedings. From that point on, his attitude to me changed totally. At a reception at Kingsmere shortly afterwards, he praised my conduct in the Chair to my wife in uncharacteristically extravagant terms. Up to this point I had been attending Liberal caucuses, an option open to a deputy Speaker but certainly not to a Speaker. If I were to preside over sessions like The Assault on the Chair, it would be better to avoid all party functions and I did not attend any others in the Thirty-second Parliament.

Speaker Jeanne Sauvé sent me a complimentary note. After being informed of the attempts to disrupt the vote that night, she had come to the House to observe and decided to leave me with the problem, confident that I would handle it.

A few days later, she arranged for Margery and myself to join a delegation visiting the European parliament in Strasbourg, with two short diversions to Brussels and Luxembourg. The European parliament was in an early phase and not in session while we were there. We met briefly with members of the Belgian parliament and were briefed on some of the language problems of that country, but the visits were too short to be productive.

---

105 Charlotte Gray, op. cit., quite incorrectly, gives Speaker Sauvé credit for having presided during The Assault on the Chair.

VISIT TO NORTH YEMEN

Early in 1981, I returned one afternoon to my office, to be handed a letter by my assistant. It was an invitation to attend an international development conference in Sanaa, North Yemen. Once before, I had received a similar invitation to go to Taiwan and had consulted the secretary of state for External Affairs, Mitchell Sharp, only to be told bluntly that I should not go. Many MPs did, however, accept invitations from Taiwan and some who did were later promoted to cabinet.

This invitation was for a time during the Easter break, which would not interfere with my duties. However, I did not want to take any chances. One day while the House was sitting, I took a seat beside the prime minister and engaged him in conversation.

"I hear that you recently visited North Yemen, sir."

"Yes. Why do you ask?"

"I have an invitation to visit Sanaa during the Easter recess to attend a development conference. Do you think I should go?"

"Sure. Go ahead, and I hope you enjoy the experience."

I did not ask permission from External, but simply informed them what I was doing. The communications clerk from the embassy met me at the airport in Cairo and drove me to the hotel where I stayed overnight waiting for my flight to Sanaa the next day.

In my stopover, I managed to cross a Cairo street (almost impossible without the aid of a policeman), visit the National Museum, which is full of the most incredible treasures from antiquity (including, for example, what the guide told me was the original Rosetta Stone,[106] which gave the initial clues for deciphering hieroglyphics), and take a quick look at the pyramids. After boarding Yemeni Air, I landed at two a.m. at Sanaa airport in incredibly warm temperatures, not knowing who was going to meet me or what was going to happen.

As it turned out, I need not have worried. Taha Qirbi, who resided in Ottawa and whose wife Heyam had helped in our elections in Ottawa West, had arranged everything. Taha had studied in the United States on a Fulbright scholarship and worked in the high-technology industry with one of the Ottawa firms. He then branched out on his own, founding a company promoting trade between the Yemen and North America and also consulting on projects in North Yemen. He also acted as an unofficial (later official) consul in Ottawa for his country of origin.

Up to this point, Canada had had very little to do with North Yemen and our diplomatic relations were handled from Saudi Arabia. The country had emerged from a civil war some five years previously, in which the British (normally more astute) had backed the losing side. The new regime, which was oriented towards the West, did not control the south,

---

106 The British Museum in London also claims to have the Rosetta Stone.

which included the ancient port of Aden and was oriented to the Soviet bloc. Frequent skirmishes took place on the border between the two countries. The government of North Yemen was anxious to modernize their ancient land and to get as much development aid as possible, including some from Canada. Their agriculture was limited but they had undeveloped mineral resources in their impressive mountain ranges and in a large area of geological terrain similar to the Laurentian Shield of Canada. In the desert of the interior, there were possibilities of oil.[107]

The city of Sanaa claims to be the oldest city in the world, older than Damascus. It is a study in contrasts. Paved streets lead to modern hotels in the suburbs, but in the centre of the city narrow, unpaved lanes are lined by mud brick structures. In the ancient *souk*, or marketplace, you can see smiths forging the curved ceremonial daggers that every adult male carries at his waist. Outside the city, I remember climbing an escarpment to watch a shepherd come down to water his flock at a spring. Judging by the appearance of the sheep, his homespun clothes and his crook, I concluded that nothing in his work had changed from the time of Christ.

The conference brought together one hundred people from Europe, America and a host of agencies affiliated with the United Nations. Two, in particular, I recognized from my days at Wisconsin, as men who had both done their PhD theses under Professor Witte, who had supervised my own thesis. One of them was then the secretary of the Arab Organization of Petroleum Exporting Countries. From UNESCO came Rowell Bowles, who had lived with us in the Student Co-operative Residence at Toronto. I told Rowell how I had come to be there and about the strong motivation of men like Taha Qirbi to help their native land.

I told Rowell also about Taha's brother-in-law, who had left his position as a full professor of medicine at Dalhousie University to come back to the Yemen, at considerable personal sacrifice, to develop a medical school. Rowell's face turned ashen. Yemen did not need North American professors of medicine, he shouted. It needed health workers, recruited from the villages, to serve their own people in a more modest way. The Chinese model would be much more helpful to them. You could not build a medical school out of thin air. You needed an infrastructure, from hospitals, to secondary schools, and a host of related services. As it turned out, Rowell was right, and the brother-in-law (a most likeable man) returned to Canada some three years later.

We made two fascinating trips out of Sanaa. On the first, we travelled some 250 kilometres south to the second city, Taiz, along a modern highway constructed with European aid funds. This had been the capital

[107] The two Yemens are now united with Sanaa as the capital. With the end of the skirmishing, a Canadian company has made significant discoveries of oil, which is exported by a pipeline to the Red Sea.

of the last Imam, and what a strange creature he must have been. In a small museum created out of a three-storey structure that served as his palace was a collection of Mickey Mouse watches, which had fascinated him. Wheelchair-bound due to a failed assassination attempt by some students, he had a series of ropes (still there) installed on the first floor of the "palace." These enabled him to pull himself in his wheelchair (also on display) from one window to the next, at each of which he kept loaded rifles, in case he needed them. Yellowed clippings from American newspapers show him personally chopping off the heads of criminal and political prisoners on a block installed in front of the palace.

It seems incredible that such a regime could have survived into the 1970s.

The second trip took us east across the desert in Jeep-type vehicles to the town of Marib. The ancient fortified town was built on the top of a hill perhaps thousands of years ago. Not far away we visited the remains of a prehistoric dam, with inscriptions in an ancient tongue that no one today can understand. The dam had trapped the seasonal flow of water in a *wadi* (Yemen has no permanent rivers flowing year round), which served to irrigate an adjacent area. The remains of some one hundred dwellings were clearly visible, each a pile with the remains of a stone fireplace chimney in the middle. What a paradise for an archaeologist! Who were these people, what did they do, and what happened to them? Why was the dam abandoned? Why was there no modern effort to restore cultivation?

On the way back, we were taken to a site in the desert with a few carved stone pillars standing in what was obviously the middle of an ancient ruin. Our guide told us that it was the site of an ancient palace of the Queen of Sheba. (At this stage, I would have believed anything. Who knows, he may have been telling me the truth.)

Agriculture had been developed in the river valleys in terraces carefully built up over the centuries. Unfortunately, many terraces were not being maintained, since the young men had gone to work abroad, sending remittances home that are a significant source of foreign exchange.

One evening I was invited to dinner at the home of one of Taha's uncles. We sat on carpets, after I removed my trousers and wrapped a loose-fitting Arab gown around my waist. Our meal consisted of boiled mutton and many vegetables, followed by a sweet dessert, eaten in a room with no women present. Members of the extended family doing business in countries bordering the Red Sea were introduced. One man had spent thirty years in Ethiopia, only to have his business confiscated by a communist government. Another had met a similar fate after fifteen years in Somalia. As far as I could gather, they had all come back home to Yemen and helped each other in some traditional way by pooling their resources. Taha's uncle, an old man said to be in his nineties, was alert and missed nothing.

I cannot leave Yemen without some reference to *qat*, the mild narcotic used by nearly all the men I met. Every taxi driver kept a wad in his cheek. The leaves of the tree are plucked while young and chewed. Branches with *qat* leaves are for sale in nearly every market and I was told the cultivation of the *qat* tree was more profitable than growing coffee. The magnificent *mokka* coffee for which the Yemen is known is declining as a result.

On my return to Ottawa, I made a report to External Affairs describing my visit and the issues raised at the development conference.

THE TRIP TO MEXICO

In January 1982, the Speaker planned a visit to Mexico and invited my wife and me to join her. At the very last minute, Margery came down with what we thought was a bad cold and felt she could not travel. She urged me to go without her and I did.

The party, which included many of Jeanne Sauvé's House of Commons staff, flew to Mexico City and had an audience with President de la Madrid. Members of the staff of the Canadian embassy showed us their beautiful new chancery, and gave us a tour of Mexico City, which is huge. The National Archaeological Museum was an eye-opener for me. I had heard of the ancient Mayan civilisation, but had no idea of the number of civilisations that had preceded it. From the capital, we flew to Oaxaca in the south, where we saw the results of archaeologists' efforts—a pyramid where human sacrifices had once taken place and treasures of jade, gold and silver had been unearthed.

On my return, I was shocked to learn how sick Margery had been with viral pneumonia. She went to the hospital, but the treatment she received never really restored her health. She had a permanent cough, which was at first diagnosed as sarcoidosis. Eventually it was recognized as pulmonary fibrosis, but more about that later. She had urged me to go ahead with the trip, but I felt guilty on my return for having left her.

THE LONG BELLS

In early 1982, the government introduced Bill C-94, an omnibus bill that incorporated the measures that comprised Marc Lalonde's National Energy Policy. On March 1, Mr. Harvie Andre, MP for Calgary Centre, raised a point of order, arguing that the bill as drafted violated requirements as to form.[108] Extensive debate took place, with precedents from Speakers Jerome and Lamoureux cited to suggest that the contents should be redrafted and introduced in a number of separate bills. The omnibus bill, which contained tax proposals, would go to Committee of the Whole, whereas at least some of the separate bills could have gone to special committees.

---

[108] Hansard, pages 15479, et seq.

On the next day, March 2, Madame Speaker abruptly ruled against Harvie Andre's point of order. Under the guise of seeking clarification of her ruling, MPs Andre and Nielsen took up several minutes of House time. Eventually, Harvie moved, seconded by John Thomson, MP for Calgary South, that the House adjourn (a traditional motion to head off a vote). At 4:20 p.m. Madame Speaker called for a vote and the bells started ringing.[109]

For nearly sixteen days, the bells rang to summon MPs for a vote. (Actually, some of the bells outside of the Centre Block burned out and were not replaced until March 17. Madame Speaker, however, made sure that the bells outside the offices of the party whips kept ringing.) To my knowledge, this had never happened before in any parliament of the Commonwealth. The bells normally stop ringing when the two whips, one from the government and the other from the official opposition, line up before the Speaker and walk the length of the House to face the Chair. The government whip appeared from time to time, but stood there alone.

I do not believe that it was the intention of the Official Opposition to have the bells ring as long as they did. From conversations with individual MPs, I had the impression that they initially just wanted to make their point of protest. The press reported events in detail and the Opposition felt that they had much public sympathy, especially in Western Canada. As a result, they just let the bells go on, until it was clear that the public wanted them to end.[110]

It was my responsibility, as deputy Speaker, to make sure that someone was presiding in the Chair at all times, day and night. Éthier, Blaker and I took the graveyard shifts and appealed to MPs of all parties to help us by taking turns. Some NDP MPs did help and one or two Conservatives. Some Liberal MPs were most helpful, and Ursula Appoloni even took part of the graveyard shift. A member of my staff spent most of her time keeping a duty roster.

The Liberal whip, Charlie Turner, set up a sleeping cot in the Government Lobby. When reporters asked him why, he replied that he was making sure someone was always in the Chair. That was my job, not his. The suggestion that a party whip was holding himself responsible for the occupants of the Chair was grossly offensive as far as I was concerned. Senior Press Gallery reporters wrote stories, with photos, about the devotion of the government whip and some of them inferred that he was keeping the duty roster, pressing Liberal MPs into service. After this story

---

[109] Hansard, pages 15532, et seq. The official Hansard of March 17, 1982 reads as follows: "And the division bells having rung from 4:20 p.m. on Tuesday, March 2, until 2:28 p.m. on Wednesday, March 17, 1982 . . ."

[110] For example, see the editorial entitled "Belling the Cat," in the *Edmonton Journal* of March 6, 1982.

was repeated a few times, I took a junior reporter into my office and showed her exactly whose office was keeping the roster. When I asked her to set the record straight in a story, she demurred, saying she did not want to contradict what more experienced reporters had written. Finally, to placate me, she did write a general description of what was going on in Parliament, and buried the story on who was keeping the roster in the second last paragraph.

We had frequent discussions in the Speaker's chambers on what we should do. Blaker and I felt that the bells should not be rung all night, but the Clerk refused to agree that they should be suspended at any time. The Speaker agreed with Koester, saying that the continuing bells would add to the pressure on Opposition MPs, and public opinion would force them to come in and vote. She said to the press that Parliament had got itself into the mess and Parliament would have to find its own way out of it.

It was my opinion that the Speaker should have publicly stated that the vote would be taken at a definite time, and that she should have proceeded with it. This would have involved the risk, if the Opposition had not shown up, that the Chair had not acted impartially and, in effect, favoured the government by forcing a decision. I believed that after the bells had rung for a few days, any MP who did not show up for the vote would have had a lot of explaining to do to his or her constituents and that most if not all of the Opposition would have appeared. Madame Speaker decided that she did not have the authority to force the vote and quoted the parliamentary authority Redlich as follows:

> Protection of a minority against obstruction and protection of a minority against oppression are both alike functions of the Chair. It is hardly too much to say that they exhaust the duties of the high office held by the impartial guardian of parliamentary law.[111]

In other words, by intervening she would have invited criticism from the minority Opposition, and by not intervening, from the government majority, who would have accused her of failing to act to permit the House to do its business. She pleaded to the House to set rules to guide the Speaker should such a situation arise again. It was my impression that to some degree she was intimidated by Nielsen, who was reported to have threatened a motion of censure against her if she stopped the bells.

---

[111] Philip Laundy, a table officer at the time, when shown a draft of this part of my text, made the following comment: "The quote from Redlich is conveniently selective. At the time, I assembled quotations from Redlich and other parliamentary texts, which showed clearly and categorically that one of the Speaker's first duties is to make sure that Parliament is able to conduct its business. Allowing the bells to ring indefinitely and insisting that the Chair and the Table were manned around the clock on the pretense that the House could be ready to vote at any time, turned a serious situation into a farcical one . . ."

Finally, negotiations between the parties produced an agreement to end the bells. McCain's amendment was defeated and the motion carried. The omnibus bill was then split into eight separate bills and time limits were set by agreement for all of them. Splitting the omnibus bill was what the Opposition had requested in the first place.

Some years previously, when Mr. Speaker Michener was presiding, one of the whips did not appear to put an end to the bell. At a Government House reception, I asked him about it. He replied that he recalled the event vaguely. He simply had called the offending whip into his chambers, told him bluntly that the vote would be taken at a certain time the next day and he had better be there or have to explain his absence to the people of Canada. The whip appeared. As far as Mr. Speaker Michener was concerned, it was no big deal and it was hardly a precedent for what we had experienced.

I cannot leave this discussion without referring to subsequent events. On May 9, 1983, when the bells started ringing at the end of the day, Madame Speaker was informed that all parties agreed to have the vote taken the next morning. She then suspended the bells until 9:00 a.m. the next day.

On March 19, 1984, I suspended the bells in a similar situation. I had a clear indication from the government side that they wished to delay the vote and thought I had a similar indication from the Official Opposition. Erik Nielsen, however, later raised a point of order denying that the Conservatives had consented.

On March 28, I again suspended the bells, this time with the consent of all parties. The next day, March 29, I suspended the bells on a dilatory motion, which in effect made the motion expire.

On March 30, I commented at some length on the problem: Had the Speaker (on May 9) ordered the bells to stop, she would have been accused of partisanship on behalf of the government. By not stopping the bells, she was exposed to criticism for failing in her duty to ensure that the House was able to function.

I went on to say that an unlimited ringing of the bells was a serious threat to the functioning of Parliament, and called attention to what had happened in Manitoba where an opposition had forced the prorogation of the provincial house by this tactic. Three courses of action were available to Parliament: The situation could be left with the timing of votes in the hands of the whips, with the obvious result; the Speaker could be given the power to exercise discretion on timing the vote; or a much better solution would be to draft an amendment to the Standing Orders of the House. A subsequent parliament chose this third option.

Mr. Bill Yurko, MP for Edmonton East, made further reference to the dangers to parliamentary democracy through abuse of the bells and in particular to occurrences in the legislatures of Manitoba and Saskatchewan.[112]

---

[112] Hansard, page 3370, May 3, 1984.

NIELSEN AND COMMITTEE OF THE WHOLE

On June 21, 1982, I was presiding over the House in the Committee of the Whole for the purpose of voting supply. Erik Nielsen raised a question concerning the duties of the minister of State, the MP for Hochelaga-Maisonneuve, suggesting that he had no defined duties and would have a pecuniary conflict of interest if the item were passed. Nielsen had raised the matter with Madame Speaker earlier that day but she had ruled the item admissible in the estimates.

The debate dragged on until after one o'clock in the morning. Nielsen and the leader of the Opposition, Joe Clark, were raising points of order. House rules specified that, at that stage of proceedings, all questions should be put "forthwith successively, without debate or amendment." I could not see any valid points of order and put the question, with Nielsen once again shouting that he should be recognized. At this point, he pulled all MPs of the Official Opposition out of the chamber. The NDP MPs on the other side of the House, however, remained and I simply put the remaining questions to those MPs present and the estimates carried.

The next day Nielsen rose in the House to complain about my conduct. He argued that he should have been permitted to appeal my ruling. In that case, the Committee of the Whole would have been suspended and the Speaker called to decide the matter. Reading the Hansard report, it is hard to avoid the conclusion that this was just another obstructive delaying tactic by Nielsen. It did not work.

RESIGNATION OF MR. DENIS ÉTHIER

The House frequently carries an item on its agenda with the Speaker's words "on division," but if any MP wishes a recorded vote of the yeas and nays, the bells will ring. The House rules at that time provided for a fifteen-minute limit on the bells. I was sitting in the Chair on one occasion, and Mr. Sinclair Stevens, the MP for York-Peel, approached for an informal chat. Had the bells ever exceeded fifteen minutes, he asked. I thought for a minute, then answered, yes, they had, but it was overlooked by the House. This was confirmed by one of the clerks at the Table. Stevens then reported to his caucus that the deputy Speaker had told him that the time limit could be disregarded!

On one bell the Conservative MPs stayed out of the House beyond the fifteen-minute limit, provoking Denis Éthier, who was presiding at the time, to threaten resigning over the disrespect for the House they were showing.[113] (In fairness to the Opposition, Erik Nielsen had offered to have the item pass "on division," without a recorded vote. Government MPs, for reasons best known to themselves, had insisted on one.) Madame Sauvé was reluctant to accept Éthier's resignation and explained to the

[113] Hansard, July 8, 1982, page 19165.

House that I had merely reported as a matter of fact that the fifteen-minute limit had been exceeded, but that did not mean the rules had been changed.

In the same debate, Walter Baker twice referred to Sinclair Stevens' misinterpretation of the rules, suggesting that Éthier reconsider his decision.[114] The House Leader of the NDP, Ian Deans, also suggested that Éthier should not resign.[115] After the leader of the Opposition, Mr. Clark, and Erik Nielsen objected to what they considered to be Éthier's intemperate remarks, he resigned on July 21.[116]

It was most unfortunate that the outcome was the resignation of a man who had served well in the Chair and was generally liked on both sides of the House. He was replaced by the MP for Madawaska-Victoria, Mr. Eymard Corbin, on July 27, 1982.

In September 1982, my mother died of cancer in her ninety-fourth year. She had had the satisfaction on one occasion of seeing me, from the Visitors' Gallery, preside over the House of Commons. A strong and vigorous woman, she had stayed in a difficult marriage to raise her three sons. At no time did she have a bank account of her own and she never learned to drive a car. My father enjoyed his poker games, and inviting his friends to the house over mother's objections. In later years, she enjoyed her games of euchre with neighbouring women of her generation. In their last decade together, however, my parents spent pleasant summers at their cottage on the Big Rideau Lake and winters in Florida.

VOTING AS DEPUTY SPEAKER

Rarely during the time I spent as deputy Speaker did I vote, and only when I felt I had to do so in the interests of my constituents.

In 1982, the government announced a program of limiting wage and price increases to control inflation—the so-called six and five formula, indicating the maximum percentages allowed for two consecutive years. The public service had previously agreed to contribute an extra percentage of their pay to go into a special fund out of which full cost-of-living supplements to basic pensions would be paid. Setting arbitrary caps, as the six and five formula would have done, would have been a clear violation of the terms of public service employment contracts and made a mockery of the supplemental contribution. Four of us from the Ottawa area, representing constituencies with significant public service voters, namely Gaston Isabelle from Hull, Jean-Robert Gauthier from Ottawa Vanier, Len Hopkins from Renfrew-Nipissing-Pembroke, and myself, voted against third reading of the *Supplementary Retirement Benefits Act* on

---

[114] Hansard, pages 19165 and 19323.
[115] Hansard, page 19323.
[116] Hansard, page 19525.

January 25, 1983. John Evans of Ottawa Centre voted for it. I think that I can take some credit for taking the initiative with my fellow MPs on this matter.

Len Hopkins[117] tells me that he had a conversation later with the government whip, Charlie Turner. Prime Minister Trudeau turned to Charlie after the vote, asking him whether or not, he, as whip, had been informed that four of us were going to vote against the government. Charlie replied that not only had he been informed, but he, as a good union man, would have voted with us had he not been whip!

MADAME SPEAKER'S TRIPS

Madame Speaker took trips abroad every year while the House was not sitting. In 1981 she had gone to Brazil and I was not invited to accompany her. In 1982 she had included me in her visit to Mexico and again when she went to Europe during the Easter break of 1983. I cannot recall all the names of those who accompanied us on the 1983 trip, but do remember MPs Walter Baker, Ian Deans and Stanley Knowles, as well as the Clerk, Bev Koester.

At one point we stayed in a hotel in Zürich, Switzerland. Margery and I were in the elevator with an American. Recognizing a North American accent, he asked if we were from the United States. No, we replied, we are Canadians. From what part of Canada, he asked. Ottawa. The only people he knew in Ottawa were his brother-in-law, Walter Baker, and his family. Did we know them? He could hardly believe us when we told him that Walter was with us, in the same hotel. He travelled in Europe for an American company and had no knowledge of Walter's travels. This was surely a one-in-a-million coincidence.

We proceeded to the West German capital, Bonn, where we met the Speaker of the Bundestag and a number of senior officials. John Halstead was still our ambassador. He and his wife, Jean, received us in their official residence and briefed us on events in that country. From Bonn we flew to a resort on the shores of the Baltic Sea, Timmendorfer Strand, in a Luftwaffe aircraft. (I wondered what the boys of 96 Squadron of the Royal Air Force would have thought about it.) Not far away was the city of Lübeck, which had been heavily bombed in the war. We visited an old church whose bell had been blasted out of the tower in a bombing raid and was being preserved in its damaged condition. Not far away was the border of East Germany, which we approached to view the sentry in the distance.

From Germany we flew to Spain. In Madrid, the Speaker of the Cortes gave us a tour of the buildings. Clearly visible in the roof of the main

[117] In the subsequent election of 1984, Len survived, after a recount, by 38 votes out of a total of 48,000 cast. Len believes that he would have gone down if he had not voted as he did on the pension issue. Isabelle and Gauthier were also re-elected, but John Evans and I were defeated.

chamber were the bullet marks from shots fired by a military group attempting a coup a few months before. The king had gone on the air to condemn the coup and to appeal to all Spaniards to resist it. As a result, he enjoyed immense popularity with all political parties, including the communists. We strolled through the famous el Prado Museum and admired the priceless works of art on exhibit.

The king received us in the royal palace in the middle of a park in the suburbs of Madrid. After the usual speeches and translations, came an exchange of gifts. Madame Sauvé offered a beautiful Eskimo soapstone carving. I could see that the translator (I had a limited knowledge from studying Spanish in high school) was having difficulties translating the word soapstone. A curious expression came over the king's face. Did he think he could wash his hands with the carving? He recovered promptly and made the appropriate gracious remarks, but I would have loved to know what he was really thinking.

In August 1983, Madame Speaker made a trip to Russia as the guest of President Mikhail Gorbachev. Her party included, among others, Ian Deans MP, the Government House Leader Yvon Pinard, the Opposition House Leader Douglas Lewis, the minister of Economic Development Donald Johnston, as well as the Clerk, Bev Koester, and the administrator, Arthur Silverman. I was not included. During this period Madame Sauvé fell seriously ill with what was reported to be Hodgkins Disease.

THE DEATH OF WALTER BAKER

When Parliament resumed in the fall of 1983, Walter Baker was often absent from the House, which was most unlike him. Rumours circulated about his health. After one absence of more than a week, he took his seat and I went over to ask how he was. He looked up, and asked if I was going to return to my office. On learning that I so intended, he said he would come to see me.

Walter entered, smiled and sat down. With perfect composure, he announced that he had an inoperable cancer of the lung, but was doing his best to fight it. He had been a pipe smoker for many years. I was stunned and did not know what to say. Although from different political parties, we had developed a strong personal friendship.

I do not believe that I ever spoke to Walter again. He died on November 12, 1983. I presided over the session at which the Rt. Hon. Joe Clark, Mr. Brian Mulroney, the recently chosen leader of the Conservatives, Yvon Pinard, Ian Deans, Alvin Hamilton and all the local Ottawa MPs paid tribute to him. From the Chair, I paid my own respects[118] emphasizing his integrity, his warm human values, his exemplary personal life and his extraordinary contribution to Parliament, to which he had succeeded as a protegé of my old rival Dick Bell.

---

[118] Hansard, page 28821.

I did not know at the time, but Dick had lost his only son in a car accident at an early age. Walter was like a second son to him and I had been the only one to link the two in my remarks. At the funeral parlour, Dick came over to thank me. I remarked that I had merely recognized the fact that he, Dick, had taught Walter his ABCs. Tears came to Dick's eyes and he turned away, unable to speak.

The time would come when Dick would return the compliment on my behalf.

CONFERENCE OF COMMONWEALTH SPEAKERS

In 1969, Mr. Speaker Lamoureux sponsored the first Conference of Commonwealth Speakers in Ottawa and trees were planted to mark the event on the Speaker's estate at Kingsmere. Mr. Philip Laundy, at the time on the staff of the Parliamentary Library, served as executive secretary until his retirement in 1994. Conferences were held generally every two years.

In 1980 it was Canada's turn again. The Speaker spent time with them in Ottawa but requested me to accompany the delegates to Niagara Falls. It was a thoroughly enjoyable experience. In spite of the enormous differences in the stages of development of the countries represented, and the ethnic and cultural diversity, it was surprising to discover how many problems were common to all of the parliaments.

In February 1983 (there was a problem and the conference was not held in 1982), Mr. Speaker Jack of the Gambia was our host for a standing

Lloyd speaking to Governor General Edward Schreyer (Margery and Lily Schreyer in the background) at a reception at Rideau Hall

committee to prepare the agenda for a full conference scheduled for New Zealand in 1984. I attended in place of Madame Sauvé.

This was my first visit to equatorial Africa and quite a shock it was. The climate was benign and the costs of food and shelter minimal, but there seemed to be no jobs for the hordes of young people we saw everywhere. The country was now Muslim and I had the impression that there was not a celibate female over the age of fifteen, perhaps younger. A Catholic priest explained to me why, after thirty years, he had lost nearly all of his flock. As the men left to seek employment abroad, or to participate in one of the African conflicts, other men would assume responsibility for their families. Christianity would permit only one wife, but Islam up to four. They converted to Islam. Plural marriages were a form of social security for the wives and children.

Banjul, the capital city, has modern hotels that attract European tourists, one of the few sources of employment. It was hard to avoid noticing that the white European women went topless in the swimming pools, but not the black women.

Some months previously, there had been an attempted insurrection based on arms allegedly provided by Libya. Insurgents had released prisoners from the jails. The Senegalese army had been invited to restore order and Senegalese troops, well behaved from all accounts, were visible in all public places. An attempt to unite the two countries into a Senegambia Federation, however, failed.

OTHER DUTIES OF A DEPUTY SPEAKER

From time to time, distinguished foreign visitors came to Ottawa and Margery and I met with them when it was not possible for Madame Speaker to do so. Jeanne Sauvé had personally invited Madame Simone Veil, then presiding officer of the European parliament, and at her request I accompanied Madame Veil from Mirabel to Ottawa. She had survived a concentration camp and risen to carve out an outstanding career in the Assemblée Nationale de France, a remarkable achievement in a country in which female parliamentarians are less than half the percentage in the Canadian Parliament.

In September 1983, Vice-President George Bush of the United States addressed the Canadian Parliament, and Margery and I spent nearly a full day with him and Mrs. Bush. They made us feel totally at ease as we toured the Gatineau and the parkways of Ottawa. Also in 1983, the Speaker of the Lokh Sabha of India, Mr. Bal Ram Jakhar, visited Ottawa and again it was a pleasure to show Ottawa in all its fall colours to a stranger. At the end of the day, Mr. Jakhar inquired whether, by chance, I would be going to the Commonwealth Speakers Conference in New Zealand in January. As it happened, Madame Speaker had asked me to attend, since she could not do so herself. On learning that I would be going, he invited Margery and myself to travel the eastern route and to stop off for a few days in New Delhi. We were pleased to accept his invitation.

JEANNE SAUVÉ'S LAST DAYS IN THE CHAIR

Jeanne Sauvé was never, in my opinion, comfortable in the Speaker's Chair. She had difficulty remembering the names of Opposition MPs. NDP Members discovered that they could totally disrupt proceedings by presenting an endless number of petitions at the appropriate time in Daily Proceedings.[119] Outside of the House, on the other hand, she could make short, gracious and charming speeches in faultless English as well as French, as I had seen her do in Mexico, Spain and Germany. This she seemed to enjoy doing.

In 1982, she was offered the post of United Nations High Commissioner for Refugees and was sorely tempted. She mentioned it to me, without indicating what her decision would be. At the same time, Prime Minister Trudeau told me that he knew of the approach to her from the UN, but he had advised her to refuse. He then added that he had something else in mind for Jeanne. What could you offer to a Speaker, other than governor general? And why did he tell me? Was I going to be named Speaker?

[119] One example of this tactic by the NDP was on October 28, 1983.

Lloyd and Margery with Governor General Jeanne Sauvé and Maurice Sauvé

In the fall of 1983, Jeanne Sauvé's illness entered an acute phase. She was totally incapacitated for some time and I presided over a month's sittings beginning on October 31. She made a slow, but good recovery and was able to preside over the speech from the throne on December 7, but left the House to me again on December 8. Fortunately, after Christmas the disease went into remission, and permitted her to function as governor general for a full five years. After the death of her husband Maurice in 1990, the disease was reported to have returned, ultimately taking her life in 1993.

NAMING A MEMBER

On the whole, my sessions in the Chair during 1983 were uneventful with two major exceptions. May 20 was an Opposition Day for the Conservatives and at the end of question period the NDP leader, Ed Broadbent, rose on a question of privilege. He alleged the prime minister had stated that, at a dinner in the prime minister's residence during the recent Conference of First Ministers, all provincial premiers, including Premier Howard Pawley of Manitoba, had agreed to the government's proposed changes in the Crow's Nest freight rates. Broadbent denied that Premier Pawley had agreed. Clearly this was a difference of opinion as to facts, not a matter of privilege, and I so ruled. Broadbent then said that the prime minister had lied to the House.

Alleging that a member has lied is clearly unparliamentary and four times I appealed to Broadbent, as an experienced MP who generally respected the rules, to withdraw his remarks. He bluntly refused to do so unless Prime Minister Trudeau changed his version of what Premier Pawley had said. I had no choice but to name him and actually started the process. At this point, Erik Nielsen intervened, asking the prime minister to do something to salvage the Opposition Day. The following exchange took place:[120] Mr. Broadbent: " . . . if [the prime minister] is now saying that he might be mistaken, then I am prepared to withdraw my remark . . ." Mr. Trudeau: "Mr. Speaker, one can always be mistaken. In this particular case, I do not think that was the case . . ."

Further exchanges took place, with the prime minister stating that if Mr. Pawley and the other premiers agreed that he was under a misunderstanding, he would be prepared to admit it.

Broadbent took this to be an admission by Trudeau that he had misinformed the House and withdrew his remarks. Trudeau rose to deny that he had misinformed the House but I quickly passed to the next order of business. Naming a senior and respected MP such as Broadbent was not what I wanted to do, but if necessary I would have done so.

On October 31, I actually did name a member, Ian Deans, MP for Hamilton Mountain. The House was debating the *Western Grain*

---

[120] Hansard, May 20, 1983, page 2563.

Transportation Act, and the NDP MP for Kootenay East-Revelstoke, Sidney Parker, was attacking the Liberals for modifying the famous Crow Rate and favouring the railroads over the farmers. The parliamentary secretary to the minister of Transport, Jesse Flis, started to read from the minutes of the Transport Committee, quoting the remarks of a mayor in Parker's riding attacking their MP. I challenged the relevance of Flis's quotation, but before I could rule on this point, Parker and Ian Deans raised points of order. Tempers flared and six times I requested Deans to take his seat while I was attempting to sort matters out. Deans became quite angry (the only time I have seen him in such a state) and used most unparliamentary language towards me, as the occupant of the Chair. I had no alternative but to name him. As he cooled down, Deans did apologize, but only after the House leader, Yvon Pinard, had moved to have him suspended for the rest of the day's sitting.[121]

---

[121] This event in no way affected my personal friendship with Deans. When we meet now, we often joke about it.

Part 4

VISIT TO INDIA AND NEW ZEALAND

SHORTLY AFTER THE HOUSE adjourned for the Christmas recess in 1983, Madame Sauvé was named to the post of governor general. Early in the new year, Margery and I left to attend the Commonwealth Speakers Conference in New Zealand with a few days' stopover in India to take advantage of Mr. Bal Ram Jakhar's invitation.

There is so much to see in New Delhi—the parliament buildings, Red Fort, the Qutab Minar ruins and its pillar dating back to the Bronze Age, the monuments to Mahatma Gandhi and other revered figures of the struggle for independence. We accompanied Mr. Speaker Jakhar to a conference of Speakers of Indian States in Bombay. Margery was able to shop for some exotic Indian fabrics in that huge city with its splendid waterfront and its high points overlooking the blue tropical sea.

By motorcar we travelled to the spectacular caves carved out of a cliff of solid black basalt rock at Elora and Agenta by Buddhist communities centuries ago. They had been covered with debris and only rediscovered in the twentieth century. I remember a huge chamber, so acoustically perfect that a whisper could be heard at any point, and other chambers with magnificent Buddhist statues.

From New Delhi we flew to New Zealand with stops at Perth and Sydney, Australia. When we landed at Sydney there was a message requesting I telephone Ottawa. Joyce Fairbairn of the prime minister's staff

Margery at Gandhi Memorial, New Delhi, 1984

Margery being carried by porters, Elora, India, 1984

told me that Mr. Trudeau had decided to nominate me as Speaker when Parliament reconvened later in the month. You can imagine what the news meant to us.

Sir Richard Harrison, the Speaker of the Parliament of New Zealand, greeted us at Wellington. It was exciting to renew acquaintance with men like him and Jack Weatherall, deputy Speaker (and later Speaker) of the British House, Douglas McClelland, president of the Australian Senate, and Condor Laucke, Speaker of the Australian House. I had met all of them at previous conferences in Ottawa and the Gambia.

The conference sessions were held in the parliament buildings in Wellington. Each parliament of the Commonwealth has evolved in its own way and yet there is a common bond among them. Precedents from one country are frequently cited in another, especially those from the United Kingdom. The parliament of India had a feature that fascinated me—a committee on ministerial undertakings. When a minister, in response to an oral question on the floor of the House, said he or she would look into a matter, that subject was automatically referred to the committee and there was no way that the minister could avoid a report. How often have I heard a minister in our House make only a private response, or none at all, despite having undertaken to do so.

We did not spend much time in Auckland, the largest city, but toured South Island. At the foot of a mountain was a plain of perhaps five acres, a solid mass of wild lupine flowers. New Zealanders told us they were an import, escaped from someone's garden and a curse, as they harmed sheep. I thought the many coloured lupines were one of the most spectacular displays I had ever seen! We were flown by helicopter to a glacier at the top of the mountain to watch the children from another party gambol in the snow they were seeing for the first time. (They should have come to Canada.)

We did not visit many cities in New Zealand but did spend a day in Christchurch, which to me was more English than any other town I have seen outside of England. People were friendly and unhurried. We were taken for an exciting white-water ride on a mountain stream and visited a replica of an old mining town. Agriculture was clearly the basic industry and I remember seeing herds of domesticated deer in the fields, something we would not see at home.

ELECTION OF A SPEAKER

On January 16, 1984, the Clerk of the House of Commons, Dr. Koester, informed the House that Madame Sauvé had resigned. The prime minister, Mr. Trudeau, then nominated me to succeed her as Speaker of the House of Commons. It is traditional to make a few complimentary remarks on such an occasion, but I particularly appreciated his emphasis on my fairness and proven ability to handle the post.

Mr. Mulroney seconded the nomination and Mr. Broadbent also made some complimentary remarks. Broadbent and Ian Waddell, NDP MP for Vancouver-Kingsway, felt that they had no objection to me personally but believed, as a matter of principle, that the Speaker should be elected by a secret ballot of MPs. I felt they had a point and would have been delighted to be the first elected Speaker. Walter Baker and I had actually discussed that possibility prior to his death.

Former New Zealand Speaker Sir Richard Harrison and Margaret Harrison

Alan Fotheringham wrote a dreadful column to the effect that Trudeau had insulted parliament by nominating a party hack! His chief complaint was that I lived in Ottawa and defended public servants. Douglas Fisher, the former NDP MP and now a columnist himself, answered Fotheringham, stating that being a party hack was the last charge that anyone should make against me and that in fact I had been a thorn in the side of the Liberals for years. He offered the opinion that I could do the job.

My old rival, Dick Bell, wrote a letter to the press saying that he lived in Ottawa West and would vote against me, but that I was an honourable, independent and competent person. He stated bluntly that Fotheringham's charges were grossly untrue. This was the mark of Dick, a man with his own strong code of honourable behaviour.

FIRST DUTIES IN THE CHAIR

My first responsibility as Speaker was to preside over a joint session of the Senate and House of Commons addressed by the premier of the State Council of the People's Republic of China, Mr. Zhao Ziyang, on January 17, 1984. Following the session, he invited me to make a return visit to China.

Lloyd in Speaker's Chair, 1984

At the first opportunity I paid an official visit to the National Assembly of Quebec at the invitation of its Speaker, the Honourable Richard Guay. We had met at a conference of provincial Speakers hosted by Madame Sauvé in Ottawa some two years previously and were on good terms. Guay told me that he was proud to fly the flag of Canada on this occasion in my honour. Not by intention, it turned out that this was my only visit to a provincial Speaker.

Some time later a crazed member of our armed forces burst into the Quebec Assembly buildings with a machine gun and killed four persons, before being disarmed by the sergeant-at-arms who bravely confronted the man.[122] I telephoned Guay, who said none of his security staff was armed to confront such an emergency. Our sergeant-at-arms, Major General Gus Cloutier, reported the situation was exactly the same with our staff. I issued instructions that he should immediately have men trained to handle weapons and that a few armed security guards be always on duty.

Presiding in the Chair did not create too many problems and I could spend time with Arthur Silverman, who was busy reforming the administration and improving the services available to MPs. The Clerk, Bev Koester, introduced new people into his department and, of necessity, displaced some older ones. Arthur Silverman made even more changes. Those pushed aside followed the time-hallowed procedure of the House by appealing to MPs to help them. Charlie Turner, the Liberal whip, who had been a long-time union officer with the Railroad Brotherhoods, listened to their complaints and took them up with the Management and Members Services Committee. It was most unusual for a whip to take a regular committee assignment but his purpose soon became clear. He used his committee, on which the Speaker was not formally represented, to lambaste the administration of the House of Commons in in camera sessions, citing every complaint brought to his attention, and repeatedly threatened to resign his seat to organize a union of House of Commons employees. While this was a laudable objective, he did nothing about it.

When I became Speaker, I invited the three party whips—Chuck Cook of the Conservatives, Charles Turner of the Liberals, and Ian Deans of the NDP—to lunch and complained about this practice. I stated my own clear preference for a regular grievance procedure, with employees represented by bargaining agents and both sides, management and employees, present. To his credit, Ian Deans was excellent. He not only agreed, he expressed his opinion about the government whip trying to act this way as a grievance channel for all House of Commons employees and abusing the committee, which was intended for another purpose. Turner rose and left.

---

[122] Mr. René Jalbert, the Quebec sergeant-at-arms at the time of the above incident, later served as the Gentleman Usher of the Black Rod in the Senate of Canada, 1985 to 1989.

There was so much to do, but time did not permit it. To get a real grievance procedure, we needed to recognize unions of Hill employees. To my pleasant surprise, members of the Board of Internal Economy, including Herb Gray and André Ouellet, agreed. New legislation would be necessary but there was still resistance to the principle of collective bargaining in some quarters. It would take some stick-handling to get the legislation passed. Recognising unions of Hill employees would also, in my opinion, have solidified the administrative reforms we had introduced.

VISIT TO CHINA

During the April Easter break I decided to accept the invitation of Mr. Zhao Ziyang, premier of the State Council of the People's Republic of China, to visit that country. Mr. Ian Imrie, head of the Parliamentary Relations Branch of the House, made the arrangements. The Speaker of the Senate, Maurice Riel, heard about our plans and asked if he could join the delegation. I agreed, which turned out to be a serious mistake.

We were quite a delegation, with the two Speakers, two Clerks, three House leaders and whips, and others. We visited Beijing, with its zillions of bicycles in the streets. Margery and I were accommodated in a guesthouse used by President Nixon of the United States not long before. The Great Hall of the People, Tienanmen Square, the Forbidden City and the Great Wall bring the very old and the very new into sharp contrast in the incredibly busy capital of China.

From Beijing we went to Shanghai and toured that ancient port. Outside Shanghai we visited a well-run collective farm, housing perhaps 20,000 people. The farm, among other things, produced flowers for the Shanghai market. Plants in the fields were uniform, plastic sheets controlled weeds, and the operation was professional by any standard. The manager explained that he had surplus manpower and had started a construction co-operative to provide employment, but there were limits to how far he could go to provide jobs. Members of the co-operative were reluctant to leave, as they received housing, education and health care for their children at the co-operative's expense. I remember visiting a health centre to see dozens of people sitting around with needles protruding, and must confess that the sight turned me off acupuncture.

In reply to my specific question, the manager stated that his salary was approximately one hundred times that of the lowest-paid employee in the co-operative. That seemed excessive to me, but corporate salaries in Canada have now exceeded that ratio. In 1984, a normal ratio for Canada was about thirty.

We then proceeded south by rail to Guanzhou (formerly Canton) and spent a day at their world-famous trade fair. I purchased a lovely jade carving, which I am looking at now as I type. After visiting a beautiful lake resort, we travelled north, noting how the semi-tropical landscape gradually changed on the way to the Special Economic Zone of Shenzhen adjacent to Hong Kong. My memories of Shenzhen consist of row on row of new skyscrapers under construction, many financed, we were told, by residents of Hong Kong to produce electronic and communications products for export.

Cartoon by Donato, *Toronto Sun*

At every stop there were official dinners and conferences with local officials. According to the official Table of Precedence for Canada, the Speaker of the Senate has priority over the Speaker of the House. Riel insisted that he was the head of the delegation and treated me as a junior at all times. He was the first to ask questions and did not hesitate to interrupt me, frequently citing his parliamentary experience. This from a

Cartoon by G.B. Brown, *The Herald*

man who had never contested an election in his life, was two years my junior and had little more than ten years in the Senate compared to my sixteen in the House! Not being the most patient man to endure slights, I finally exploded on one occasion and we have hardly spoken since.

LIFE OF A SPEAKER

In the course of his duties, the Speaker has to face many different situations. Here are a few from my experience.

In the spring of 1984, the Business Council on National Issues held meetings in Banff, Alberta, and invited me as Speaker to attend a session on the government of Canada. In order to do so and return to Ottawa promptly, it was necessary to use a government aircraft, the one and only time I used this perquisite normally reserved for cabinet ministers.

It came as a shock to discover that a few MPs were running up large bills in the Parliamentary Restaurant. The sergeant-at-arms, Gus Cloutier, had the unenviable job of trying to collect them and had to write off a few after every election for MPs who did not come back. In one or two cases, the bills were for thousands of dollars. I felt that I had no choice but to cut off all credit. Some MPs who were in the habit of paying their bills on a monthly basis protested and the press got hold of it. A cartoon in the *Toronto Sun* showed MPs washing dishes to pay their bills.

Gordon Taylor, the MP for Bow River and later Lieutenant-Governor of Alberta, introduced a private member's bill to have the notorious child murderer Clifford Olson put to death. I had to call him into my chambers to explain that he could not do this: introduce a Bill of Attainder of the kind that had been used by the Stuart kings in the United Kingdom centuries ago. In our society with the rule of law, punishments are imposed on individuals for crimes by the courts, not by Parliament. Taylor quickly got the point.

About this time, Prime Minister Trudeau had taken his famous walk in a winter snowstorm and resigned. The Liberal Party held a leadership convention, in which I, of course, played no part. All of the delegates from my constituency of Ottawa West were pledged to John Turner, including Bill Lee who served initially as Turner's campaign manager when the election was called.

One of Turner's early actions was to call Bob Chiarelli, who had served as my campaign manager in four elections, and ask him to arrange an evening to honour me in Ottawa West. Bob cleared the date with Turner and went ahead with the preparations. Bob reported that he sent two reminders to Turner and arranged for one of them to be marked urgent and placed on Turner's desk. Turner did not appear or even send a message to be read to the gathering. He never apologized. I find it hard to believe that this was done deliberately and put it down to the inefficient way he ran things.

Cartoon by Rusins, *Ottawa Citizen*

As Turner was picking his cabinet, I pondered my responsibility with regard to two prominent Liberal MPs and whether or not I should inform him. Madame Speaker Sauvé had taken action bluntly with one of them. His constituency office, for which a high rent was being paid, had been a booth in a parking lot. His constituency secretary had been the parking lot attendant, who presumably was drawing two salaries. Madame Sauvé promptly put an end to it, without publicity.

The second instance was an MP who had placed his wife on his Ottawa payroll, although she seldom came to Ottawa as far as we could determine. I had just learned of it and had not yet confronted the MP.

After hesitating, I decided that it would be best, on the whole, to inform the prime minister. I need not have worried about it. John Turner simply never returned my telephone calls. Both of these MPs featured in Turner's subsequent appointments.

ADJOURNMENT OF THE HOUSE

The last sitting of the Thirty-second Parliament of Canada occurred on June 29, 1984. At four o'clock in the afternoon my office suddenly became busy. To resign, a member must to do so in writing to the Speaker, who must accept the resignation and then pass a warrant to the chief electoral officer.[123] After receiving one, then another and another, I called in my assistant, Joyce Erskine, asking if she could stay late because something clearly was going on. She checked with her husband and arranged to stay.

By six-thirty, it was over. I received 19 resignations from Members of Parliament who planned to move to other posts. Thus we learned of the famous list of patronage appointments, which was to feature so prominently in the election campaign that followed.

MR. STANLEY KNOWLES

In early 1984, the veteran MP Stanley Knowles suffered a severe stroke that affected his mind. Prior to that unfortunate event, he had been one of the most respected members of the House, an expert on its rules and a staunch defender of pensioners, of Medicare and of people who benefited from social welfare programs. The House of Commons was his life and he had been offered the post of Speaker by Prime Minister Diefenbaker, but declined. MPs of all parties spontaneously expressed their sympathy and Stanley was promptly elevated to a political sainthood.

In June 1984, Stanley went to Prime Minister Trudeau to ask that something be done to permit him to stay on the floor of the House. It was a most unusual request and I doubt that his condition at the time would have permitted him to take such an initiative on his own. Moreover, it was

[123] *Parliament of Canada Act*, Revised Statutes of Canada, Chapter P-1, Section 25(1).

Lloyd with Prime Minister Pierre Trudeau and Joyce Fairbairn, 1984

not in keeping with his character to make such a request for himself. Gossip on the Hill had it that his secretary wanted a few more years to improve her pension and that it was really her idea.

Joyce Fairbairn of the prime minister's office called Jerry Yanover, a veteran strategist on the staff of the Liberal House leader, to ask what could be done. After reflecting, Jerry suggested that a seat at the Table could be provided. There was a precedent of sorts with the former Clerk, Alistair Fraser, who had been so rewarded. Fraser, however, never took his place. There was one big difference: Fraser had been a Table officer and Knowles an MP.

Joyce called me to ask if, as Speaker, I had any objections. Bev Koester, the Clerk, felt it could be dangerous and, in any case, it would be a bad precedent. Meanwhile, the suggestion that Knowles might be appointed had leaked and a member of the Press Gallery had asked him what his duties would be. Knowles replied that he would listen to what was going on, then speak to MPs of the government and Opposition. This was exactly what Koester did not want to happen, as it would inhibit free consultation among the Table officers when the Speaker needed advice.

From talking with Knowles, it became clear that his mind was so impaired that he was not capable of causing the kind of trouble that Koester feared. The prime minister wanted to appoint Knowles. Who would deny this small favour to a seventy-six-year-old House veteran who had suffered such a severe stroke?

For almost thirteen years, Stanley occupied an office in the Centre Block with a full-time secretary who, in later years, doubled as an attendant. If you take her salary and the costs of maintaining the office over the years, the total comes close to a million dollars by my rough calculations. In addition, of course, he drew his well-earned MP's pension.

I made one mistake. There should have been a time limit of, say, five years for this appointment. At the time, no one expected him to live this long. Stanley said he would have died without his appointment, but public policy, unfortunately, has to be based on more material calculations. Despite the high regard held for Stanley by all MPs, myself included, I do not think that anyone would have objected to such a limitation.

KINGSMERE

In July 1984, Margery and I managed to spend some time at our summer place in the Rideau Lakes, which we loved. This was fortunate, as it turned out to be our last opportunity. Margery's health was not good and her frightful cough persisted, but we made the best of it. While it had bothered her during our travels in China, I know she enjoyed the trip. We did sleep at Kingsmere, the official residence of the Speaker, a few times but, being Ottawa residents, preferred our own quarters.

Actually, we did not enjoy Kingsmere that much. At the time, only part of the house on the estate was available, since the caretaker and his family lived in the rest of it. The stables for horses and the tennis courts were attractive features, but we much preferred boating on the Big Rideau Lake. I understand that the whole house is now available for the Speaker's use, as it should be.

When Mackenzie King learned of the bombing of Westminster during the Second World War, he requested that some stone fragments be sent to Canada.[124] This was done in 1943 and some of the stones were probably incorporated into a tourist curiosity known as the Ruins not far from the Speaker's residence. The Ruins have also built into them odd pieces of stone and sculpture assembled by Mr. King from buildings wrecked in Ottawa over the years.

Kingsmere is, however, an excellent location for the Speaker's annual reception. Its location in the Gatineau Hills provides a beautiful setting for every season of the year.

Beside the Speaker's chambers in the House of Commons is a small apartment. It is most useful when Parliament has emergency or long night sittings and the Speaker has to face the next day at an early hour. I used it once or twice but, being an Ottawa resident, much preferred to go to my own home. Other Speakers have made better use of it.

A SPECIAL GIFT TO PIERRE TRUDEAU

Just before leaving 24 Sussex Drive, Mr. Trudeau held a reception for the Liberal caucus. I did not want to attend a party function, but decided to call on him at the end of the afternoon. Our relations were more than cordial and I wanted to express my thanks for the way he had nominated me in January. He proudly showed me a bronze sculpture embodying some of the stones I had polished, and which occupied a prominent place on a mantelpiece.

The sculpture had been a gift from the Liberal caucus in 1970. At the time, I had been deputy whip and suggested the gift (the price was right—a donation). Lois Betteridge, who has since won the Governor General's Award as a silversmith designer, cast the stylized bronze tree. Another member of the Lapsmith Club and I selected stones from across Canada that we polished into shapes that Lois fitted into her bronze. The stones, of different sizes, colours and textures, could be taken out for examination. We found a special stone for each province except Prince Edward Island.

Some five years later, Lois asked me about the bronze and I could not say what had happened to it. She then wrote to the prime minister, asking if she could borrow it for display in an exhibition of her work. At the same

---

[124] *Mike, the Memoirs of the Rt. Hon. Lester B. Pearson*, Volume I, University of Toronto Press, 1972, pages 187, 188.

time, she had been commissioned by the Bronfmann family to design a silver bowl for presentation to Mr. Trudeau and he probably recalled the name.

The prime minister called me into his office to show me a green, streaked bronze that had been stored in some attic or other and asked me if this was Lois's item. It clearly was. He then pulled out a bag with dozens of tumbled stones (that I suspect his sons had played with) and asked if there were any of the stones belonging to the sculpture. I found two and assured him that I could create duplicates of the missing eight.

Lois polished up the bronze and showed it at exhibitions across Canada, giving me credit for the stones. At one point it was shown in the National Museum on McLeod Street in Ottawa. After some weeks, Mr. Trudeau had asked for it back and there it was in a prominent place in the prime minister's residence on Sussex Drive! I had added a chart, naming and describing the stones with their provinces of origin, and this was framed and displayed alongside. He seemed as proud of it as I was.

THE 1984 ELECTION

John Turner called an election for early September 1984. The polls were favourable and the early campaign went well. As Speaker, I endeavoured to avoid a partisan campaign, although I was the official candidate of the Liberal Party. My Conservative opponent, David Daubney, a young, likable lawyer, attracted swarms of enthusiastic volunteers. We clearly had to canvass door-to-door to hold our ground.

The anchor for Global Television, Peter Truman, went on prime time to complain that, as a resident of Ottawa West, he was disenfranchised since he was represented by the Speaker, who could not vote. This, of course, gave a slogan to my opponents: "Don't be disenfranchised." The problem of a Speaker seeking re-election is bad enough under our system, without being singled out by a senior news editor. Was it too much to expect him to show just a little more understanding of my problem?

The staff associations representing the public service prepared a joint questionnaire that they presented to all parties. They were interested in our views about amendments to the *Public Service Staff Relations Act*, especially amendments that would call for employer contributions to a dental plan they were sponsoring. One day I received a telephone call from an old friend in the Professional Institute. Conservatives and NDPers had responded, but there was nothing from the Liberals. John Evans from Ottawa Centre, Jean-Robert Gauthier from Ottawa Vanier and I drafted discreet replies to the questions asked, but we were told that they had to be approved by a cabinet minister. Time was running short. I put urgent calls to John Turner's office and Bill Lee assured me that they were placed on Turner's desk. Again, Turner did not return my calls and the staff associations printed the responses with a big blank for the Liberals.

John Turner's surprise hostility came as a severe personal blow. To this day, I cannot explain it. When he became the cabinet minister for the Ottawa area, he had invited me to act as secretary of his weekly caucus of local MPs. For the nomination convention that elected him, all of the delegates from Ottawa West pledged to him. I am not aware of any issue or, for that matter, any occasion, on which we had locked horns.

I have since learned, from someone close to Turner at the time, that he relied heavily on Marc Lalonde in forming his cabinet and I can only conclude that Lalonde had something to do with the change in Turner's attitude toward me. After reflection, I have come to the conclusion that Turner was simply a good example of the Peter Principle: promotion to the point of incompetence.

Towards the end of the campaign came the famous television exchange between Turner and Mulroney over the June patronage appointments. Turner stated that they were forced on him and he was not responsible. (As it turned out, he was responsible for some of them.) Mulroney's classic response: "You had a choice. You could have refused!" sounded the death knell for one hundred Liberal candidates, myself included. This incident surely belongs in any study of the effects of television on our politics.

From that point on, the campaign was hopeless. In an effort to salvage what I could, I accepted invitations to all-candidates meetings and, as a Liberal, defended the government's record. Reception at the door was hostile.

The results of the election on September 4, 1984, were as follow:

DAUBNEY (Conservative)	26,591
FRANCIS (Liberal)	19,314
CHAPMAN (NDP)	8,304
TURMEL (Independent)	285

Liberal representation in the House of Commons declined from 135 at dissolution (after the famous June resignations) to 40. Conservatives under Brian Mulroney increased their numbers from 100 to 211. The NDP declined by one seat from 32 to 31. In a landslide of these proportions, Ottawa West was a hard seat for a Liberal.

Referring to the defeat of Mr. Speaker Michener who sought re-election in Toronto-St. Paul's in 1962, Mr. Speaker Jerome observed:

> Had Roland Michener had the good fortune, as both Lucien Lamoureux and I did, to represent a single city constituency, I am sure he would have stayed on as Speaker.[125]

[125] Op. cit., page 135.
Michener was defeated by a distinguished Toronto lawyer and Rhodes Scholar, Ian Wahn. Wahn must have had mixed feelings when his leader, Pearson, named Michener governor general. In spite of being elected to four parliaments between 1962 and 1972, Wahn received no promotion to the cabinet, nor even a parliamentary secretary's post.

The results in Ottawa seemed to confirm Jerome's observations. In a city such as Cornwall or Sudbury, with no cabinet ministers representing adjacent constituencies, the prestige of the office of Speaker counts a great deal more. In a metropolitan area, the partisan campaign spills over to all constituencies. In the campaign of 1984, however, I do not think that anything could have changed the result in Ottawa West.

Stanley Knowles, recognising this problem, had suggested a decade previously that a special constituency of Parliament Hill be created for the Speaker. In that way, the Speaker could be spared the obligation of participating in a partisan election campaign. Lucien Lamoureux had actually been re-elected once in Cornwall, running as an independent, with the Official Opposition declining to nominate a candidate against him. In the subsequent election, the Conservative Party declined to give Mr. Speaker Lamoureux an acclamation and he was obliged to seek re-election, not as a Liberal, but with Liberal support. Fortunately for Lucien, he was successful.

On the whole, I believe Stanley Knowles' suggestion of a special constituency for Parliament Hill has merit.

LAST DAYS IN OFFICE

According to Section 45 of the *Parliament of Canada Act*, a Speaker continues in office until replaced, even though ceasing to be an MP. One

Executive committee, House of Commons, 1984: Bev Koester (Clerk), Lloyd, Arthur Silverman (administrator), Major General "Gus" Cloutier (sergeant-at-arms)

day in October, George Anderson of my staff reported that the Turners would be moving into Kingsmere. My reply was instinctive: "Go back and tell whoever gave you that news that Kingsmere belongs to the Speaker and no one has spoken to him."

Within an hour, I received a telephone call from Fred Doucet of the prime minister's office. "It seems that there has been a slip-up. The Mulroneys do not want to move into Sussex Drive until it is redecorated, and will be staying on at Stornoway for a while. Meanwhile, the prime minister would like you to make Kingsmere available to the Turners." "Tell the prime minister that the Speaker will do as he wishes. Please have Mr. Turner call me."

I must confess that I could not resist having Turner call me, and this time he did, inviting me to have lunch at Madame Berger's in Hull. We talked about inconsequentials and finally got around to Kingsmere. When did he want to move in? As soon as possible. With anyone else, I would have agreed, but in the circumstances I suggested that we would need at least two weeks since Margery was not in the best of health. (My wife was indeed not well but we had very few of our things in Kingsmere.) How long would the Turners be staying? Likely a couple of months. For the benefit of my successor, I indicated it would be proper to put a memo on file stating that, as Speaker, I had consented to the use of Kingsmere by the Turners for a period not exceeding four months, to end in February, 1985.[126]

In October 1984, Pope John Paul II made an official visit to Ottawa and, since I was still Speaker, it was my pleasure to be part of the official party that greeted him at Government House and in the open ceremonies on LeBreton Flats.

One day I received a personal call from the prime minister. "Lloyd, how would you like to be an ambassador?" I could hardly believe my ears. "Very much, sir." "We have an opening in Portugal. I'll see what I can do."

Bryce Mackasey's appointment as ambassador to Portugal had been one of the names on the June patronage list. The Portuguese, however, in a rare gesture, refused "agrément," which meant they would not have him. The Portuguese ambassador in Ottawa, Luis Navega, a capable and shrewd observer whom we had come to know, no doubt had something to do with the attitude of his government. I had been invited to functions in the Portuguese Embassy on a number of occasions.

Mackasey had gambled on the stock market and lost a considerable amount of money. An accountant friend of his arranged a series of transactions involving numbered companies which relieved Mackasey of his debts but left the bank with loan guarantees that it had to write off.

[126] I read with interest while I was in Portugal that the Turners were still in Kingsmere in the spring of 1985 and the wife of my successor, John Bosley, was not pleased. John Bosley tells me that my memo to file of October 1984 could not be found.

During this period Mackasey was a member of the Banking Committee of the House. Had he brought pressure on the bank to get out of his debts? The *Montreal Gazette* seemed to think so and accused him of irregularities. Charges were laid against him in the Quebec courts that were eventually dismissed.

Mackasey had a frightful press in the period prior to the 1984 election and his name kept coming up to embarrass the Liberals at all-candidate meetings during the campaign. By a curious twist of fate, thanks to Luis Navega, the rejection of Bryce Mackasey, and the kindness of Brian Mulroney, I received an appointment.

In November, I was named as the Canadian ambassador to Lisbon but did not assume my post until January 20, 1985. Meanwhile, I took Portuguese lessons and found my previous knowledge of Spanish helpful. Two people in External Affairs, Raymond Chretien, a nephew of Jean Chretien and later ambassador to Washington, and Julie Loranger, later ambassador to Spain, were most helpful in briefing me on my new duties.

The Speaker's staff, 1984. Front row: George Anderson, Joyce Erskine, Lloyd, Frank Marchington; middle row: Lillian Lamy, J. Maziglia, Madeleine Valeé, Audrey Maloney, Joan Murray, Lilian Chatterjee; back row: Satnam Vaid, Norman Hall, Dana Angus, John Milloy

Among other things, I visited Newfoundland and Nova Scotia to learn how we shared cod catches with the Portuguese in the various zones off the Atlantic Coast.

REFLECTIONS ON MY TERM AS SPEAKER

I cannot leave my term as Speaker without thanking a number of people. Arthur Silverman as administrator did a superb job, as did the Clerk, Bev Koester. My relations with the sergeant-at-arms, Gus Cloutier, were smoother than had been the case with my predecessor. Ian Imrie of Parliamentary Relations was always helpful. Madame Claudette Chemla is an excellent French teacher and I reached the point under her tutelage where I did not need to use the awkward translation earphones while in the Chair. My steward, Leo Robitaille, had served many Speakers, starting with Roland Michener, and was indispensable, guiding my way through many formal situations. Joyce Erskine, my assistant, and Audrey Maloney in my constituency office went the extra mile to keep things in order. Frank Marchington, George Anderson and Norman Hall looked after a wide range of constituency and other matters. Madeleine Vallée's talents have been recognized by three succeeding Speakers whom she has served as secretary. Satnam Vaid was a faithful driver.

Unfortunately, I was not able to get the post of administrator confirmed in the organization chart of the House. The auditor general had recommended in 1980 as follows:

> Appoint a top-flight administrator, with deputy minister status, reporting directly to the Speaker, to provide leadership and direction for administrative functions. This means clearly separating procedural from administrative responsibilities... The Clerk would remain the senior permanent deputy head, devoting his entire efforts to advising and supporting the Speaker and the House on procedural matters. The sergeant-at-arms would be responsible for all ceremonial duties, as well as control of security and access to buildings and a variety of related building services. The administrator would direct and co-ordinate the administrative affairs and support services of the House. The Clerk, the sergeant-at-arms and the administrator, with the Speaker as chairperson, would constitute an executive committee for the general, financial and personnel administration of the House.[127]

This recommendation made sense to me. With the encouragement of Speaker Jeanne Sauvé, Arthur Silverman, no doubt relying on the strong wording of the auditor general's report, had accepted the post. At the time,

[127] Op. cit., page 5.

the Management and Members' Services Committee, as well as the Board of Internal Economy, had agreed. My successor, John Bosley, also agreed with the recommendations concerning the administrator and during the tenures of Sauvé, myself and Bosley, the executive committee functioned as the auditor general had envisaged.

I had always been concerned about the influences brought to bear on the Management and Members' Services Committee, however, and something happened to change their views. Frankly, I believe the old boys network, inspired by senior employees of the House who felt that their privileges were threatened, went to work. It was no surprise that Arthur Silverman finally left the House of Commons for another post as senior assistant deputy minister in the public service of Canada. Under the current organization chart, the Clerk is still in charge of administrative and procedural functions and, together with the sergeant-at-arms, reports directly to the Speaker.[128]

The talent for being an expert adviser on parliamentary procedure to the Speaker is quite different from that of a good administrator. In my experience, the Clerks were good on procedure and weak on organization. Dr. Bev Koester was a scholar, who studied all the books on the arcane procedures of the House and offered excellent advice. Arthur Silverman knew finance, human resource management and procurement and the whole world of communications based on modern computers.[129]

The Speaker is responsible for a substantial budget, which in my day exceeded $100 million annually. Mr. Speaker Jerome found himself in deep trouble when he tried to implement budget cuts and had to go through the Clerk in an endeavour to get the facts from lower levels of administration. I believe most strongly that the Speaker can only stay on top of matters when administrative decisions are fully reviewed by the executive committee, which affords the sergeant-at-arms as well as the Clerk an opportunity to explore the implications of administrative proposals before they are implemented, with the Speaker present and listening. In my time all three members of the committee functioned well and, as each reviewed the operations for which he was responsible, the comments of the others led to a good deal of cross-fertilization.

Most but by no means all of the problems arose in the administrative area. To cite one example: MPs now have larger personnel staffs that they direct, but it is essential that there be some uniformity in hiring practices,

---

[128] The position of administrator continued for some time at the deputy minister level, but has now been abolished and replaced by a position designated as deputy clerk, corporate services.

[129] Under the present Clerk, Robert Marleau, the structure has reverted to what it was previously. Marleau appears to have better administrative skills than his immediate predecessors, but I still believe the senior administrative officer should have direct access to the Speaker.

pay scales and classifications. We had to be constantly on guard against abuses such as the hiring of relatives with little or no responsibilities, and the administrator had to have direct access to the Speaker to deal in a timely way with situations. In my opinion, the elimination of the executive committee can only make the job of the Speaker more difficult.

The Public Service Commission has no responsibilities whatever for the selection or promotion of House of Commons staff, which is unfortunate.

I had hoped to do something about the growing number of agencies reporting directly to Parliament and not supervised by a minister of the Crown, nor, as far as I could observe, by anyone else. This family keeps growing—the auditor general, the elections commissioner, the privacy commissioner, the human rights commissioner—and I have by no means exhausted the list. As I write, the leader of the Opposition has suggested the addition of some kind of science supervisor. Theoretically, these report to Committees of the House, but in practice, the auditor general seems to be the only one to appear regularly as a witness. The others are called infrequently, every two or three years or so. Who approves their budgets? The auditor general has had a huge expansion of staff and I am not saying it was unjustified, but someone should have an independent look at his operations.

I wanted Parliament to approve a position on the staff of the Speaker that would report each year on the activities of a named list of agencies reporting to Parliament. It would call attention to any unusual personnel practices, adoption of new policies, and expansion of activities, so that Parliament could judge its priorities for examination. In a general way, such a person would parallel the work of the auditor general for other branches of government.

It was also a matter of regret that my period in office was too short to be able to further develop collective bargaining and grievance procedures for employees of the House of Commons.

Those who implement a revolution do not always get recognition for their efforts. The House of Commons is now better administered and the MPs have a modern range of office services, thanks to the reforms initiated by Speaker Jeanne Sauvé and Administrator Arthur Silverman that incorporated the majority of the auditor general's recommendations. Modern personnel procedures and systems are now in place.

I had accepted the appointment as deputy Speaker in April 1980 hoping to do something to reform the administration of the House of Commons. At the time, I had only the vaguest knowledge of the work of the auditor general and even less of the contents of his report, or of the concerns of Mr. Speaker Jerome that had led him to invite the auditor general to undertake a special study. It was a pleasure to have been part of the team that changed things.

There is a military saying that you never know the quality of a soldier until he has been under fire. It is also true of a Speaker: you never know his or her mettle until tested in a crisis. I believe that I came through in a few hard tests, such as the Assault on the Chair. It is for others to judge.

PORTUGAL: THE COUNTRY AND ITS PEOPLE

The two years and eight months that we spent in Portugal were the most pleasurable and exciting of my life. Margery, in spite of her illness, was able to share them. This nation of ten million people on the Iberian peninsula has a history going back thousands of years, with settlements dating from Phoenician, Greek and Roman times. Its proudest moment came when Portugal's navigators of the fifteenth, sixteenth and seventeenth centuries explored Brazil in the West, rounded Cape Horn to make contact with India, found the Spice Islands in the South Pacific, and eventually travelled to Japan.

The Monument to the Discoveries on the Lisbon waterfront symbolizes the nation's pride in its past.

The people—friendly, courteous and gentle with few exceptions—reflect their Mediterranean origins with the mixtures that came from the invasions over the centuries. One evening at a dinner the guest beside me, a tall, blonde woman with almond-shaped eyes who occupied a Chair of Biology at the University of Lisbon, told me that she and most of her

Gordon Osbaldeston, Clerk of the Privy Council, administering the Privy Councillor's Oath, January 1985. In the background: Governor General Sauvé, Prime Minister Mulroney, Maurice Riel (hidden); beside Lloyd, "Tommy" Douglas, Saul Cherniak, Paule Gauthier

village were descendents of the Visigoths, whose regime collapsed over a thousand years ago. The Moors occupied the country for many centuries and the province of the Algarve in the south was the last part of the country to be liberated. Many place names begin with the letters "al," indicating their Moorish origin.

Eleven ancient provinces range from tall mountains in the north to rich plains in the south. Portugal's seashore has long stretches of the finest beaches in the world. Those on the Atlantic can be stormy and their waters are usually colder. However, the beaches in the southern Algarve—some as long as fifty kilometres—are sheltered and attract tourists in large numbers during the winter season.

Prior to 1974, Portugal had been ruled by the dictator Salazar for more than four decades. During the Spanish Civil War of 1936-39, he had actively supported General Franco and was reported to have summarily executed fleeing Spanish Loyalists who crossed the border seeking asylum. The official version of the present government is that his regime was a brutal fascism, and prison cells from his time at Peniche are now a museum. I did, however, meet some Portuguese who revered his memory (including a woman reputed to have been his mistress). Salazar died in office, but his successors became involved in attempting to suppress liberation movements in the African colonies of Mozambique and Angola. The wars that ensued bled the Portuguese Army severely. In April 1974, General Ramalho Eanes, in command of a division in Lisbon, put an end to the dictatorship in a coup d'état. The Portuguese Army, to its credit, supervised the transition to a democratic state, with Eanes as its first president.

Between April 1974 and the election of July 1987, which finally brought a majority government under Cavaco Silva to power, Portugal had ten governments. Political instability was matched by economic mismanagement. The country was obliged to accept over 600,000 *retornados* (equal to six per cent of the total population), many in desperate circumstances, from the former colonies of Angola and Mozambique. Communists were significantly represented in the *Assembleia* and the newly adopted constitution described the country as socialist, with a clause prohibiting the denationalizing of state industries. All of the banks and the most basic industries were nationalized.

In January 1986, Portugal and Greece entered the European Common Market, although it was generally agreed that they had the lowest per capita incomes of the member countries. Cavaco Silva, a former professor of economics, guided the country in a shift to a market-oriented economy and Portugal has become more prosperous.

ARRIVAL IN LISBON

Margery and I arrived in Lisbon in January 1985, some seven-and-a-half years after our visit with the Inter-Parliamentary Union. The chargé d'affaires, Frank Chandler, met us at the airport. Frank had been acting in charge since Lucien Lamoureux, the former ambassador and also a former Speaker of the House of Commons, had left some three months previously.

We were taken to the official residence on Rua de Buenos Aires, in the old quarter of Lisbon called Restello, which reminded me of Rockcliffe in Ottawa. The beautiful old house had been constructed some decades ago by a wealthy family from the Azores. The first floor included a large dining room with a table that would seat fifteen persons comfortably, a small dining room where we usually took our meals, and a spacious drawing room that opened out on a small, but beautiful, back terrace. The walls of the terrace were bordered by beautiful flower plots and to one side some flowering tropical shrubs, including a banana tree that Lucien Lamoureux had brought back from Madeira. The banana tree actually produced a stalk of small, sweet bananas, which tells you something about Lisbon's climate. The second floor contained three bedrooms and a study with a television set where we usually relaxed in the evenings, enjoying particularly English and Canadian productions with Portuguese sub-titles. The basement included a huge (by my standard) wine-cellar and a small room that I was eventually able to transform into a lapidary workshop. It also had a luxurious kitchen with a work surface that included a marble slab ten feet long.

Helena, a widow in her late fifties, ran the household, super-vising Olinda, the cook, and Celesta, the maid. In addition, we had a full-time chauffeur, Rodrigues (I never did know his first name), an excellent fellow with a military background. None of them spoke English, but Rodrigues spoke fair French and Helena some French. Nevertheless, we got along famously, especially after Margery and I learned some Portuguese.

Our official car was a huge Chevrolet Caprice, the only one of its kind in all of Portugal, as far as I could determine. It was conspicuous and ill suited to the narrow, old streets. A few months before our arrival, Armenians had stormed the Turkish embassy, killing four persons. Not long after we had settled into our new quarters, there was a nasty incident in Ottawa involving an Armenian terrorist, who had been seized and imprisoned. Therefore, at the first opportunity, I purchased a new small German Mercedes, which was much less conspicuous on Portuguese roads and seemed to be the favourite car for Portuguese taxis. We used it for our personal travel and put more than 50,000 kilometres on it.

WORK OF THE EMBASSY

Staff in our office included some fifteen Canada-based and perhaps twenty locally engaged positions. Most active was the immigration section, followed by the consular, trade and cultural sections. A lone member of the Canadian Security and Intelligence Service was attached to us for administrative purposes. While he was a most pleasant associate and the kind of person you would welcome at your side if you were ever in trouble, I had no knowledge of his work. In addition, we had the usual Canada-based communications and office supervisory personnel.

Immigration from Portugal to Canada at the time was about 1,500 persons per year. While the Lisbon office was also responsible for immigration from Spain, this was covered by infrequent trips to Madrid and was not onerous. Spaniards preferred to emigrate to Central and South America, whereas the well-established Portuguese communities in Canada—some 300,000 strong—gave our country a good name. Applicants for admission to Canada were numerous, so much so that a previous ambassador had transferred the entire immigration section to a separate building some five blocks away. I could hardly believe that he was able to get away with it, involving as it did duplication of reception areas, telephones and office services. To interview applicants, our staff regularly visited the Azores and Madeira.

One of my last acts before leaving Portugal was to move our staff to new quarters on Avenida da Liberdade and combine the immigration section with the rest of our operations. My experience with real estate in Canada was of no help whatsoever. In my opinion, we should have constructed a new building, but local circumstances made that choice impractical. Although excellent sites were available on most reasonable terms, we would have had to purchase the leases of the tenants at prices some four times that of the site. Decades of rent controls had created value for holders of leases: some of our own staff were paying the equivalent of ten dollars a month rent for apartments that would have fetched a thousand dollars in a free market. Construction was monstrously inefficient, since contractors had to pay a couple of years' wages for every one that they laid off. As a result, the contractor kept a small crew who did the excavating, the forming, the plastering, the carpentry work, the electrical and plumbing—all the trades. You can imagine what that did to productivity. From the balcony of our residence, I watched the construction of a four-storey apartment building. It was half-finished when we arrived and barely finished when we left two years and eight months later.

We purchased two storeys in a new office building on Avenida da Liberdade, which I judged to be almost completed. Foolish me!

My successor, Geoffrey Bruce, told me of the problems he faced in an uncompleted building, which had not been finished when I checked three years later.

Back to the immigration section, which presented by far the most problems, or should I say challenges. The head of the section had been our ambassador to Senegal some time previously. One evening he came home to find his charming and capable wife dead of a heart attack. We did our best to console him, but he had no wish to stay. His assistant and I had serious differences and I requested that he be replaced. The department then sent me a superb fellow, Gordon Whitehead, who promptly took charge, to my intense relief.

ALLEGED SALE OF VISAS

At seven o'clock one morning in March 1987, I received a long-distance telephone call from a Toronto journalist. What did I have to say about the charges by a Toronto MP, Sergio Marchi, that the Canadian embassy in Lisbon was selling immigration visas? Marchi, accompanied by a dozen Portuguese immigrants, had called a press conference to announce that all of those present had been obliged to bribe their way into Canada. This news came as a bombshell and I refused to comment until I could get details of the charges and check them out. Reporters from the Portuguese press received the same answer and the local headline read: "Canadian Ambassador refuses to comment on scandal."

After checking carefully with every person in the immigration section, I was satisfied that there was not a grain of truth to the story. But how could we answer the charges? The reputations of not only Whitehead and myself, but also at least two of our competent junior officers, were at stake. Fortunately, we got a break. The *Toronto Star* sent a Portuguese-speaking journalist, Dale Brazao, who had the names of the individuals mentioned by Marchi, to investigate. All told the same story. They alleged that they had gone to a consultant in Cascais. For a fee, he interviewed them, filled out their application forms (many were illiterate) and told them to ask for Jorge in the immigration section. The consultant told them that these application forms were coded with some special dots to ensure priority treatment.

I was persuaded that the reporter was professionally competent and felt I had to trust him. It was undoubtedly against regulations, but I stood with him while we pulled each of the files he requested. We answered all of his questions, confident that we had nothing to hide. No codes or special dots of any kind could be detected in the files. Jorge, by the way, was the receptionist in the immigration section, and since he greeted every applicant, there was nothing special about asking to see him. Moreover, he denied any acquaintance with the immigration consultant and I believed him.

Brazao then went to Cascais to seek an interview with the consultant, who refused to speak to him. Brazao watched his house and took a photo of the man from a distance. While he was in a restaurant, Brazao's car was broken into and his camera destroyed. Conversations with locals produced the information that the so-called consultant was regarded as a thug who had managed, by one means or another, to get permission to carry a gun at all times. He probably knew enough about Canadian immigration regulations to deal only with those clients likely to be selected in any case.

Brazao went home and wrote a story completely absolving us from the charges. Sad to say, the *Toronto Star* story did not get the attention that the initial charges in the *Globe and Mail* received. The RCMP also sent a man to conduct an investigation who came to the same conclusion as the *Star* reporter. The RCMP report, as far as I know, was never made public.

PROBLEMS WITH IMMIGRATION CASES

Whitehead sometimes just spent time at the airport, randomly checking people going to Canada. One party of several persons was travelling with what appeared to be valid Canadian passports, but had no elementary knowledge of English or French. Suspecting that something was wrong, he talked the Portuguese authorities into delaying their departure. When the passport numbers were sent by telex to Ottawa, it was quickly confirmed that the passports were fraudulent. The quality of the forged documents was such that they easily fooled experts. It is the policy of Canada to hold the transportation companies responsible when they carry passengers to Canada who lack valid travel documents, but in my opinion this is not fair to the companies in view of the excellent quality of some modern forgeries.[130]

Canada has an excellent record for accepting refugees, but it is often difficult to detect fraudulent claims. Many people in this world, sadly, have a well justified fear of persecution in their homelands and we wish to treat them with all the sympathy they deserve. What do you do, however, with arrivals who destroy their documents en route, by flushing them down the toilet, for example, and then apply for refugee status in Canada? (Sometimes they were advised by "consultants" to do this.) I cannot resist the conclusion that Canada has become an easy mark for a number of undesirables, such as money launderers, terrorists and even criminals. They choose the refugee route since it is a much simpler and quicker way to get into our country. Our system permits appeal to a refugee board and ultimately, if they have the financial resources (which many undesirables have), to the Federal Court of Canada. Our Supreme Court, in a decision written by Madame Justice Bertha Wilson, has ruled that the protection of the Canadian Charter of Rights and Freedoms extends to any human being in Canada, regardless of whether they are in the country legally or illegally.

One scam that emerged in my time was the claim for refugee status by Portuguese saying that they were Jehovah's Witnesses who were fleeing from persecution. This excuse was invented by "consultants." There are only a few thousand Jehovah's Witnesses in Portugal and I never heard of

[130] This policy has had a recent tragic application, in the case of a Taiwanese ship whose captain is alleged to have cast Romanian stowaways adrift at sea rather than face fines from the Canadian authorities for carrying unauthorised persons to Canada.

a single one of them making a charge of persecution. Portugal, at this time, does not persecute any minority. I understand that some initial claimants actually succeeded with this flimsy claim, but the facts were soon established.

I would like to describe one further incident. Lisbon, according to an agreement worked out between the governments of Canada and Quebec, included an immigration officer whose salary and accommodation were paid by the province. This man, an amiable and pleasant fellow, was included in our receptions and other events. One day, he gave us the name of an applicant that he had approved, who had proved ownership in Montreal of properties valued in excess of $1 million. Whitehead interviewed the applicant and requested the completion of a routine questionnaire. One question asked if the applicant had ever spent time in prison or been convicted of a criminal offence. The man was reluctant to complete this part, but did so eventually. Whitehead got suspicious, and a bit of research revealed that the man had spent time in a California prison for illegal arms sales in Central America. He was a well-known arms dealer, with a passport authorising entry into the United States. Needless to say, we rejected him.

This incident illustrates the problem of any province attempting to set up its own immigration service. Frankly, the Quebec officer lacked the resources or sophistication for the job. Federal officers had the right to veto his selections, and there was no argument about this particular case. What would have happened if we had not been able to prove a criminal conviction, but were forced to rely on information offered to us by investigators in friendly countries? If the case had not been clear beyond any doubt, would we have had a nasty dispute over it?

Quebec justifies its separate immigration officers on the grounds that it needs to make special efforts to encourage French-speaking immigrants. Francophones were well represented in our own immigration section and in most of the exchanges promoted by our cultural affairs staff. Frankly, I doubt that Quebec's efforts in Lisbon produced one more immigrant to that province. For that matter, many of the Portuguese emigrating to Canada went first to Montreal, then to Toronto, attracted by the better economic prospects in that city.

In July 1986, Canada was obliged to impose a visa requirement on all residents of Portugal, the Azores and Madeira seeking to visit Canada. The purpose was to prevent illegal immigrants, but on the surface it was offensive and discriminatory towards the Portuguese, as we did not have the same requirement for other member states of the European Community. We administered the visitor's visa most carefully, doing our best not to offend Portuguese sensitivities, but issuing 20,000 visas per year took a lot of staff time. The visa was, however, necessary and we rejected some fifteen per cent of applicants.

CONSULAR WORKLOAD

Work of the consular section, which was Chandler's responsibility, remained constant most of the time, but exploded during the tourist season from January to April. A few hundred Canadian citizens were registered with us, but no one could guess how many Portuguese had emigrated to Canada, taken out citizenship, and returned to the land of their birth for their retirement years. These people occasionally came to us to renew passports, secure copies of documents, or for various other reasons, but on the whole they generally left the embassy alone.

The problem with tourists was that many agencies recruited tour parties without asking any questions about the health of the applicants. I recall one tour that brought four heart attacks that resulted in two deaths! Each case, needless to say, required hours of staff work involving hospital admissions, renegotiation of dates for return (the travel agencies were not always the most helpful), and sometimes counselling. Arrangements to ship a dead body back to Canada could not help but involve the embassy. In the case I mentioned, one of those suffering a heart attack was an old friend and I made a special trip to the Algarve to see him and to arrange for his move by ambulance to the British Hospital in Lisbon. Fortunately, he recovered. One of the others on the tour wrote a nasty letter to my minister, the Rt. Hon. Joe Clark, complaining that I gave special treatment to my Liberal friends!

One of the saddest cases involved a young couple from Montreal who came to Portugal for their honeymoon. After renting a car at the airport, they proceeded to a hotel on a beach on the Atlantic coast. Arriving just after dark, they went for a stroll at high tide. A wave swept the bride off the rock on which she was standing carrying her to sea to be drowned on her wedding night! Going after dark on the rocks of a foreign shore is reckless, but people do strange things.

One Sunday morning I received a call from the man at the embassy entrance desk. A woman wanted to speak to the ambassador and came on the line.

"You will think that I am very foolish and you are right. I am thirty-five, unmarried and a teacher in Canada, now taking a course at the University of Coimbra. Frankly, I got bored and came by train to Lisbon to have a good time.

"I met some people who took me to two or three places and had too much to drink. When I came to, my friends were gone and so was my purse with my money and travel tickets back to Coimbra.

"I found my way back to the railway station, which was nearly deserted. A man offered to find me accommodation for the night at a pensao (a kind of Portuguese boarding house). After I was set up in my room, he appeared and wanted to spend the night with me. As a result, I spent the night on the street."

A duty officer met the woman and took her to the railway station. She seemed to remember she had rented a locker and left some things in it, but of course she had no key. With the co-operation of the railway station officials, a number of lockers were opened and eventually hers was found. In it she had left some travellers' cheques. We saw her safely on the train back to Coimbra.

The Canadian embassy is your friend if you get into trouble. In my experience, purse snatches occurred, but not as frequently as in some other countries. Rented cars were often broken into in tourist areas, usually by youths who live by their wits on the beaches. In Portugal, stolen passports are usually recovered, often after a delay. In such cases, we were authorised to issue replacements.

THE TRADE SECTION

Our trade section, under the direction of James Feir and later Luis Bustos, with Manuel Lima locally engaged, provided services to Canadian businesses attempting to sell in Portugal. This was an uphill battle, although Canada's balance of trade with Portugal was better than with the rest of the European community. They earned Canadian dollars from tourism, emigrants' remittances and the sale of such products as wine and cork. We sold them dried codfish (we still had some for sale at that time before the collapse of the fishery), seed potatoes, dairy breeding stock, software and high-technology products. However, after Portugal entered the European Common Market in 1986, we discovered the length to which European countries would go to exclude Canada by non-tariff barriers.

Portugal's telephone system was antiquated by any standard and the government invited proposals to modernise it. The two contenders with clearly superior technology were Ericksson from Sweden and Nortel from Canada, but they could not even get on the short list. Eventually, after much negotiation, the Portuguese market was split between Thomson of France and Siemens of Germany. Siemens had its own technology of sorts, but Thomson had to go to the United States to make a deal with AT&T. The Swedish ambassador was furious, but to no avail.

Canada has two companies producing banknotes, and for a time they had a technological lead over their competition, since their notes were much harder to forge. The Bank of Portugal decided to issue for the first time a note for 10,000 escudos[131] and called for proposals. The Canadian Bank Note Company was chosen from the list of applicants.

---

[131] When I visited the Azores, I was shown a gold coin recovered by divers from a wreck, denominated for one escudo. At the time of its issue there were 1,000 reis to one escudo. Today, reis have disappeared and one escudo is worth about a tenth of a Canadian cent! Such is the measure of price inflation over the years.

Unfortunately for Canada, the firm of Thomas de la Rue of London has printed Portugal's banknotes since time immemorial. The salesman for Canadian Bank Note called on me to complain that he had been reliably informed that the British ambassador had written a letter to the governor of the Bank of Portugal saying that if Thomas de la Rue did not receive the contract for the 10,000 escudo note, the British representative in Brussels might have to reconsider his vote on Portugal's agricultural credits from European Community funds.

I wrote a letter to the governor of the bank stating that the Canadian Bank Note Company was thoroughly reputable and printed asubstantial amount of Canada's currency. Canada was anxious to develop this kind of business and looked to Portugal for fair treatment. We had, admittedly, a superior technology. I went so far as to say that the Canadian government would be disturbed if the contract was awarded on any ground other than merit.

Some weeks later, I left Portugal without having received a reply. From enquiries, I understand that Thomas de la Rue got the job.

One of our specialties in agricultural exports is seed potatoes. The Department of Agriculture and Agri-Food has a fascinating film showing how our geneticists develop new varieties to meet special climate and soil conditions. For some years we had been selling to Greece, Italy and Portugal, but growers in Germany, Holland and the UK were determined to displace us.

An outbreak of potato blight in Prince Edward Island brought a blanket prohibition by the European Community of all seed potatoes from Canada. We protested that we were a big country and were taking measures within our own borders to quarantine the small areas affected, but our representations fell on deaf ears. Portugal and Greece worked hard to get a derogation (as it was called) from the ban, but were only successful for a year or two at a time. The handwriting was on the wall.

My last story had a different outcome. Another of our export specialties is Holstein breeding cattle. Representatives of a Portuguese co-operative from the old province of Tras-as-Montes visited Canada and decided that they wished to buy a herd from us. Northern Europeans heard about it and made the usual behind-the- scenes representations. The co-operative had friends, however, across the border in Spain who purchased the cattle in Canada, imported them and drove them over to their friends.

I have described the Portuguese as gentle, but the Spaniards are less so. Certainly the European Community did not intimidate them. Spain, however, was bigger, wealthier and less dependent on European Community subsidies.

Each year Canada took a booth at the trade fair at Santarem in Ribotejo province, about one hundred kilometres north and east of Lisbon. In many ways it reminded me of the Ottawa Exhibition that I had known as a child with its exhibits of fruits, vegetables, flowers and agricultural implements. The fair was a festive occasion attended by families who patronised the food booths and midway attractions. We were a popular spot, with many coming to ask all sorts of questions about Canada.

THE CULTURAL SECTION

Our cultural section kept busy promoting the distribution of Canadian films and educational materials, attending film festivals and occasionally sponsoring showings by Canadian artists. Unfortunately, I was out of the country when Dr. and Mrs. Jack Firestone opened a showing in Lisbon of works of the Group of Seven from their famous collection. Historically, French has been the second language of Portugal, and film producers, musicians and other artists from Quebec visited more frequently than similar persons from English-speaking Canada. In the last two decades, however, largely due to American influence, English has displaced French as the second language in the schools.

TRIAL OF TERRORISTS

One curious tie between groups in Canada and Portugal undoubtedly existed. Portugal developed a small group of terrorists who had friends in the Front de Libération du Québec in Canada. Their beliefs were essentially anarchist, as far as I could determine. Some sixty-five were brought before the courts in a mass trial, including a young priest in whose house terrorists had stayed. Evidence was produced that members of the group had fired mortars against NATO warships visiting Lisbon from a mobile launcher of some sort, likely a truck. The operators were, however, inexperienced and missed their targets. Banks were robbed to provide funds and a few bombs actually caused casualties, including deaths.

These acts had taken place over some years and the Portuguese authorities had painstakingly accumulated their evidence. Meanwhile, petitions were circulated in Canada asking that all charges be dropped against the young priest and many thousands of signatures were secured, including that of a bishop. The petitions suggested that the whole trial was a fraud.

At this stage, I went to the Papal Nuncio, who was the head of the diplomatic corps in Lisbon, and asked his opinion about the case against the young priest. Had he, as the representative of the Vatican, made any representations to the Government of Portugal on the trial? No. Did he intend to do so? Again, a firm no. Finally, he turned to me, saying in a clear voice: "This rash young man will have to face the consequences of his actions."

I reported the conversation to Ottawa, with the recommendation that it would be offensive for the Government of Canada to suggest in any way that it was supporting the petitions. That seemed to end the matter as far as Canada was concerned. The young priest was convicted of abetting the terrorists and served a term in prison.

LIFE IN LISBON

Occasionally in Lisbon, we suffered from minor annoyances. The garage of our official residence in Restello opened on a side street and signs (called *placas*) were placed to prohibit parking blocking our entrance. One day they disappeared. How could this be? I went to city hall to be told that it was a temporary inconvenience as the *placas* were being repainted.

Meanwhile, street parkers totally blocked the garage and we could seldom use our cars. If we did get one out, frequently it had to sit on the street overnight, a most inadvisable procedure in Lisbon. I went to the mayor, to be greeted with apologies and assurances that matters would be set right. The dean of the diplomatic corps was no more helpful.

A week later, in dire frustration, I telexed Ottawa, asking for advice. A formal protest was lodged with the ministry of foreign affairs in Lisbon. Again, nothing happened.

I mentioned my problem to my good friend Admiral Antonio Andrade Silva, who directed me to his friend the chief of the national police. The *placas* were restored the next morning.

A few days later, I received a telex from Ottawa. It seems the ambassador for Portugal in Ottawa had been having problems with parking for his embassy on Island Park Drive. A partial solution had been worked out. Tit for tat? Or was it just coincidence?

I have already mentioned that we had no count of the number of Portuguese who had emigrated to Canada, taken out citizenship and returned to their homeland for their remaining years. However, they could easily be spotted. To indicate to their neighbours their prosperity, they often constructed the biggest house in the village. But, on their passing, no member of the family was left in the village to occupy it. Such a structure could be easily recognised in small communities and was known as one of the *casas dos emigrantes* (houses of emigrants). Returning workers from many countries, including others in the European Union, did the same thing.

Two expatriate Canadians became good friends. Dorothy Osborne (a cousin of Walter Gordon, who had been the minister of Finance) had served her career in the foreign service of Canada. Just as she was contemplating retirement, she fell in love with an American career diplomat, Ted Xanthaky, and married him. Together they built their dream home some twenty kilometres south of Lisbon, near Azeitao. It had everything—spacious open rooms, a swimming pool, a hectare of land on which they had planted orange, lemon and fig trees. A live-in Portuguese couple looked after the garden in which she grew North American corn, the only time we tasted it in Portugal.

Dorothy and Ted had a few years together, but he had died prior to our arrival. She had bouts of ill health, and stayed with us for a few days following one admission to the British Hospital. After we left the country, a succession of strokes wore her down and she died in January 1993.

Collette Wilson was born in Ottawa, the sister of Charles Le Royer, who had worked with me in the Department of National Health and Welfare in the 1950s. She had married an Australian pilot who worked for an international airline. For some years they were based in Geneva, where they raised a family of two girls. For retirement, they built a home in the Algarve ("Casa Collette"), near Porsches Velho, in a semi-rural area about a kilometre from the sea. Like Dorothy, she had lost her husband prior to our arrival but had taken up with a retired British army officer. Collette died in 1991.

For Canadians contemplating retirement in Portugal, the language is a formidable barrier. A knowledge of French is helpful and Spanish even more so. For those with the talent to learn Portuguese, no country offers more pleasant accommodation at reasonable cost, as Dorothy Xanthaky assured me. Our CSIS officer in Lisbon, Ken Perkins, and his Argentine-born wife, Lucinda, for example, have recently retired to a country place in the Alentejo.

I believe that the Portuguese gave Canada its name. When the Corte Real brothers sailed up the St. Lawrence River they were really turned off by the bleak and rocky north shore and wrote on their charts "*ca—nada*" (translation: "here—nothing"). I joked with my Portuguese friends saying that, if the brothers had travelled further up the St. Lawrence, they would have written: "*ca—tudo*" (translation: "here—everything"), and I would have then been known as a CATUDIAN instead of a CANADIAN.

To this day the word "*canada*" is used in the Azores for a cul-de-sac, a street that does not go anywhere.

The diplomatic community in Lisbon represented about ninety nations. We made many friends. Some names I can remember, but others, because of language, I cannot recall exactly. Ita and Jim Perkins of Ireland and Leopold Quarles van Ufford of The Netherlands as well as the ambassador for Greece, were close to us. The jovial Italian ambassador and his Swedish wife always made us welcome. The ambassador for Turkey on our arrival was a retired general of my age who had survived the Armenian assault and it was easy to establish a bond with him. His successors, a young couple who appeared to be recent graduates of the French Sorbonne, were a total contrast and we saw little of them. The Swiss ambassador, M. Moret and his Ottawa-born wife, Betty, were charming. The wife of the Swedish ambassador was, like myself, an amateur lapidary and we shared this interest. The Mexican ambassador, Sr. Casanova, was a retired professor who told delightful stories.

We enjoyed the best of relations with a number of countries of the Commonwealth: Australia, Nigeria, Zambia, Pakistan and India and, of course, the United Kingdom, to many of whose events we were regularly invited. The Burgis Khans of Pakistan and the Haksars of India were the best of friends, and I suspected they had studied in the same schools before the partition of their sub-continent.

South Africa was also represented by an older couple, Mr. and Mrs. Pretorius. Because of apartheid, they were ostracised in many circles. Margery and I got to know them and both indicated discreetly to us that they felt their country had to change its ways. When it came time to leave and their tour was over, we attended their farewell party. One officer of our staff who knew the Pretoriuses as well as we did, refused to attend, citing departmental policy. I was embarrassed. We maintained formal relations with South Africa and surely we should at least be polite on such occasions.

In 1986, Queen Elizabeth and Prince Philip made a state visit to Portugal on the royal yacht *Britannia*. Along with other members of the diplomatic corps, I was presented to them at a formal reception in one of Lisbon's palaces. It was not easy to explain to the ambassador for Colombia beside me that she was also my queen, although she never travelled outside the United Kingdom in that capacity.

The queen invited representatives of the Commonwealth to a state dinner on board the *Britannia*. Prior to the dinner, we were presented to her. She had been informed of my previous experience as Speaker, and we agreed that any Speaker, unlike the recent example in the United Kingdom, should wait a discreet interval before publishing his memoirs. (I hope fifteen years is enough.) She made one feel completely at ease. As I passed to Prince Philip, he commented on my tie, which had been given to me by the Speaker for the legislature of the Northwest Territories, and depicted a polar bear. "You kill those bears and you should not."

"Your Highness, our northern indigenous peoples have been killing them for thousands of years. We now have them on a permit-to-kill system. We carefully monitor the numbers of the bears, and they are not declining. We believe that we are acting responsibly."

"You also kill whales and you should not."

This was too much for me and I blurted out: "Your Highness, it is difficult for me as a North American to accept a moral lecture from a

European. You have killed off so much of your wild life. There is not a single bear left on this Iberian Peninsula."

He turned and walked away. The conversation ended.

Back to the diplomatic corps in Lisbon. For some time, the American embassy had a chargé d'affaires, Alan Flanigan, whose wife Beverley was born in Winnipeg. A thoroughly competent career officer, he was widely respected and liked. The ambassador that was subsequently appointed proved to be a most curious fellow.

Frank Shakespeare was named by President Reagan. Previously, he had been head of the United States Information Service. A fanatical anti-communist, he refused to shake hands with representatives of countries behind the Iron Curtain. On one occasion, he solemnly told me that the Russians were systematically destroying their churches according to formula. They would target a church, then arrange for it to be demolished within a twenty-four hour period before any protest could be raised.

The United States Embassy carries a great deal of prestige in Lisbon, as it does elsewhere, and Shakespeare was invited to address the diplomatic corps at a luncheon. News had just leaked to the press how President Regan had found the means to purchase arms for the "contras" in Central America without having to seek approval for the funds from Congress. Shakespeare proudly cited these events as proof of America's devotion to the fight against communism. Many of my Latin American colleagues were clearly uneasy and the silence that greeted his words spoke for itself. I decided to speak up.

"Mr. Ambassador, I represent Canada, your ally in two world wars, in the Korean campaign, your partner in the North Atlantic Treaty Organization and North American Air Defence. We are your best customer and I believe your best friend, but I must set the record straight for those assembled here today. Canada has not participated in your contra operation and does not approve of it. America has embarrassed us."

Later that afternoon, the Portuguese minister of Foreign Affairs called our embassy to express his approval of my remarks. Had my minister, Joe Clark, been there, his words would have been even stronger.

Shakespeare was a devout Catholic and on one occasion told me he attended mass every morning. He was, however, divorced. Not long afterwards, he was appointed envoy to the Vatican, which must have pleased the embassy staff in Lisbon as much as it did him.

The ambassador for the USSR was, like myself, a grandfather. He and his wife kept their grandson with them in Lisbon, rather than have the boy stay with his parents who were on duty in Lebanon. On one occasion, he asked me about unemployment in Canada. I replied that regretfully, it exceeded ten per cent of the labour force. No doubt he was going to tell me that there was no unemployment in his country.

The USSR ambassador paused, then replied carefully: "I would not put it that way. Officially, we have no unemployment, but we have many people who do not work. For example, the last man posted to me from Moscow does not know the meaning of the word."

"Why do you not simply have him sent home?"

"I cannot be that foolish. This man is sly and capable of finding his way into the section to which I have to report."

For some strange reason, it made me think of one or two cabinet ministers in Ottawa, whose success was due more to wits than to industry.

We counted the Polish ambassador and his wife as good friends. Olga, a Russian, had met her big teddy bear Boguslaw, a Pole, while they were students in China. Like us, they had a grown family that they had left behind in Poland. On one occasion, I offered her a gift of a small stone cross that I had polished from pink British Columbia rhodenite, which could be worn as a pendant. Her reaction was a quick smile, a thank you and a simple statement: "I am a Christian."

I reported the incident to Frank Shakespeare, hoping that it might persuade him to change his ways a little. Not all diplomats from behind the Iron Curtain were devils. Shakespeare had a simple response: "Do you think that they will defect?"

The Chinese ambassador and I shared the experience of having taken classes from the same man, Professor Frank Coe. An American, he had taught economic theory in our second year at Toronto. Although he gave no indication of having radical opinions, for some reason he had been called before Senator McCarthy's Committee on Un-American Activities, and received a dreadful press. Coe then simply resigned and accepted a post at a university in China where he spent the rest of his days.

We had numerous visitors from overseas, which I place in three categories. The first and by far the most numerous were our family and friends from Canada and the United States, whom we were delighted to see. Paul and Marie, with their children Elizabeth, David and Marnie, were followed by Elaine and her twins, Casey and Andrew, and Donald and Helene with their two, Margo and Michael. Margery's cousin, Marion Beale, and her husband Bob, who had given the wedding reception for us in 1943, also came. Vivien Dzau and a friend visited, as well as my cousin Irene Hannahson. We greeted Charles and Pauline Scott from Ottawa, Frank and Eleanor Genovese from Massachusetts, Ed and Phyllis Young and Bob and Jo-Ann Lampman from Wisconsin.

We were honoured to host Madame Léger, the widow of a former governor general, Mitchell and Jeanette Sharp and Jean and Aline

Son Paul Francis and family: daughter Marnie, wife Marie, son David, daughter Elizabeth

Chrétien, as well as a number of MPs and former MPs. Our good friend from Inter-Parliamentary Union days, Steve Paproski, chaired a delegation. John Fraser visited as minister of Fisheries. Mel Jack's son, Don, stayed with us for a weekend on his honeymoon.[132] The list went on and on.

In 1986, my old friends from University of Toronto days, Don and Barbara Blackley, came to see us. Don was a professor of medieval history at the University of Alberta in Edmonton. By coincidence, our older son Paul, whose undergraduate degree had been in history, was in Lisbon at the same time. Don and Barbara, Paul, Marie and their daughter Marnie (who had been injured in a near-tragic accident in a swimming pool), took off in our Mercedes for a "castle crawl" (as they called it) in the north of Portugal.

In the second category, I place a number of people who just showed up, in some cases bluntly asking if they could stay with us, although we scarcely knew them. If we could accommodate them, we did, although prior commitments to other people sometimes obliged us to refuse. A

132 Mel Jack, well known as George Hees's assistant, had been a friend since our introduction by Robert McKeown in the 1960s. He lived within the boundaries of old Carleton. In one election, a Liberal attempted to ingratiate himself by describing his strenuous efforts to neutralise Mel. Little did he know that Mel had made a financial contribution to my campaign that day and never lifted a finger against me. Politics has a seamy side!

daughter of a senator arrived with two male friends, who left us with some horrendous long distance telephone bills, which we paid personally. The divorced wife of a former colleague at Buffalo stayed for over three weeks, with constant stories of how her plans to travel in Spain were upset.

On another occasion, the daughter of a former colleague on Ottawa City Council arrived with three male friends on bicycles before Christmas one year, cold and exhausted after their long ride from Spain. We were pleased to accommodate all four over Christmas and New Year's, expecting them to move on. Instead, they made short trips out of Lisbon, coming back to the embassy each time. After a further three weeks had passed, I indicated that it was time to move. The last to go, after returning from a trip to the Azores, had to be told bluntly that he was no longer welcome.

Son Don Francis and family: wife Hélène, daughter Margo and son Michael

You may remember that my mother came from a large family in England. One of her sisters had married a Welshman and raised four daughters. Two of these, Grace and Mabel, had visited Ottawa. One sister died. The remaining three asked to come to Lisbon and we accepted them, although it overlapped with a visit from Bob and Marion Beale. It was a pleasant visit, but a bit of a shock when one of Mabel's sons, whom we had never met, asked to come with his wife. At this time Margery was very ill and we were overloaded with visitors. He repeated his request, saying that they would pick up a rented car in Lisbon. I met them at the airport (after paging them) brought them to the embassy for dinner and the night. After breakfast the next morning, I suggested that they should pick up their rented car. Some weeks later, we received a note thanking us for the "short stay" and have never heard from them since.

In February 1987, I received a note from my minister, the Rt. Hon. Joe Clark, suggesting that he would like to create some vacancies at the ambassador level, and what would be my reaction to terminating my appointment in six months? Lisbon was a most desirable post and I was a political appointment. Clearly the date was negotiable and I had to think about it.

At this stage, my wife's health was a major concern. Her illness had been diagnosed as sarcoidosis, a condition that could remain stable for a long period. She coughed incessantly, however, and I began to have doubts about the diagnosis. In January, on returning from a trip to the north, I hit an obstacle in the road and we had to make the rest of the journey back to Lisbon by bus. Margery caught a bad cold, which lingered for months.

With great reluctance, I made the decision to terminate as Joe had suggested. The wisdom of this decision became quickly apparent. In the spring, we returned to Canada as part of the celebration of the first direct flight by TAP,[133] the national Portuguese airline, from Lisbon to Toronto. While I was speaking to the Portuguese community in Toronto, Margery consulted with her doctors in Ottawa. She returned to Lisbon with me, but I later discovered that Dr. Peter MacLeod had done his best to dissuade her, preferring to put her in hospital immediately in Ottawa.

Margery's health deteriorated rapidly. By June it was an effort for her to walk any distance. On July 1, she stood beside me as we greeted our guests

133 The inaugural flight was the result of a treaty which had been negotiated into the small hours of the morning in our residence in Lisbon. Randolph Gherson was the Canadian negotiator. Prior to 1987, TAP flew directly to Mirabel only, serving basically the Portuguese community in Montreal. As the community in Toronto grew larger, TAP was understandably anxious to fly to that city.

at the reception for our national day, but it was clearly an effort. We had agreed on a departure date of August 31, and our daughter Elaine came to Lisbon to help Margery with the packing. By the end of July, she was counting the days until her return. In August, she counted the hours.

In this period we received a request from a reporter for the *Ottawa Citizen*, whom I had known since city hall days, to visit us with his wife. I had to telephone him in London, saying that we were preparing to return to Canada and could not accommodate his visit. Why were we going back, he asked. Basically, because of my wife's health. Clearly, he did not believe me. Had I had a difference of opinion with the Government of Canada? No. What was I going to do? I was not sure, but among other things I

Daughter Elaine Francis with twin sons Andrew and Casey

wanted to reflect on some things that had given me concern in Europe, such as our immigration and trade policies.

The reporter wrote a scurrilous article saying that Joe Clark was firing me because I disagreed with basic policies of the government. Nothing could have been further from the truth. I prepared my exit documents, and extensive briefing notes for my successor, Geoffrey Bruce. The department had assessed my performance as above average and given me bonuses over my basic pay. As far as the Rt. Hon. Joe Clark was concerned, our relations have always been cordial, and remain so to this day.

Part 5

RETURNING TO CANADA

AS THE AIRCRAFT carrying us back to Canada took off, we looked down on Lisbon. We followed the beaches west of Cascais, where we had spent many happy hours, and the roads around the mountain of Sintra. Below us we could still imagine the nasturtiums and geraniums that grow wild in the fields of Portugal and which people so carefully cultivate in their gardens in Canada. The solid blue masses of morning glory flowers that cover every wall and rock face with a southern exposure are taken for granted by the Portuguese and are an unforgettable sight to us. We had many pleasant memories.

Our family rented a bus and took us from the airport at Mirabel to Ottawa. Margery was quickly taken to hospital, where her illness was diagnosed as fibrosis of the lungs, not sarcoidosis. After discharge, she was immediately placed on oxygen, which brought relief, especially to her coughing. I was present when she asked Dr. MacLeod when she would be rid of the oxygen. The answer: Never. She then asked how much time she had left to her. His reply: Hopefully, three years.

Margery took the news calmly and thanked her doctor. We made our plans. Hospital is a lonely place, especially at night and we agreed that she would spend her last days at home. This involved a large oxygen tank, replenished at first every three days and later daily, as the dosage increased. The Victorian Order of Nurses and a visiting housekeeper were invaluable. I made sure she got her pills on time and later gave her insulin shots after the medication made her diabetic.

We did succeed in making two trips in a station wagon that I purchased, which would secure an oxygen tank. We visited Dunnville where she entered the old home at 334 Broad Street West, now inhabited by Dr. Richard Hesler and his wife Penny. She met her childhood friends, Hazel and Ewart Cass, and a distant cousin, Don Rowe, with whom I had gone fishing in Lake Erie for pickerel in our days at Buffalo. We visited the cemetery where her family members are buried. We made a trip to Toronto for the eightieth birthday celebration of Bob Beale, and to Hamilton to see for the last time the only surviving member of her mother's family, Aunt "Dot" Luxton.

It was a long, slow, downhill trip for her. In her last month, she asked to be allowed to die, not wishing to continue as she was. At 6:00 p.m. on Sunday, December 10, 1989, I left her so I could prepare a sandwich for my dinner, and when I came back ten minutes later, she was dead.

As Margery lay in her coffin in the funeral parlour of Hulse, Playfair and McGarry, Governor General Jeanne Sauvé called to pay her respects. This was the only time that I had seen her in the two years and three months since our return. Maurice Riel, the Speaker of the Senate, was a close

Lloyd and Mary with Carmo and Antonio Andrade Silva from Portugal

friend of Jeanne[134] and gave her a distorted account of our trip to China, alleging that I had made disloyal remarks about her. Riel's comments were completely untrue.

Retirement and Margery's death were a double shock from which I recovered slowly. Our house was too big and too full of memories. I had to distribute to our children her personal effects and most of the treasures that we had accumulated over our forty-six years. In addition, it was necessary to sort the mountains of papers accumulated from four municipal and nine federal campaigns. Eventually, I sold the house and moved into a new place near the Experimental Farm.

ADJUSTMENT TO A NEW LIFE IN RETIREMENT

My new home contains in the basement a lapidary workshop in which I have spent many happy hours. A hobby itself can be useful therapy and I found participating in the annual shows of the Ottawa Lapsmith Club a challenge to produce my best work for display. In this activity I was joined by Mary Penner, a woman fourteen years my junior, and the former wife of a colleague in the House of Commons. We were married in October 1992. Our extended family now includes her daughters Catherine and Eleanor, her son Ralph, and their families.

---

[134] Senator Riel delivered the eulogy at Jeanne Sauvé's funeral.

We spent our honeymoon in Portugal, staying in *pousadas* and visiting friends like Admiral Antonio Andrade Silva and his wife Carmo, and the former Social Democratic member of the *Assembleia*, Guido Rodrigues, and his wife Maria.

Mary and I enjoy salmon fishing, which my son, Paul, arranges on charter boats operating from the Port of Wellington on the Quinte peninsula on the shores of Lake Ontario. The invasion of our Great Lakes by lamprey eels almost destroyed the lake trout population and the bait fish—alewives, herring and smelt—expanded greatly in numbers. The Americans introduced Chinook salmon by stocking, first in Lake Michigan, then other lakes, to feed on the bait fish. The results were spectacular, with specimens in excess of forty pounds. Other species were then added—cohoes, steelheads, rainbows and, not least, the Atlantic salmon that had been so numerous in colonial times but had disappeared with the destruction of their spawning grounds. Meanwhile, the Canadian authorities joined the restocking program, but most of the fish we were catching had strayed from American waters. On her first trip, Mary caught a thirty-pound salmon and later the same day one over twenty-four pounds. Her brother, Hugh Gemmell, on his first trip caught a Chinook in excess of thirty-seven pounds, which he had mounted.

Fishing for salmon in Lake Ontario, July 1996: Lloyd, son Paul, Judge Yves Forest

My post-retirement activities fall into three categories: voluntary services with organizations in North America, a few international assignments, and lastly, private travel, usually associated with the lapidary hobby that Mary and I share. In addition, I assist members of my family in various business enterprises.

THE ASSOCIATION OF CANADIAN CLUBS

As I had indicated to the *Citizen* reporter, I eventually published a few articles describing my concerns about Canada's immigration policy.

In brief, the quality of fraudulent documents is now such that it is not fair to punish the transportation companies that carry illegal immigrants to our shores. While we must maintain our policy of accepting refugees, we should give a priority to those persons accepted as refugees by the United Nations High Commissioner.

Most important, Canada should tighten its passport regulations and take every precaution against becoming a haven for terrorists, drug dealers, those wishing to launder dirty money and plain criminals. A recent decision written by Supreme Court Justice Madam Bertha Wilson extended the protection of our Charter of Rights and Freedoms to any human being in our country, regardless of whether he or she had arrived legally or illegally. This meant that any applicant for landed immigrant status, if he or she had the means (and most undesirables have the means), could carry their appeal to the Federal Court, over a period of up to three years. The longer they stay, the harder it is to deport them. Frequently such a person marries a Canadian citizen, has a child, becomes an active church member and gets acquainted with the press.

I was an MP when the Charter of Rights and Freedoms was adopted. Never at any time did I think that its protection would be extended to illegal entrants, nor did any other MP of the time, to whom I have spoken. I believe this decision to be a bad one, but how can it be corrected? Not by a simple act of Parliament it seems, since this decision is now part of our constitution. Something, however, must be done.

The National Association of Canadian Clubs invited me to speak to member clubs on the subject, and I spoke to over twenty from Victoria, BC, to Grand-mère, Quebec. The first of these invitations came in 1988 and they continued after Margery's death.

After my speech, a reception was held in the Auberge Grand-mère. A woman came up to me and asked if I had been attached to the Royal Air Force in Honiley. I looked hard. It was Audrey, a motor transport driver that I had dated fifty years previously. She had married one of my fellow radar mechanics and returned to Canada with him. Her husband had gone back to university, taken an engineering degree and then worked for the paper mill. Together they had raised a family of three, none of whom made their home in Quebec. Windows from our past!

STATESMAN IN RESIDENCE, BABSON COLLEGE, WELLESLEY, MASSACHUSETTS

For the spring semester of 1992, Frank Genovese, my old friend from post-graduate days at Toronto and Wisconsin, arranged an appointment for me at Babson College in Wellesley, a business school not far from Boston. At that time Frank was the retired dean of Arts and Science and he and his wife, Eleanor, jointly edited the *American Journal of Economics and Sociology*.

Babson was founded by Roger Babson, who endowed the college with several hundred acres of land that became progressively more valuable as urban settlement extended. The college received a minimum of state grants and was largely supported by high tuition fees. The calibre of its faculty was, on the whole, superior as far as I could judge.

The appointment worked wonders in rehabilitating me from a long period of depression. It was good to attend general meetings of the faculty, reminding me of the University of Buffalo many years before. I had been away from university life too long, however. I gave a few special lectures on Canada and attended a few seminars, but did not have the careful notes for lectures that I once possessed. Part of the time I stayed with Frank and

Lloyd with Eleanor and Frank Genovese

Eleanor and the rest of the time in an apartment on campus. Mary Penner came down for a weekend and accepted my proposal of marriage.

My younger brother, Jack, was still a professor of food sciences at the University of Massachusetts in Amherst, some 250 miles distant, and we exchanged visits. Frank and Eleanor took me to Boston to visit Ed Bernays, then in his hundredth year, a nephew of Sigmund Freud. Ed had been an assistant to President Wilson at Versailles and was an acknowledged expert in public relations. His mind was still vigorous and clear.

THE OTTAWA HISTORICAL SOCIETY

For some time I had been a member of the Ottawa Historical Society, and on my return was elected for a term as president. The society sponsored public meetings with speakers that had studied Ottawa from its earliest days, and published a number of their papers. In addition, it operated the Bytown Museum in an old building that had once served as the commissary for Colonel John By, the builder of the Rideau Canal a century-and-a-half ago. The museum is beautifully located beside the locks descending to the Ottawa River, in the ravine between Parliament Hill and the Chateau Laurier.

Lloyd and Mary with Vivien Dzau

As a policy, the museum has accepted gifts of artifacts relating to local history and has been obliged to rent a substantial amount of storage space. It is physically impossible to display all of the artifacts at once and every effort is made to rotate the exhibits. Ottawa's winter, however, restricts the operation of the museum to part of the year.

The Ottawa Historical Society contributes funds for the care of Colonel By's grave in Frant, Sussex. In May 1997, Mary and I joined a tour sponsored by the society to visit Frant and nearby places in the southeast of England. We also attended the unveiling of a tablet in London to commemorate By's birthplace.

The Royal Bank of Canada chose Robert Legget, former head of building research for the National Research Council, one of the pillars of the Ottawa Historical Society and a universally acknowledged expert on Colonel By, to receive its special annual reward, worth $50,000. As one of the guests, I shared a table at the dinner with Senator Eugene Forsey, Ivan Head, former special assistant to Prime Minister Trudeau, and Dr. and Mme. François Genest from Montreal. Dr. Genest wore the insignia of Officer of the Order of Canada, as a result of his efforts in the field of medical research.

A toast to the queen was offered, but the Genests did not rise. I asked him why and he replied: "She is not my queen."

"I can understand why someone can be uncomfortable with our present arrangements with the monarchy. In Lisbon, as the ambassador for Canada, I was presented to the Queen of England on the same basis as all the rest of the diplomatic corps. She never travels outside of England in the capacity of queen of Canada. My problem is that I do not know how to change it and whom I would substitute for the head of state."

"It is simple. Quebec should be a republic. I do not care what the rest of you do."

Then Genest taunted Senator Forsey: "You are a well-known monarchist and no doubt I am offending you."

Forsey replied that indeed he was a monarchist and further, he just could not see that an elected president would fit Canada. If Quebec were to secede, what would happen to the French language in the remaining provinces? For that matter, what would happen to Quebec as an island surrounded by an English-speaking sea?

Genest replied that he was not at all worried; he had spent some years with a medical centre in Boston, and Quebec would join the United States. Americans loved French Canadians, respected them and would grant Quebec the same special language status that Puerto Rico enjoys for Spanish.

I could hardly believe my ears. "You really WANT TO BE LIKE PUERTO RICO?" I asked incredulously.

"Yes," he replied. "You have persecuted us for over two hundred years." This, from a man wearing the Order of Canada insignia. I could not resist a final parting shot. "Maybe we will all join the United States. In that case, those speaking English will have a definite advantage."

Ethnic nationalism is a disease of the mind in this decade, affecting people from Ireland to Yugoslavia and many other places. It does not respect social position, education or how people have prospered. I fail to understand it and if there are many people like the Genests, I fear for Canada. At Versailles, US President Woodrow Wilson had coined the phrase "self-determination of nations" (Ed Bernays told me that it was his suggestion), and used this as the rationale for breaking up the Austro-Hungarian Empire. Since that genie was released from the bottle, it has assumed many malevolent forms.

THE RIDEAU CANAL MUSEUM

David Baird had spent many years in the public service of Canada and, independently, developing a different concept of museums.

Essentially, they did not just display artifacts but told a story with extended use of dioramas. For this work he had received the Order of Canada.

Without question, Baird's best work is to be seen in the Royal Tyrell Museum of Palaeontology in Drumheller, Alberta. Over a period of four years he had developed the story of Alberta's Badlands, how they had changed over geological periods and how they must have looked at the time of the dinosaurs whose bones are now being exposed. The museum is an incomparable tool for the teaching of earth sciences, geology, palaeontology and biology.

David Baird had a summer place on the Rideau Lakes, where he became acquainted with Hamilton Southam, of the family that owned a series of Canadian newspapers. Hamilton, now retired, had risen to the rank of ambassador in the foreign service of Canada and had chaired the board that supervised the construction of the National Arts Centre in Ottawa and guided it through its formative years. He and David developed the concept of a museum to tell the story of the building of the Rideau Canal. Smiths Falls, halfway between Ottawa and Kingston, was the logical location and an old stone mill that once manufactured agricultural implements, adjacent to the canal itself, was available.

Hamilton invited my old friend and family lawyer, Charles Scott, and myself to join the board. The building had been abandoned for decades, but with the aid of federal and provincial grants as well as donations from the public, the Rideau Canal Museum emerged. Many of the cottagers in the Rideau Lakes live in Ottawa and responded to our appeal. Scott and I enjoyed our trips to Smiths Falls for meetings over a period of two years. For more than half a century we had been travelling the Rideau Waterway, as Legget had properly described it, and were pleased to see see its story so graphically recorded for future generations.

ELECTIONS OBSERVER IN SRI LANKA, 1993, 1994 AND 1999

I had visited Sri Lanka in 1975 with a parliamentary delegation. At the time, it was clear that the unfortunate country was eroding its democratic heritage. Terror—both from the Sinhalese majority and Tamil minority—has since become a feature of Sri Lankan life.

One day in April 1993, I received a telephone call from the high commissioner for Sri Lanka in Ottawa. Would I like to join a team of international observers for the elections to the provincial councils to be held in May?

Before accepting, I checked with External Affairs, only to learn that Canada did not like to have the expenses for such services by our citizens paid by the host country. Canada had a formula for such occasions and was prepared to send a full team at our country's expense if so requested. The high commissioner amended his request to Canada accordingly.

Unfortunately, the minister, the Hon. Barbara MacDougall, was out of Canada and the prospective team could not be officially confirmed.

Meanwhile, the leader of a major opposition party in Sri Lanka, a Mr. Athulathmudali, was assassinated. The high commissioner called to say that the elections would proceed and was I still interested? Time was running short and the government of Sri Lanka wanted to have the international team in place in time for briefings. I gave him my assurance that, in any case, I would accept the invitation.

A few days later the president of Sri Lanka, Mr. Premadasa, was assassinated. Barbara MacDougall had not yet returned to Ottawa. The high commissioner was extremely concerned, and I agreed to let him purchase my airline ticket.

A representative from External Affairs, learning of my decision, asked if I could represent Canada in the ceremony of lighting the funeral pyre in Colombo for the president. I agreed.

Within hours of my departure, I was informed that the Hon. Flora MacDonald would be Canada's representative at the ceremony. Unknown to me at the time, she had been Canada's representative on the previous observers team, but for reasons known only to the Sri Lankans, had not been invited this time.

We met at the airport in Frankfurt, where we changed to Air Lanka for the balance of the trip. As it turned out, I was the only passenger in first class while Flora was in executive class. You can imagine how that ruffled her feathers!

We were met at the airport by Canada's high commissioner, who took Flora to the official residence. An assistant drove me to the hotel where the team was assembled. To my pleasant surprise, the Chair was an old acquaintance, the Hon. Douglas McClelland, former president (Speaker) of the Australian Senate, whom I had met at least twice at conferences of Speakers of the Commonwealth.

The next day I watched the ceremonies on television. McClelland, who was representing Australia, told me that, at the moment the flame was lit, Flora had stepped out of the line, kneeled and taken pictures, no doubt for her TV program at home. To say the least, it was gauche.

The Sri Lankans had prepared excellent briefings, describing their procedures for an election based on proportional representation by province, with each party nominating a slate. Parties were identified on the ballot by symbols. Their election officials were certainly as competent as ours in Canada. Representatives of the security forces outlined their precautionary measures, with 30,000 members scheduled for duty on election day. We were each assigned to a district and, possibly by coincidence, I was assigned to Ratnapura, the gem district. I say possibly, because the student whom we had sponsored, Chantal, now Mrs. De Saram and the mother of a small son, had called me after arrival and verified my continuing interest in lapidary. In Sri Lanka, a handful of families know each other and have their own ways of getting things done.

There were no further incidents of terror, although the possibility was on everyone's mind. The official report of the election observers for the 1991 election mentioned that in one poll with no votes recorded by noon, terrorists had shot the first three persons in line and strung up their bodies for all to see.

Chantal entertained me at a dinner party with a number of local people, including journalists. Gradually, I pieced together a story. Foreign observers had erroneously assumed that the political assassinations were the work of the Tamil Tigers. It seems that President Premadasa had started well, from humble beginnings, but took kickbacks from construction contracts and amassed wealth abroad. When his colleagues found out, he eliminated them one by one, becoming ever more ruthless and finally resorting to assassinations. Some of his cabinet colleagues tried to bring an impeachment motion,

Lloyd with the former president of the Australian Senate, The Hon. Douglas McClelland and his wife, Lorna

but the Speaker ruled it out of order and the courts refused to act. They then formed a new political party, the Democratic United National Front, to contest first the provincial elections, then others. When they started to achieve success, Premadasa had their leader assassinated. The opposition then knew they had no option and assassinated Premadasa. Shades of Robespierre, the Terror and the French Revolution! Since then, the Terror ceased, peace returned and the government party had chosen a new and respected leader.

One of the United States observers, James Lowenstein, had hinted to me of this. He pulled out a notebook listing 200 suspicious assassinations in the previous eighteen months. Lowenstein and his colleague Gilbert Sheinbaum knew Sri Lanka well and were a great asset to the international team.

Each of us had an armed bodyguard and liaison officer. My liaison officer was a university professor who did not want to have his name mentioned in any document or report. My bodyguard was a career member of the security forces. Some three years previously, during the suppression of an attempted Buddhist insurrection, he had been shot four times and spent six months recovering in a Japanese hospital. I came to like him, finding him to be trustworthy, serious and good company.

Shortly before election day, a team comprising the chief elections officer of Ontario and a worker in Barbara MacDougall's constituency office arrived. They were too late for most of the briefings and, as far as I could judge, not much help to the Sri Lankans. Our high commissioner held a reception in his residence for them but did not invite me. This was a most unusual act for a career diplomat and I suspected Flora's fine hand in it. She clearly resented the decision by the government of Sri Lanka to invite me to join the observer team, instead of her. I was the only member of the international team not to be hosted by the representative of his country.

The team comprised, in addition to the two Americans, three Canadians and McClelland from Australia; two capable retired diplomats from India, Gurbachan Singh and Eric Gonsalves; a retired supreme court justice from Pakistan and another from Bangladesh; two members of the British parliament; and others from India, Bangladesh, Nepal, France and Germany, who were less experienced, for a total of twenty-five persons. We were compatible and I thoroughly enjoyed the experience.

For two days prior to the election, we visited polls to see what preparations had been made. On a tea plantation high on a mountain, a colony of Tamils whose ancestors had been brought from India over a hundred years ago were scheduled to vote some six kilometres or more away. It bothered me, but I was assured that every single voter would walk the distance to vote and, according to their elections act, it would have been an offence for a political party to offer them transportation. I made as much contact as possible with representatives of the political parties.

One man who was on the slate of a minor leftist party refused to come to see me, but was reported to be full of complaints. I made a special trip to visit him in his home in the middle of a large rice paddy to ask about his concerns. He was speechless to see me go to such efforts to meet him.

On election day, the turnout of voters was high, almost eighty per cent. No attempt was made to conduct the election in the Tamil-held areas of Jaffna in the north and Trincomalee in the east. In my district, only a few minor incidents were reported, involving alleged impersonation of voters, destruction of posters, and illegal use of government vehicles. There were no incidents of intimidation or terror, in spite of allegations before the vote that some parties had access to firearms. I visited as many polls as possible from the hour of opening to the close. The count of ballots took place in a large centrally located building that was so hot I could scarcely stand it, with scrutineers from all parties present.

The team took some three days to prepare its report. The results of the election largely favoured the ruling party, but we were unanimously agreed that the results were as free and fair as anyone could expect. Indeed, the elections had been conducted remarkably well considering what had happened in the preceding weeks. We recommended that more television time be allocated to opposition parties, since the government had a clear advantage in this respect, and that efforts be made to reduce the number of spoiled ballots. Douglas McClelland assigned me one section, perhaps a third of the report, to collect from the delegates and to edit.

Before leaving Sri Lanka, my bodyguard, Suresh, took me to visit some of his friends in the gem pits. Men were working in pits perhaps thirty or forty feet deep, dug by hand and reinforced by hand-hewn timbers. Buckets hauled the gem gravels to the surface with the aid of winches. Fortunately it was the dry season because the pits must have been swamped during the monsoon. Another crew was busy washing the gravels from a stream bed. By invitation, I entered an auction for buyers of the stones sorted out of the gravels. On advice, I bid for a nicely coloured blue sapphire that just might have contained a star. If so, I would have been a real winner. My bid on the stone was successful, and I then had it cut. The result was a cabochon of about four carats, clear but with a star too weak and not centred. A silversmith from our Lapsmith club in Ottawa later made it into a distinctive ring for Mary, my wife.

Chantal arranged for me to visit the moonstone pits in the south of the island. The operation was more professional with better equipment. I witnessed the extraction of stones from the host rock and visited the cutting room.

Chantal's parents, Mr. and Mrs. Obeyesekere, took me for a weekend to their chalet in Nuwara Eliya in the mountains. The entire town was a relic of colonial days, with its cricket field and a racetrack that no longer seemed to have a regular season. Their chalet had been constructed decades ago.

Complete with a large overhead fan and period furniture, it would have made a good Hollywood set for a Gunga Din movie. The scenery on the way was spectacular, but the traffic on the roads totally unpredictable. We met elephants, for example, moving at a slow but steady pace, difficult to pass.

In 1994, I was again invited to join an international team, this time to observe a federal election to be held on August 16. I accepted without clearing with External Affairs, in view of the snub I had received at the hand of our high commissioner the previous year. As it turned out, he was on holidays for the elections, which seemed strange to me. (In Portugal, I would never have dreamed of being out of the country on election day.) Doug McClelland was again the Chair. A remarkable and most likeable fellow Canadian, Air Commodore Leonard Birchall, joined our team. Birchall had been posted to a flying boat squadron based in Sri Lanka during the Second World War and spotted a raiding Japanese fleet heading for the British battleships in the harbour of Trincomalee. He managed to get a signal back to base before being shot down and taken prisoner. When the Japanese bombers arrived they found a squadron of Hurricanes in the air ready for them and the British fleet at sea heading for Madagascar.

Sir Winston Churchill paid public tribute to Birchall's efforts, and Birchall was also decorated for his conduct during his three-and- a-half years as a prisoner in Japan, defending others in prison camps. The Japanese were furious with him because a dozen of their best pilots were lost in the aborted raid.

Our delegation also included the Hon. Walter McLean, a former member of Mulroney's cabinet, who had served as an elections observer in Africa. In addition to many who had served the previous year, the team was enlarged by a British member of the European parliament and a number of academics.

We arrived in Colombo on August 10. By this time, Sinhalese Buddhist terror had subsided but the Tamil Tigers were starting a civil war. It was not possible to hold elections in Tamil-held territory in the north. The team met with representatives from the government, opposition parties, Muslims and four separate organizations of Tamils. The commissioner of elections and inspector general of police briefed us. We held a press conference and most of us were surprised at the brutal criticisms levelled against us to the effect that the election would be rigged and our assignment was to whitewash it.

It soon became apparent that our observer team was split in two groups. On August 12, we debated at length a proposal to increase the number of observers to send to Jaffna in the north. The election would only be held in some fifty polls on government-held islands, since the rest of the territory where some five hundred polls might have been held was controlled by rebel Tamils. Only a small helicopter was available to the observers and their mobility was, to put it mildly, restricted. McClelland proposed to send two of our most experienced people, Sheinbaum of the United States and Lord Redesdale of the United Kingdom, and did not see how more observers could add anything. The motion was defeated, but we were surprised at the support it received.

This time I was assigned to Anuradhapura district in the north, bordering the territory held by the Tamil terrorists. For five hundred years (roughly AD 500 to 1000) it had been the centre of an island kingdom and contained many famous ruins. My bodyguard spoke little and I did not feel that I got to know him. My liaison officer, the matriarchal middle-aged wife of a retired government employee, Mrs. Asoka Jayasena, held a PhD from an Australian university and had studied in the United States. She held a chair in the local university and knew the district well. She insisted, however, in stopping for religious exercises at every Buddhist temple we came even close to, meanwhile giving me elaborate explanations of the symbolism in each temple. Clearly, she did not share my views on the priority of the election.

On remarking that I liked to see ruins, she arranged a side trip to Sidiriya, a magnificent site with temples carved out of its volcanic core, moats and gardens. We visited the temple of the Bo-Tree which had been brought from India 2,000 years ago and is now supported by steel posts and protected by an iron railing. She offered saffron cloth for the monks, purchased lotus flowers whose petals were ceremoniously plucked, and paid for Buddhist chants to which we were obliged to listen. By my count, she prayed at six points in our tour of the temple.

Back at the hotel, we met my fellow observer assigned to Anuradhapura, Mr. Justice Subhan, a retired justice of the Supreme Court justice of Bangladesh, whom I came to like and respect. He had received complaints about four murders allegedly committed so far in the election campaign and intimidation by the police and military. A retired deputy inspector general of police said that the number of DIGs had increased from six to fifty-four since his retirement. Similarly a retired army brigadier said that there were now forty-two of his rank, compared to six on his retirement. It was baldly alleged that these promotions were for the purpose of buying favours for the government.

Clearly, we had to take these complaints seriously. On election day, we agreed to the itinerary that each would follow in visiting polls, so as not to overlap. Beginning in the morning, I visited ten adjacent to the rebel-held area, then eight other rural polls and six in the urban areas prior to their closing at four p.m. Approximately thirty persons, including representatives of the parties as well as election officials, were present in each. In all polls the pattern was the same: Heavy voting at the outset, with sixty per cent of votes cast by noon and many polls with a vote exceeding eighty per cent of the names on the list. Subhan and I were pleasantly surprised that we had no serious incidents to report.

Counting of the ballots took place in an overcrowded and incredibly hot room. We witnessed the count of nine polls, with more than 10,000 ballots, which were simply dumped in one container and handed out to some thirty persons for counting. Scrutineers for all parties were present.

My liaison officer, Mrs. Jayasena, was obviously in some distress due to the physical conditions of the room and I saw no point in staying beyond 10:30 p.m. Getting back to the hotel in Colombo over 200 kilometres distant was not easy, since a curfew had been imposed at seven p.m. on August 16 extending till eight a.m. on August 18. On the way we were stopped twenty-eight times for road checks by military teams who examined our credentials carefully. Near Colombo they waved us through, but looked as though they meant business, with armed machine guns at the ready. Mr. Jayasena remarked: “Sometimes our young men are excitable and one must be careful.”

I had been named chair of a subcommittee to co-ordinate the district reports from observers and drafted a short report, based on what I had been told, concluding that, apart from the rebel-held areas of Jaffna and Vanni, the elections had been free and fair. My report was immediately torn to pieces. Eight observers cited the complaints received, many before the voting, and considered it their job to report them all. They made no effort to hide their sympathy for the opposition and antagonism to the government.

When it appeared to McClelland and myself that a minority report was inevitable, the results of the election were announced. The government had been defeated! Were these people prepared to say that the party they favoured had won in a fraudulent election? Hardly. Finally, I was able to get agreement on my section of the report and McClelland was able to sign the complete document on behalf of all of us. A few individual members of the team who felt they had to say something, but were not formally dissenting, added their observations.

When I returned to Canada, Chantal sent me copies of interviews printed in Colombo papers by these same people a few days later, criticising our report.

In 1999, I was again invited to join an international team to observe elections held on December 23. Tamil Tigers by now have developed the most sophisticated terrorist organization in the world, based on suicide bombers. The eloquent and charming president, Mrs. Chandrika Kamaratunga, whose father and husband had both been assassinated while in office, met the team at 4.00 p.m. one afternoon, then attended an election rally that evening. A suicide bomber killed twenty-two persons and Mrs. Kamaratunga lost her left eye. Shortly afterwards, she appeared on television, imploring the voters to be calm. The television camera then focussed on the grisly severed head of the woman suicide bomber.

My district was Ampara in the southeast. While I detected some shenanigans in a few Muslim polls, the election was on the whole as fair as one could expect.

To a foreign observer, the occupation of Jaffna and other Tamil territory in the north by Sinhalese forces has not solved anything. The Tamil Tigers seem to be able to recruit numbers of suicide bombers and to train them in techniques that are impossible to counter. Sri Lanka has trained staff capable of holding democratic elections, but the background of terror makes their task difficult.

VISIT TO MOZAMBIQUE WITH CIDA PROJECT, 1996

Peter Dobell, a former career officer in External Affairs, organized the Parliamentary Centre in Ottawa. As an MP during the seventies and as deputy Speaker later, I had served as a member of his board of directors. The centre undertook special assignments for parliamentary committees and also served Parliament in other ways, such as assisting with exchange visits with members of the United States Congress.

In the spring of 1996 the Parliamentary Centre put together a project for the Canadian International Development Agency (CIDA) in Mozambique. That unfortunate country had just emerged from over a decade of civil war. Partisans of the leftist government went under the acronym of FRELIMO and the South African-supported rebels by RENAMO. While in Portugal, I had met with representatives of RENAMO who wanted a Canadian news team to visit their areas, so that their side of the struggle could be better reported in America. (My superiors refused the request.) I had also met in Lisbon a Portuguese married to the daughter of a chief in the RENAMO-held area. He seemed to make a good living selling rubellite tourmaline in Germany, which he managed to get out of Mozambique.

Under the auspices of the United Nations, elections were held, bringing representatives of FRELIMO and RENAMO together in a parliament. Apart from the problems of writing a constitution and establishing new institutions, rules and procedures had to be developed permitting an elected body to function. Our delegation included Catherine Stewart, who had spent some time as a student volunteer in Mozambique and was fluent in Portuguese. Catherine's mother was Christine Stewart, a minister in Chrétien's cabinet and responsible for Canada's aid programs. Stephen Langdon, also in our delegation, had been an NDP MP for the Windsor area but now held a university post in Canada. Stephen held a PhD from the University of Sussex in England and was a specialist on development problems of the Third World.

We took turns making presentations to seminars that included two groups that only months before had been killing each other in a civil war.

Both sides seemed anxious to make their new parliament work and to learn the roles of elected representatives. They acted respectfully toward each other, but were not inhibited in asking questions. Langdon described the successes of model states in Asia, such as Singapore, Malaysia, Taiwan, South Korea and Indonesia, indicating the policies he believed were successful and those that were not. In his second presentation, he talked about the problems of development, such as inflation, balance of payments, stability of the currency and sources of capital. I spoke of the role of Parliament in economic development, illustrating from the Canadian experience how we had worked out a trade agreement with the United States, how we had, after prolonged debate, adopted a new and significant tax, the goods and services tax, and of Parliament's role in influencing the current policy of budget restraints. In my second presentation, I went through the steps to adopt a budget and just what the budget itself involved.

We did our best to make our talk as relevant as possible in a country with much of its agricultural land blighted by untold numbers of land mines, and which suffered from extreme poverty. We met a number of representatives of international aid programs in Maputo and could not help but notice a strong South African influence, due to its geographical proximity. President Nelson Mandela spoke to the *Assembleia* just after our arrival.

One subject interested me a great deal. Mozambique has many tribes speaking a host of languages with no single one dominating. I was told that they now had only one official language, Portuguese. The curricula and all the textbooks used in the educational system were in Portuguese and many of the deputies with whom I spoke said that they could no longer speak their ancestral tongues. Chico Francisco, a member of the party of the official opposition, RENAMO, and the chair of an economic development committee of the *Assembleia*, assured me that this policy had been adopted to combat the problems of tribalism. They all recognised that the legacy of tribalism had been devastating for Africa, especially for countries like Rwanda where the most horrifying massacres have taken place. Some day I would like to go back to see how their policy of unilingualism worked out.

The men and women that I met, newly elected members of their *Assembleia*, were trying desperately to make a democratic system work. Mozambique at present is one of the poorest countries in the world, but has good resources in agriculture, fishing and possibly mining. Eighty per cent of their labour force is engaged in subsistence agriculture and the hundreds of thousands of land mines left over from the civil war make life in the countryside most difficult.

They need all the help we can give them.

THE CANADIAN ASSOCIATION OF FORMER PARLIAMENTARIANS

In 1979, after being defeated in the election, I accepted the invitation of some former members of the United States Congress to attend their annual meeting held that year in Milwaukee, Wisconsin. Their agenda was fascinating and I flirted briefly with the idea of helping to form a similar organization for former Canadian members of Parliament. In 1980, however, I was re-elected.

Lloyd with Senate Speaker Gil Molgat

Lloyd and Mary with House of Commons Speaker Gib Parent

By 1987, when I returned from Portugal, John Reid and others had formally established a Canadian Association of Former Parliamentarians, with a constitution that was finally confirmed by an act of Parliament in 1997. I joined the CAFP in 1988 and was elected to the board of directors shortly afterwards.

Jack Ellis, the former Conservative MP for Prince Edward-Hastings and previously the mayor of Belleville, Ontario, took over from John Reid. Jack had been a member of the Management and Members' Services Committee and strongly supported our reform of the administration of the House. We were good friends and it was a pleasure to work with him.

The annual meeting of the CAFP brings together old colleagues, usually in the spring of the year when Ottawa's tulips are blooming. The Speakers of the House and Senate hold a joint reception for us and usually the governor general also. Jack Ellis, before his death in 1995, established an educational foundation in an endeavour to make the best use of the experience and talents of many men and women who have served in the parliaments of Canada.

A former minister of National Defence, Mary Collins, suggested that the names of all MPs since Confederation should be recorded in the Parliament Buildings, possibly in the Peace Tower. Speaker Gilbert Parent carried the proposal further and solicited funds from the private sector for a series of bronze plaques with the names of all who served in the House

Speaker Gib Parent hosts former Speakers of the House of Commons, 1998. Left to right: John Bosley, Lloyd, John Fraser, Alan Macnaughton, James Jerome

and the Senate of each parliament since Confederation. These were unveiled in a moving ceremony in 1996 and are now on display in rooms beneath the Hall of Honour in Centre Block.

Ellis had worked out a program of reciprocal visits with the Peoples' Republic of China. In October 1996 I acted as chairman of a Canadian delegation which included Mr. and Mrs. Reynald Guay of Québec, Mrs. Edna Anderson and her daughter from Ontario, Mr. Harry Olaussen from British Columbia, as well as my wife, Mary. We visited two cities I had visited previously, Beijing and Shanghai, but this time also included three interior cities, Nanchang, Jiujang and Changsha.

Visiting the Great Wall, the Forbidden City and Tienanmen Square are highlights for any tourist in Beijing and they are impressive. This time I noted fewer bicycles and many more cars. People on the streets were smartly dressed in Western styles and I did not see a single Mao uniform. Many apartments had air conditioning units in their windows.

Everywhere we went the level of construction activity had to be seen to be believed. The interior cities were clearing broad swaths (I estimate fifty metres wide) right through their centres for modern thoroughfares; in the process they had to destroy many old buildings. From my hotel room in Shanghai, I counted twenty-five major construction projects. Harry Olaussen had been born and raised in Shanghai and could still speak the local dialect. We walked the streets of Shanghai together at eleven o'clock at night and saw construction crews rivetting steel girders twenty stories

Twenty-fourth anniversary of MPs elected in 1968. Left to right: Robert Kaplan, Steve Paproski, Les Benjamin, James Jerome, Lorne Nystrom, Maurice Foster, Lloyd.

up. I shudder to think of what the record must have been for industrial accidents!

Across the river from Shanghai, the city of Pudong has a hundred skyscrapers, in an area that was a swamp a decade ago. I was pleased to note that Canadian businesses occupied a few of them.

Our guides talked freely with us explaining how China imposed strict discipline on public affairs. Differences of opinion are permitted up to the point when a decision is made, but not after that point. China is determined to have economic development before permitting political freedom. The example of Russia was cited, where they attempted political freedom first and suffered economically. One person put it bluntly: "In Russia, the army shelled the parliament. It will not happen here."

We were extremely well received and I know that every member of the delegation enjoyed the visit.

RADAR MECHANICS CONVENTIONS, 1996, 1997, 1998, AND 1999

In 1996, a group of former radar mechanics from World War II decided to hold a national convention in Calgary, Alberta. I had last visited the city during the 1990 Liberal Convention that elected Jean Chretien; our delegation from Ottawa West had supported him solidly.

Organizing a convention of veterans fifty years after the end of hostilities was not an easy task. No mailing lists existed and it was necessary

Lloyd with Pierre Trudeau at the unveiling of plaques with the names of former parliamentarians, 1996

Lloyd with Beryl Gaffney and Gordon Blair

to track down as many addresses as possible of the survivors from the 5,800 men who had been trained.

Bob Linden has been writing the story of these men who served on every continent except Antarctica. Angus Hamilton has written about those who served in South East Asia Command.[135] Many individual stories have been written. Most, like myself, were attached to the Royal Air Force and in the Canadian celebrations of the fiftieth anniversary of the end of the war in 1995, no mention was made of the radar mechanics.

Using the Access to Information Laws, Linden discovered that the UK authorities had proposed in 1945 to present a certificate of appreciation on their behalf to every mechanic who had served with their forces. They mailed a sample of the form they intended to use and later followed it with 5,000 copies. Officials in the Canadian Department of National Defence promptly destroyed them. Linden, however, found the original sample form in the archives and suggested that it be replicated and a copy be presented to every mechanic at the Calgary convention.

[135] Angus Hamilton, *Canadians on Radar in South East Asia*: 1941-1945, by ACH Publishing, 1092 Highway 105, Douglas, New Brunswick.

What followed would make a good plot line for a comedy show. (*Royal Canadian Air Farce*, please note.) A letter was written to the minister of National Defence, David Collenette, inviting him to present the certificates. He promptly referred it to the secretary of state for Veterans Affairs. He referred it in turn to his officials who, after due consideration, pronounced the original decision of 1945 valid, therefore it would not be possible to present the certificates. The original "reasons" were that people not eligible for certificates would be jealous and, further, it would not be possible to locate all of those eligible, who were now geographically scattered in civilian life.

At this point Linden, after learning that I had been a radar mech, came to me for assistance. I interviewed the secretary of state for Veterans Affairs and pointed out that we would be responsible for the names of eligible persons. Anyone we missed could come forward and claim their certificates later. If any other categories of men and women who served and were not recognised emerged, they could surely fight their own battles. For any politician it was a win-win opportunity. All that had to be done was to go to Calgary, shake hands as the certificates were presented, and smile at the cameras.

Following the interview, I thought everything was settled, but I did not count on the Department of Veterans Affairs bureaucrats. They drafted a letter repeating their spurious reasons for refusing to present the certificates and eventually had it signed by the minister of National Defence. I could not believe it!

Irving Aaron, Marlene Catterall, MP, and Ron Catterall at Lloyd's birthday celebration

Cpl C. Lloyd Francis

Can. R132837

Royal Canadian Air Force

was One of those who, in the hour of England's greatest need, came forth voluntarily to man the vital Radar stations upon which the air defense of Great Britain so signally depended.

By their selfless and devoted services these men not only had an indispensable share in the defense of this country but also contributed in great part to the development of this new branch of science, to the general benefit of the Allied cause.

Air Ministry, 1946 — Secretary of State for Air

Certificate of Appreciation from the Air Ministry, London, 1996

This time Linden and I went to Douglas Fisher, my old colleague in the House of Commons and now a columnist for the *Sun* newspapers. Doug wrote a scorcher of a column blasting the stupidity of the DVA officials. The very day that column appeared, the minister of National Defence called me on the telephone. What was the fuss all about? While a facsimile of the minister's signature was on the letter we received, he had apparently not read it.

To make a long story short, the Liberal MP for my old seat of Ottawa West, Marlene Catterall, asked a question in the House of Commons on the policy of the government concerning the award of certificates of appreciation. The minister of National Defence undertook to have representatives of the federal government make the presentations at our convention in Calgary. His parliamentary secretary, Major General

Richardson, who represented an Ontario seat, Major General McGillivray of the Department of National Defence, and a junior from the Department of Veterans Affairs handled the situation with aplomb.

The convention was a great success. The City of Calgary presented white Stetson hats to Linden, myself, and two others. Thanks to Doug Fisher's column, we received good radio and press publicity. Words fail to describe how you feel on meeting old comrades that you have not spoken to for over half a century.

Because of the distances involved, many from Eastern Canada did not make it to Calgary. In addition, many others did not learn of the plans for Calgary until the last minute and could not make it. A group based in Ottawa made plans for a second convention to be held in October 1997 and were able to build upon the mailing list so painstakingly accumulated by our Calgary friends.

Bob Linden and I co-chaired the Ottawa committee. As it turned out, we had over 550 veterans in attendance, certainly as many as one could expect. An additional fifty paid their registration fees, but did not show up, presumably for health reasons. Come to think of it, our average age must have been close to eighty years! We were recognized by Mr. Speaker Parent as we sat in the galleries and attended a reception with the minister of National Defence, Art Eggleton; his parliamentary secretary, John Richardson; deputy whip and MP for my old seat of Ottawa West, Marlene Catterall; and a number of other MPs.

Ottawa displays its colours in October as the maple trees receive their first touch of frost. My wife, Mary, and I proudly accompanied delegates that took the tourist train through the Gatineau to Wakefield, one of our most dramatic autumn experiences.

These were the first reunions of Canadian radar mechanics since 1945, but a committee in Vancouver managed to sponsor a third in October 1998. A fourth was held in London, Ontario in 1999 and a fifth was held in Sept. 2000 in Montreal. The Royal Air Force radar mechanics in the United Kingdom have held several reunions, some of which were attended by Canadians. Mary and I attended one in Bournemouth in May 1999.

EPILOGUE

You have read my story. Having now passed my eightieth birthday, I cannot say that there will be that much ahead, but I hope so. My health is good and I have a partner that has helped me overcome the great loss in 1989 that so disrupted my life. Without her help, this book would not have been written. I have been fortunate. In the words of Tennyson's Ulysses:

> For my purpose holds
> To sail beyond the sunset and the baths
> Of all the western stars, before I die.

One or two brief voyages I have not described, such as being an elections observer in Macedonia in November 1998, this time being named by the Government of Canada. Hopefully, there will be others. Looking back, I think of the high points of my public career and also some of my failures.

By the time I left the Research and Statistics Division of the Department of National Health and Welfare in 1960 to embark on a career in public life, I had developed a set of beliefs and a political philosophy. Parliamentary government in Canada is based on traditional nationwide parties that encompass in their ranks many points of view. The parties are pragmatic; they compromise to bind together this huge country, with its many diverse economic regions and cultures. The central government uses its fiscal powers to develop a national safety net, doing its best to promote national standards and to assist poorer provinces. This is not to deny the role of ideology in political thinking: issues such as the role of governments and tax policy are always in the background.

I had seen Paul Martin, Senior, as the minister in charge of my department, initiate new social programs and expand others. He believed in health insurance and under his guidance the foundations for hospital insurance, followed later by Medicare, were laid. I decided to join his party, the Liberals.

At Bob McKeown's suggestion and with his assistance, I had an exciting municipal career over a period of six years. The school sidewalks program and the fund to reconstruct the sewers in the older central parts of the city, were, I believe, the results of my suggestions.

When elected to the House of Commons in 1963, I naively believed that I might make a contribution in a number of areas. As Shakespeare put it, there is a tide in the affairs of men, but the turn I took, thanks to bilingualism in the public service and the Pearson Pledge, did not lead me on to fortune. My efforts to defend the careers of long-term unilingual public servants incurred the wrath of senior francophone cabinet ministers and I was labelled a maverick.

Firstly, I hoped to continue with the Department of National Health and Welfare, where I had spent nine years in a position that gave me an overall view of its operations. In this, I failed, not even being named to the committee of the House dealing with this department.

Secondly, perhaps I could have worked with a department setting policies for the public service. After all, I had served as the national president of one of the public service unions. The nearest I came in this field was when Jean Chrétien, the president of the Treasury Board, entrusted me, his parliamentary secretary, with guiding amendments to the *Superannuation Act* through the House.

The third area arose out of my municipal service. Municipal affairs were now assuming greater importance to the federal government. In addition, there was the special problem of the nation's capital and the need to make changes to the operations of the National Capital Commission (NCC). On this one, I kept trying, but to no avail.

THE NATION'S CAPITAL

Something will surely have to be done about our nation's capital, whose structure is probably the most complicated in the world. With two official languages, two systems of property and civil law, two provincial education systems and, until recently, a host of municipalities on both sides of the Ottawa River, the wonder is that any overall view of the development of our National Capital Region is possible. A federal statute defines a territory in Ontario and Quebec over which a crown corporation, the NCC, does what it can.

I have detailed the abuse of power exercised by Douglas Fullerton in wasting $20 million on an ill-conceived land assembly in a swamp and in failing to construct proper approaches to Portage Bridge, as well as the apparent conflict of interest by the present chairman, Marcel Beaudry, because of his land holdings. The problem lies in the weakness of current appointments to the NCC Board of Directors, who simply do not know enough about the operations. The NCC is the only body that concerns itself with the entire National Capital Region; however it must be strengthened and preserved until something better can take its place.

A good start would have the regional chairs of Ottawa and the Outaouais serve ex officio as directors of the NCC. These people are well informed on what is taking place in the region, and are backed by competent staff.

KEEPING CANADA TOGETHER

Mr. Pearson's appointment of the Royal Commission on Bilingualism and Biculturalism in 1964 marked a new phase in the life of Canada. To meet the growing separatist threat in Quebec, new policies were devised.

Bilingualism meant the official recognition of two languages, English and French. It meant that the public service had to be transformed if the two languages were to be fully and equally respected. Ottawa West, with the highest proportion of anglophone public servants of any constituency in Canada, was a good testing ground for the policy. It repudiated its sitting MP in nine successive elections, but the sitting Liberal, Marlene Catterall, has now won three successive terms. The bitter remnants of the opponents of bilingualism now vote for the Reform Party in that riding, while the Conservatives, as a result of their disillusionment with Mulroney, trail a poor third.

On the national scene, more Canadians have embraced a second language. Our schools offer many options, going as far as total immersion at elementary levels. A large number of Canadians have shown good will and accepted bilingualism. All this is positive.

Biculturalism has disappeared, to be replaced by multiculturalism. Communities like the Ukrainians under the leadership of the late Senator Paul Yuzyk promoted the concept of a Canadian mosaic, to which a great number of other ethnic groups also contributed. French Canadians have not responded to multiculturalism with the same enthusiasm, many of them believing that it offers anglophones an excuse to downplay the role of French in Canada and treat them as just another ethnic group.

Multiculturalism is now an essential part of Canada. In our public life, politicians bridge the gaps between different groups. It was truly a pleasure to work with the Chinese, the Germans, the Italians, the Lebanese, the Ukrainians, people of Caribbean origin, people from India and a host of others.

I never did like the term mosaic; a mosaic is static and multiculturalism is anything but static. It is dynamic in the extreme and our Canadian Parliament and provincial legislatures are now reflecting the changes.

I have had no difficulty accepting multiculturalism, which replaced biculturalism, but must say, frankly, that it has not done much to keep Quebec in our political union.

In the last category, I place a number of policies coming from the fertile mind of Pierre Trudeau: patriation of the constitution, the Charter of Rights and Freedoms. These were designed to raise our self-esteem as a nation, or country, or whatever. They were part of our maturity process. As far as I can judge, they were well accepted across Canada, including Quebec. The charter is changing our legal system and giving the courts powers not conceived under British common law, but now cannot be reversed.

How successful have these policies been in meeting the challenge so aptly described by the B & B Commission? Judging by the results in federal and provincial elections in Quebec, not very. Official bilingualism has not been enough to satisfy Quebec, which has declared itself to be officially unilingual. Two referenda on separatism have come dangerously close to being adopted. We have stalled for time, hoping that the problem will go away. It has not. A hard core of something over thirty per cent of Quebec's population want to separate, and I have no idea of how to cope with this form of ethnic nationalism.

If Quebec were to separate, the rest of Canada would not be viable. The western provinces could hardly tolerate a union with Ontario comprising more than fifty per cent of the whole. Atlantic Canada would seek American muscle to defend its fishery and power transmission rights. In short, we would be pulled by an economic gravity on north-south lines to the United States of America.

MY CONTRIBUTION

Over the years, I became familiar with the operations of Parliament, and its rules and procedures. It was some satisfaction to have chaired the committee that revised the Veterans Charter for the one and only time before it passed into history. The compliments from men like Cliff Chadderton, president of the War Amps and a recipient of the Order of Canada, meant a great deal.

Working on the Public Accounts Committee introduced me to an outstanding and pioneering auditor general, James MacDonnell; I believe that my work was helpful to him and he also was complimentary.

I have mixed feelings about my service on the committee that failed to show up the weaknesses in Bryce Mackasey's disastrous amendments to the *Unemployment Insurance Act*. I just did not get my act together in time to be effective.

Without question, my most important contribution was as deputy Speaker to Jeanne Sauvé and later Speaker of the House of Commons. Madame Sauvé was shocked to discover the level of corruption in the administration she had inherited. It was a pleasure to have been part of the team that cleaned it up. I believe that my account is the only one available from the point of view of the actual administration in this period and have tried to set out events as I recall them, without pulling any punches.

I believe that I was a competent presiding Speaker. There is, however, a recorded tape of events for others to see and to judge.

I thoroughly enjoyed my term as ambassador in Lisbon. My successor, Geoffrey Bruce, a career foreign service officer, was complimentary about the briefing notes I left for him and the tidy state of the post in general.

THE SENATE

Lastly, I would like to say something about the Senate of Canada. There is a move to abolish it, which I think would be a mistake. Over the years, many senators were helpful when I had a problem. Senator Eugene Forsey would put aside whatever he was doing to advise me on a matter before a committee or when I wanted to say something about our constitution. Senator Paul Yusyk was always eager to discuss multiculturalism. Senator John Connolly was one of the very few to understand how the bilingual policy in the public service was hurting in Ottawa West. Senator Carl Goldenberg was a recognized expert on collective bargaining and the public service. I could cite many others who did their utmost to help an MP regardless of political affiliation.

There are good and bad senators, as there are good and bad MPs. In my opinion, the Senate does good work on committees, especially when long, time-consuming hearings are required across the country and MPs are simply not available. Admittedly, there are abuses, conflicts of interest and recent publicized cases of chronic absenteeism, but the Senate is still a repository of a great deal of talent.

CAMPAIGN WORKERS WHO WENT ON TO OTHER OFFICE

I believe that my campaigns inspired a number of our workers to run for public office. Bob Chiarelli became a member of the Ontario parliament and chair of the regional municipality of Ottawa Carleton. Alex Cullen became a regional councillor and later a member of the Ontario parliament. Frank Marchington became reeve of the Township of West Carleton and a provincial candidate. Gordon Hunter became a councillor of the City of Nepean and a federal candidate. Al Loney became a councillor of the City of Nepean. There were others. All of them, in my opinion, served the public interest and are the kind of people that bring respect to politics.

You have read my story. If you are a historian, you may wish to compare my record of certain events with that of others. If you are an aspiring politician, you will want to try avoiding some of my mistakes. If you are just a curious reader, I hope you enjoyed my anecdotes. Years ago, in high school, I memorized a poem that went as follows:

In after days, when grasses high
O'ertop the grave where I shall lie,
Though ill or well the world adjust
My slender claim to honoured dust,
I shall not question nor reply . . .
I shall be mute, as all men must
In after days.

Lloyd and Mary with Lloyd's cousin, Irene Hannahson, 2000

Lyle, Jack and Lloyd Francis, 2000

INDEX